W9-BBS-058

VATICAN IMPRESSIONS

VATICAN
IMPRESSIONS

EDITED BY
Francis Sweeney, S.J.

SHEED AND WARD – NEW YORK

262.13
Sw V

© Sheed and Ward, Inc., 1962

Library of Congress Catalog Card Number 62-9107

Manufactured in the United States of America

To
His Lordship
John J. McEleney, S.J., D.D.
First Bishop of Kingston in the West Indies

FOREWORD

🌾 GATHERED HERE in one place and bound in one swatch of buckram are the spoils of innumerable hours of reading in the literature of the Papacy. Most of these selections I have read many times, with a pleasure proof against the narrowing tolerances of middle age, and I have thought that they might be talismans of equal delight to those of my fellow mortals who enjoy the local color of Catholic life or who share my affection for the baroque glamor of papal Rome.

Anthologists are supposed to identify the inspiration which moved them, or to mention some gap in the library shelves which their book will fill. I am anxious at the outset to explain what I mean by the title I have chosen for this collection. My purpose is not to offer a dogmatic or devotional tract, nor to make any but quick and rheumatic obeisance to the Muse of History. I have attempted to assemble here a bookful of descriptive reading on the Popes, something on their personalities and public occasions, but more on the climate of custom and folkway in which the papal monarchy has flourished since the first century. "Vatican" here means what it means in the newspapers: not only the fabric of St. Peter's and the Apostolic Palace, not only the wearer of the Triple Crown and his court, but the four-square mystery of the papal fact, the *Romanitas* of the Church of Christ.

The reactions of some fifty writers to the unique vitality of Rome are recorded in many accents and attitudes, and in styles varying from the chaste gemmary of Henry James to the rough-cast journalism of Salvatore Cortesi. I have copied out a sheaf of impressions from the letter books and memoirs of the English travelers of the nineteenth century (when the English aristocracy was Italy's *cavalier servente*), and rifled the wallets of pilgrims from Montaigne to Sean O'Faolain.

Reportage, memoirs, descriptive essays—but not much fiction. I have found little among the novels and short stories using a Vatican setting which would satisfy my easy-going preference for writing "with a bit of style to it." Booth Tarkington's sketch of Saint Pius X, though listed as a short story, is really an essay. The only other item of fiction (who could doubt the candor of Cellini's raffish memoir?) is Patricia Collinge's perplexed account of the mixture of protocol and jostling democracy at a papal general audience.

Anthologies rarely win unmixed approval, and perhaps this one can claim only to be good in parts, like the curate's egg. I send it into the world, however, with the hope that, over the shoulders of the pilgrims and reporters and gossips gathered here, the reader may catch some occasional glimpses of the sacred humanity of the Papacy. It gleams out in a thousand instances in the Roman story: Peter's tears and Gregory's *Non Angli sed angeli*; and for me most touchingly in the incident which Bishop Francis Clement Kelley relates of Pius XI. "You must be glad it's over, Holy Father," a visitor said to him at the end of the Holy Year of 1925. "What with receptions for pilgrims from all over the world Your Holiness must be tired to death and glad to have a little time to yourself."

"I shall be dying of loneliness," the Pope answered.

ACKNOWLEDGMENTS

"The Pilgrim's Vow"; quoted from *The Path to Rome* by Hilaire Belloc with the permission of George Allen & Unwin Ltd.

"GO!" by Lord Acton; quoted from *A Writer's Recollections* by Mrs. Humphrey Ward with the permission of Harper & Brothers.

"St. Peter's"; quoted from *Transatlantic Sketches* by Henry James, published by Houghton Mifflin Company.

"City of Joy" by Romain Rolland; quoted from *Winged Sandals* by Lucien Price with the permission of Lucien Price.

"My Friend Cipolla"; quoted from *A Summer in Italy* by Sean O'Faolain, published in 1920 by Devin-Adair Company, New York.

"Painter to the Pope" by Giorgio Vasari; quoted from *The Lives of the Painters* (1896), ed. E. H. and E. W. Blashfield and A. A. Hopkins, published by Charles Scribner's Sons.

"Mr. Morse Grows Weary"; quoted from *Letters and Journals* of Samuel F. B. Morse (1914), ed. Edward Lind Morse, published by Houghton Mifflin Company.

"A Critical Guest"; quoted from *Italian Journeys* (1901) by William Dean Howells, published by Houghton Mifflin Company.

"Skyline"; quoted from the book *Cities of Italy* by Arthur Symons. Copyright, 1907, by E. P. Dutton & Co., Inc. Renewal, 1935, by Arthur Symons. Reprinted by permission of the publishers.

"The Odor of Sacrifice"; quoted from *The Puppet Show of Memory* by Maurice Baring. Copyright, 1923, by Maurice Baring. Reprinted with the permission of the author's Executor.

"Emporia Invicta"; reprinted with the permission of The Macmillan Company from *The Autobiography of William Allen White*. Copyright, 1946, by The Macmillan Company.

"A Roman Holiday"; reprinted from *Heathen Days* by H. L.

Mencken, by permission of Alfred A. Knopf, Inc. Copyright 1942, 1943 by Alfred A. Knopf, Inc.

"Castelli Romani"; quoted from *An Italian Holiday* by Paul Wilstach. Copyright © 1928 by The Bobbs-Merrill Company, 1956 by Arthur Hellen, reprinted by special permission of the publishers.

"Arrivederce, Roma" by John Cogley; reprinted with permission from *The Commonweal*, 232 Madison Avenue, New York 16, N. Y.

"Sanctuaries"; quoted from *My Unknown Chum* by Charles Bullard Fairbanks, published in 1912 by The Devin-Adair Company, New York.

"When the Pope Dies"; quoted from *My Thirty Years of Friendship* by Salvatore Cortesi. Copyright 1927 by Harper & Brothers. Reprinted by permission.

"The Watch on St. Peter's Square"; quoted from *Roman Fountain* (1940) by Hugh Walpole; reprinted with the permission of Rupert Hart-Davis Limited, Publishers.

"Their Ancient Places"; quoted from *The Poet's Diary* by Alfred Austin, ed. Lamia, with the permission of The Macmillan Company Ltd.

"No Shadow of Pride" by G. K. Chesterton. Reprinted by permission of Dodd, Mead & Company from *The Resurrection of Rome*.

"Father and Son" by Alfred E. Smith; reprinted with the permission of The McNaught Syndicate, Inc.

"The Pope Amid Storms" by Anne O'Hare McCormick; reprinted with the permission of *The New York Times*.

"The One Man in All the World"; reprinted from *Europe in the Spring* by Clare Boothe, by permission of Alfred A. Knopf, Inc. Copyright 1940 by Alfred A. Knopf, Inc.

"The Fifth Army in the Vatican"; quoted from *Not So Wild a Dream* by Eric Sevareid, published by Alfred A. Knopf, Inc. Copyright 1946 by Eric Sevareid; reprinted by permission of The Harold Matson Co.

"The End of the Holy Year"; quoted from "The End of the Holy Year" in *Rome and a Villa* by Eleanor Clark. Copyright 1952 by Eleanor Clark. Reprinted by permission of Doubleday & Co., Inc.

"The Pope Who Remains a Priest." Copyright 1951 by Graham Greene. Reprinted with the permission of Monica McCall, Inc.

CONTENTS

[*xi*]

V. TO THE CONSUMMATION
OF THE WORLD

ILLUSTRATIONS

1. Hjalmar von Moerner, "Il Carnevale di Roma" (Carnival in Rome), Rome 1820.

2. Giuseppe Agustino Vasi, "Basilica di S. Pietro in Vaticano" (Basilica of St. Peter in the Vatican).

3. Giuseppe Agustino Vasi, "Basilica di S. Maria Maggiore" (Basilica of St. Mary Major).

4. Giuseppe Agustino Vasi, "Basilica di S. Giovanni in Laterano" (Basilica of St. John in the Lateran).

5. Piranesi, "Piazza Navona"

6. Piranesi, "Piazza di Spagna"

7. Piranesi, "Fontana di Trevi" (Fountain of Trevi).

8. Piranesi, "Castel Sant' Angelo"

VATICAN IMPRESSIONS

ECCO ROMA

was conductor in the sand arena; that was doing rather well with the Daily Roman Courant.

I

Ecco Roma

DURING the Grand Tour of the olden time, a heart-quickening moment came when the coach had labored up the last hill on the Via Flaminia and the vetturino pointed with his whip to the walled City dominated by the dome of St. Peter's, and cried, "Ecco Roma!"

This first chapter, an omnium gatherum of articles and sketches, says "Here's Rome!" The oddly assorted company here convened offer a kaleidoscope of lenses on the Vatican. Henry James and F. Marion Crawford write their essays from the splashed palette of the novelist; the historians Lord Acton and Thomas Hughes see the present as the green room of the past; the brilliant Bostonian, George Ticknor, displays his genius for friendship and sympathy in the alien world of Rome; Father Prout, the sharp-tongued Irishman, in the dispatches he mailed to Dickens' Daily News, mingles his Roman faith and enthusiasm for Pius IX with some acid paragraphs on the Roman bureaucracy. Sean O'Faolain writes with Dublin's gentle irony of the flavor of Roman gossip.

With some regret the anthologist finally omitted a charming essay by a young halberdier of the Swiss Guard, who describes, in the simple style of any youngster writing home from an Army camp, the daily life of the picturesque company who guard the Pope. Every tourist is familiar with their striped uniforms—Sophia Hawthorne said that they looked like tulips. Once in Rome, I attempted to lo-

cate the halberdier. Tempora mutantur, nos et mutamur in illis. He was no longer in the papal service, but was doing rather well with the Gulf Refining Company.

THE PILGRIM'S VOW

❦ ONE DAY AS I was wandering over the world I came upon
the valley where I was born, and stopping there a moment
to speak with them all—when I had argued politics with the
grocer, and played the great lord with the notary-public, and had
all but made the carpenter a Christian by force of rhetoric—
what should I note (after so many years) but the old tumble-
down and gaping church, that I love more than mother-church
herself, all scraped, white, rebuilt, noble and new, as though it
had been finished yesterday. Knowing very well that such a
change had not come from the skinflint populace, but was the
work of some just artist who knew how grand an ornament was
this shrine (built there before our people stormed Jerusalem), I
entered, and there saw that all within was as new, accurate, and
excellent as the outer part; and this pleased me as much as
though a fortune had been left to us all; for one's native place is
the shell of one's soul, and one's church is the kernel of that nut.

Moreover, saying my prayers there, I noticed behind the high
altar a statue of Our Lady, so extraordinary and so different from
all I had ever seen before, so much the spirit of my valley, that
I was quite taken out of myself and vowed a vow there to go to
Rome on Pilgrimage and see all Europe which the Christian
Faith has saved; and I said, "I will start from the place where I
served in arms for my sins; I will walk all the way and take advantage of no wheeled thing; I will sleep rough and cover thirty

miles a day, and I will hear mass in St. Peter's on the Feast of St. Peter and St. Paul."

Then I went out of the church still having that Statue in my mind, and I walked again farther into the world, away from my native valley, and so ended some months after in a place whence I could fulfill my vow; and I started as you shall hear. All my other vows I broke one by one. For a faggot must be broken every stick singly. But the strict vow I kept, for I entered Rome on foot that year in time, and I heard high mass on the Feast of the Apostles, as many can testify—to wit: Monsignor this, and Chamberlain the other, and the Bishop of so-and-so—*polis in partibus infidelium;* for we were all there together.

—*The Path to Rome.*

GO!

🌵 *Go to Rome!* Never mind the journeys. Go! You will have three days there, you say? Well, to have walked through Rome, to have spent an hour in the Forum, another on the Palatine; to have seen the Vatican, the Sistine Chapel, and St. Peter's; to have climbed the Janiculum and looked out over the Alban hills and the Campagna—and you can do all that in three days—Well! Life is not the same afterward. If you only had an afternoon in Rome it would be worth while. But *three days!*

—Letter quoted by Mrs. Humphrey Ward
in *A Writer's Recollections.*

HEART OF THE WORLD

❦ WE WHO HAVE KNOWN Saint Peter's since the old days cannot go in under the portico without recalling vividly the splendid pageants we have seen pass in and out by the same gate. Even before reaching it we glance up from the vast square to the high balcony, remembering how from there Pius the Ninth used to chant out the Pontifical benediction to the city and the world, while in the silence below one could hear the breathing of a hundred thousand human beings.

That is all in ghostland now, and will soon be beyond the reach of memory. In the coachhouses behind the Vatican, the old state coaches are mouldering; and the Pope, in his great *sedia gestatoria,* the bearers, the fan-men, the princes, the cardinals, the guards and the people will not in our time be again seen together under the Roman sky. Old-fashioned persons sigh for the pageantry of those days when they go up the steps into the church.

The heavy leathern curtain falls by its own weight, and the air is suddenly changed. A hushed, half-rhythmic sound, as of a world breathing in its sleep, makes the silence alive. The light is not dim or ineffectual, but very soft and high, and it is as rich as floating gold dust in the far distance, and in the apse, an eighth of a mile from the door. There is a blue and hazy atmospheric distance, as painters call it, up in the lantern of the cupola, a twelfth of a mile above the pavement.

It is all very big. The longest ship that crosses the ocean could

lie in the nave between the door and the apse, and her masts
from deck to truck would scarcely top the canopy of the high
altar, which looks so small under the super-possible vastness of
the immense dome. We unconsciously measure dwellings made
with hands by our bodily stature. But there is a limit to that. No
man standing for the first time upon the pavement of Saint
Peter's can make even a wide guess at the size of what he sees
unless he knows the dimensions of some one object.

Close to Filarete's central bronze door a round disk of porphyry
is sunk in the pavement. That is the spot where the emperors of
the Holy Roman Empire were crowned in the old church;
Charlemagne, Frederick Barbarossa and many others received
the crown, the chrism and the blessing here, before Constantine's
ancient basilica was torn down lest it should fall of itself. For he
did not build as Titus built—if, indeed, the old church was
built by him at all.

A man may well cast detail of history to the winds and let his
mind stand free to the tremendous traditions of the place, since
so much of them is truth beyond all question. Standing where
Charles the Great was crowned eleven hundred years ago, he
stands not a hundred yards from the grave where the Chief
Apostle was first buried. There he has lain now for fifteen hundred years, since the "religion of the fathers" was "disestablished,"
as we should say, by Honorius, and since the Popes became
Pontifices Maximi of the new faith. This was the place of Nero's
circus long before the Colosseum was dreamed of, and the foun-
dations of Christendom's cathedral are laid in earth wet with
blood of many thousand martyrs. During two hundred and fifty
years every bishop of Rome died a martyr, to the number of thirty
consecutive Popes. It is really and truly holy ground, and it is
meet that the air, once rent by the death cries of Christ's innocent
folk, should be enclosed in the world's most sacred place, and be
ever musical with holy song, and sweet with incense. It needs
fifty thousand persons to fill the nave and transepts in Saint

Peter's. It is known that at least that number have been present
in the church several times within modern memory; but it is
thought that the building would hold eighty thousand—as many
as could be seated on the tiers in the Colosseum. Such a concourse was there at the opening of the Oecumenical Council in
December, 1869, and at the jubilee celebrated by Leo the Thirteenth; and on all those occasions there was plenty of room in the
aisles, besides the broad spaces which were required for the
functions themselves.

To feel one's smallness and realize it, one need only go and
stand beside the marble cherubs that support the holy-water
basins against the first pillar. They look small, if not graceful; but
they are of heroic size, and the bowls are as big as baths. Everything in the place is vast; all the statues are colossal, all the
pictures enormous; the smallest detail of the ornamentation would
dwarf any other building in the world, and anywhere else even
the chapels would be churches. The eye strains at everything, and
at first the mind is shocked out of its power of comparison.

But the strangest, most extravagant, most incomprehensible,
most disturbing sight of all is to be seen from the upper gallery
in the cupola looking down to the church below. Hanging in
mid-air, with nothing under one's feet, one sees the church pro-
jected in perspective within a huge circle. It is as though one saw
it upside down and inside out. Few men could bear to stand there
without that bit of iron railing between them and the hideous
fall; and the inevitable slight dizziness which the strongest head
feels may make one doubt for a moment whether what is really
the floor below may not be in reality a ceiling above, and whether
one's sense of gravitation be not inverted in an extraordinary
dream. At that distance human beings look no bigger than flies,
and the canopy of the high altar might be an ordinary table.

And thence, climbing up between the double domes, one may
emerge from the almost terrible perspective to the open air, and
suddenly see all Rome at one's feet, and all the Roman mountains stretched out to south and east, in perfect grace of restful

outline, shoulder to shoulder, like shadowy women lying side by side and holding hands.

And the broken symmetry of the streets and squares ranges below, cut by the winding ribbon of the yellow Tiber; to the right the low Aventine, with the dark cypresses of the Protestant cemetery beyond, and the Palatine, crested with trees and ruins; the Pincian on the left, with its high gardens, and the mass of foliage of the Villa Medici behind it; the lofty tower of the Capitol in the midst of the city; and the sun clasping all to its heart of gold, the new and the old alike, past and present, youth, age and decay,—generous as only the sun can be in this sordid and miserly world, where bread is but another name for blood, and a rood of growing corn means a pound of human flesh. The sun is the only good thing in nature that always gives itself to man for nothing but the mere trouble of sitting in the sunshine; and Rome without sunshine is a very grim and gloomy town today.

It is worth the effort of climbing so high. Four hundred feet in the air, you look down on what ruled half the world by force for ages, and on what rules the other half today by faith—the greatest center of conquest and of discord and of religion which the world has ever seen. A thousand volumes have been written about it by a thousand wise men. A word will tell what it has been—the heart of the world. Hither was drawn the world's blood by all the roads that lead to Rome, and hence it was forced out again along the mighty arteries of the Caesars' marches—to redden the world with the Roman name. Blood, blood and more blood,—that was the history of old Rome,—the blood of brothers, the blood of foes, the blood of martyrs without end. It flowed and ebbed in varying tide at the will of the just and the unjust, but there was always more to shed, and there were always more hands to shed it. And so it may be again hereafter; for the name of Rome has a heart-stirring ring, and there has always been as much blood spilled for the names of things as for the things themselves.

It is wonderful to stand there and realize what every foot means, beneath that narrow standing room on the gallery outside the lantern, counting from the top downward as one counts the years of certain trees by the branches. For every division there is a pope and an architect: Sixtus the Fifth and Giacomo della Porta, Paul the Third and Michelangelo, Baldassare Peruzzi and Leo the Tenth, Julius the Second and Bramante, Nicholas the Fifth and Alberti. Then the old church of Constantine, and then the little oratory built over Saint Peter's grave by Saint Anacletus, the third or, according to some, the fourth bishop of Rome; then, even before that, Nero's circus, which was either altogether destroyed or had gone to ruins before Anacletus built his chapel.

And far below all are buried the great of the earth, deep down in the crypt. There lies the chief Apostle, and there lie many martyred bishops side by side; men who came from far lands to die the holy death in Rome,—from Athens, from Bethlehem, from Syria, from Africa. There lie the last of the Stuarts, with their pitiful kingly names, James the Third, Charles the Third, and Henry the Ninth; the Emperor Otho the Second has lain there a thousand years; Pope Boniface the Eighth of the Caetani, whom Sciarra Colonna took prisoner at Anagni, is there, and Rodrigo Borgia, Alexander the Sixth, lay there awhile, and Agnes Colonna, and Queen Christina of Sweden, and the Great Countess, and many more besides, both good and bad— even to Catharine Cornaro, Queen of Cypress, of romantic memory. In the high clear air above, it chills one to think of the death silence down there in the crypt; but when you enter the church again after the long descent, and feel once more the quick change of atmosphere by which a blind man could tell that he was in Saint Peter's, you feel also the spell of the place and its ancient enchantment; you do not regret the high view you left above, and the dead under your feet seem all at once near and friendly.

—*Ave Roma Immortalis.*

ST. PETER'S

As a mere promenade, St. Peter's is unequalled. It is better than the Boulevards, than Piccadilly or Broadway, and if it were not the most beautiful place in the world, it would be the most entertaining. Few great works of art last longer to one's curiosity. You think you have taken its measure; but it expands again, and leaves your vision shrunken. I never let the ponderous leather curtain bang down behind me, without feeling as if all former visits were but a vague prevision, and this the first crossing of the threshold. Tourists will never cease to be asked, I suppose, if they have not been disappointed in the size of St. Peter's; but a few modest spirits, here and there, I hope, will never cease to say, No. It seemed to me from the first the hugest thing conceivable—a real exaltation of one's idea of space; so that one's entrance, even from the great empty square, glaring beneath the deep blue sky, or cool in the far-cast shadow of the immense façade, seems not so much a going in somewhere as a going out. I should confidently recommend a first glimpse of the interior to a man of pleasure in quest of new sensations, as one of the strongest the world affords.

There are days when the vast nave looks vaster than at others, and the gorgeous *baldacchino* a longer journey beyond the far-spreading tessellated plain of the pavement, when the light has a quality which lets things look their largest, and the scattered figures mark happily the scale of certain details. Then you have only to stroll and stroll, and gaze and gaze, and watch the *baldacchino* lift its bronze architecture, like a temple within a temple, and feel yourself, at the bottom of the abysmal shaft of the dome, dwindle to a crawling dot. Much of the beauty of St. Peter's resides, I think, in the fact, that it is all general beauty, that you are appealed to by no specific details, that the details indeed, when you observe them, are often poor and sometimes ridiculous.

The sculptures, with the sole exception of Michael Angelo's admirable Pietà, which lurks obscurely in a dusky chapel, are either bad or indifferent; and the universal incrustation of marble, though sumptuous enough, has a less brilliant effect than much later work of the same sort—that, for instance, of St. Paul's without the Walls. The supreme beauty of the church is its magnificently sustained simplicity. It seems—as it is—a realization of the happiest mood of a colossal imagination. The happiest mood, I say, because this is the only one of Michael Angelo's works in the presence of which you venture to be cheerful. You may smile in St. Peter's without a sense of sacrilege, which you can hardly do, if you have a tender conscience, in Westminster Abbey or Notre Dame. The abundance of enclosed light has much to do with your smile. There are no shadows, to speak of, no marked effects of shade; but effects of light innumerable—points at which the light seems to mass itself in airy density, and scatter itself in enchanting gradations and cadences. It performs the office of shadow in Gothic churches; hangs like a rolling mist along the gilded vault of the nave, melts into bright interfusion the mosaic scintillations of the dome, clings and clusters and lingers and vivifies the whole vast atmosphere.

A good Catholic, I suppose, is a Catholic anywhere, in the grandest as well as in the humblest churches; but to a traveler not especially pledged to be devout, St. Peter's speaks more of contentment than of aspiration. The mind seems to expand there

immensely, but on its own level, as we may say. It marvels at
the reach of the human imagination and the vastness of our
earthly means. This is heaven enough, we say: what it lacks in
beauty it makes up in certainty. And yet if one's half-hours at
St. Peter's are not actually spent on one's knees, the mind reverts
to its tremendous presence with an ardor deeply akin to a pas-
sionate effusion of faith. When you are weary of the swarming
democracy of your fellow-tourists, of the unremunerative aspects
of human nature on the Corso and Pincio, of the oppressively
frequent combination of coronets on carriage panels and stupid
faces in carriages, of addled brains and lacquered boots, of ruin
and dirt and decay, of priests and beggars and the myriad tokens
of a halting civilization, the image of the great temple depresses
the balance of your doubts and seems to refute the invasive vulgarity of things and assure you that nothing great is impossible.
It is a comfort, in other words, to feel that there is at the worst
nothing but a cab-fare between your discontent and one of the
greatest of human achievements.

—*Transatlantic Sketches.*

LEAR OF CITIES

❦ I LOOK OUT of the window this gray, rainy day, and see the streets all mud and the roofs all green mould, and the mists lying like a pall over the lower town, and Rome seems to me like King Lear staggering in the storm and crowned with weeds.
January 30, 1869.

—Letters and Journal.

BRIDE OF CHRIST

❧ WE HAD ANOTHER Roman scene this morning, very different from yesterday's. The young Countess Bolognetti, one of the famous Cenci family, took the veil at the Tor de' Specchi, the fashionable, rich convent of the nobility here; and as the Princess Gabrielli had made arrangements for us to see it, and as the Princess Massimo—who once passed four years of her education here—offered herself specially to show it to us, we were able to see all that such an occasion affords, under agreeable circumstances. . . . We were received in the parlor of the convent, where was Count Bolognetti, the father, apparently about seventy years old, in a full and elegant court dress of black, with a sword by his side, lace ruffles, and powdered hair; the Countess Bolognetti, his daughter-in-law, also in full dress, blazing with diamonds; several of the nuns, old and good-natured; and some of the Pope's noble guards.

The company collected fast, . . . the elite of the fashionable nobility of Rome. . . . The Princess Massimo soon proposed to us to go to the church, in order to have good places. We found military guards the whole way, the passages ample and rich, and the church itself beautiful, with marbles and velvet tapestries, great wealth on the altar and in its neighborhood, and excellent taste everywhere. . . . Soon after we were seated, Cardinal Galeffi came and placed himself at the altar, a service of beautiful silver was offered him to wash his hands, he put on his robes, and took his seat. Immediately afterwards six nuns with wax-lights came in, and in the midst the Countess Bolognetti, richly but not showily dressed in pure white, without jewels, and with a crown of white roses on her head. At her side walked a beautiful little child, four or five years old, bearing on a cushion a jewelled crown; . . . representing an angel offering her the crown of heavenly love. She advanced to the altar, knelt before the Cardinal, and having received his blessing, returned to the body of the church, where she knelt before a little *prie-dieu,* looking pale, but very pretty, gentle, and solemn. . . . The Cardinal celebrated high mass with all the pomp of his church, the guards knelt and presented arms, and there was more or less stir through the whole church, but she remained perfectly motionless. . . . When the Cardinal had partaken of the sacrament he administered it to her, and she received it with much apparent humility, after which, turning to the Abbess of the convent, an old Princess Pallavicini, she knelt to her, and asked her permission to enter the convent. This being granted, she addressed herself to the Cardinal and asked him to receive her vows, to which he gave his assent, and added his blessing; and she turned round to the audience, and in a gentle, but firm and distant voice, solicited their prayers while she should pronounce them.

The nuns now took off some parts of her dress, and put on that of the convent; she pronounced her vows of obedience, seclusion, etc.; her hair was cut off; . . . the *Miserere* was sung, the service for the dead chanted, and she was sprinkled with holy water, as the priest sprinkles a corpse. All this happened in front of the altar, as she knelt by the Cardinal. She then walked slowly and gently down into the church; knelt in the middle of the pavement of marble on a cloth spread there; a black pall was thrown over her feet; she fell graciously forward on her face, and the pall was spread over her whole person; and with a few more prayers and ceremonies, whatever belongs to an entire burial-service was fulfilled, and she rose a nun, separated from the world,

and dedicated—as she believed—to Heaven. This part of the
ceremony was very painful, and it was impossible for many of
us to witness it without tears; for she was a young and gentle
thing, who seemed to be fitted for much happiness in this world.
But she now passed down the aisle as a nun, having first received
the Cardinal's benediction and had the crown set upon her head.
Near the door the nuns received her, and she embraced them all;
a *Te Deum* was sung, and she left the church with her sister,
another very young and pretty creature, who is also a member of
the convent. . . . A tasteful breakfast and collation was prepared
in the room of the Superior; those who chose went over the
convent, and saw the room of the new nun, which was prettily
and comfortably fitted up, and the whole affair was ended. . . .
February 12, 1837.

—*Life, Letters, and Journals of George Ticknor.*

FATHER PROUT IN ROME

❦ A SAD CALAMITY has befallen our city. The Tiber, suddenly swollen by rain such as is only witnessed under the tropics, and impeded in its course towards Ostia by a south-east wind, has just flooded two-thirds of the inhabited streets, and destroyed property, both in town and country, to a melancholy extent. This century had not seen a similar inundation, that of 1805 being far less extensive or disastrous. As far as the eye could reach, from the Pincian Hill to the foot of Monte Mario, from the Ponte Molle to the contrescarpe of Castle St. Angelo, became at once a vast lake, interspersed with tops of trees and farm roofs, cattle swimming, and floating wagons. Not only the accustomed low quarters of the Piazza Navona and Pantheon, but the Corso and Condolli were submerged, and the well-known magnificent arena of the Porta del Popolo became a deep pond impassable to carriages. It was a singular sight to look down from the Pincian on this extemporized basin, reflecting calmly the surrounding churches and monuments, and receiving into its abundance the rather superfluous contributions of the four Egyptian lions who kept up the farce of their quadruple *jet d'eau* throughout. The central obelisk of Rameses, which rose in quiet grandeur over the waters, seemed, after many thousand years, to have got a glimpse of his native Nile at its work of fertilization. Unfortunately, mischief, unmixed with any compensating result, ensues from these visits of the Roman river.

The reports from the various quarters (or islands) of the city
have as yet brought no tidings of drowned men; though horses,
pigs, and kine have perished in numbers, and the misery of the
poorer classes can hardly be estimated unless by the knowledge
of their exclusive tenancy of all ground-floors, in Rome the
upper storeys being alone inhabited by the wealthy. But the unfortunate Jews are in the worst predicament of all other denomi-
nations, their disadvantageous quarter being not of their own
selection; and hence it became only an act of common honesty in
the government to behave as it has done by them—today supply-
ing them at once, and in the first rank, with food and necessaries.
For this purpose domiciliary visits were made to all bakers and
fashionable hotels and every loaf carried off to the Ghetto. If
any good could possibly be elicited from the present sad occur-
rence, it would be, perhaps, the forcing the Pope's attention to
the folly and un-Christian policy of his predecessors in cooping
up the remnant of Israel here into a space of the town so confined and so objectionable as to nearly resemble the hold of a
Brazilian slave-ship on the middle passage. To condemn a people
to perpetual dirt and disease, with the interlude of an occasional
deluge like the present, is a sorry scheme for their conversion, and
a sad lesson of Christian love. These unlucky sojourners in the
capital of the Church have just had all their property, cloths,
silks, velvets, and every commodity in which they trade, destroyed at once by no act of theirs; and in any civilized country
they would be clearly entitled to recover the amount from the
legislature. The old houses are happily falling on each other's
shoulders, and the whole rookery will be rendered soon unin-
habitable, in which case they must perforce be allowed to select
some other part of this wide metropolis to build in.

This is the moment for their brethren throughout Europe to
memorialize the benevolent pontiff on their behalf, with every
probability of success. The Pope would be too happy to find outward support against the prejudices of the lower orders and the

narrow-minded rich. 'Twas a touching sight to see these helpless sufferers, with the scanty wreck of their furniture, crowded under the roof of the synagogue, which was the only dry spot of their prison-house. By the river of Babylon well might they sit and weep when they remembered Sion!

There lived 3,600 of them in this black hole, of whom 1,900 are paupers; about 1,000 earn a livelihood by trade, and the remainder are comparatively rich. They raise among themselves 13,000 dollars yearly for the support of their own schools and other institutions. The State draws a large revenue from their commercial operations, and it is a remarkable circumstance in the case of the Roman Jews that by way of propitiating their Christian fellow-citizens they are in the habit of emphatically disclaiming any part or portion in the great misdeed visited upon them and their children. They maintain, and with considerable pretension to truth, that they are descended from a colony of Hebrew men settled in Rome long before the period of the Crucifixion—and certainly we know that Pompey brought thousands of captive Jews to Rome; and Josephus, I think, describes 8,000 of them going up to remonstrate with Augustus on some occasion or other.

I pray the assistance of your brethren of the press in London in drawing the attention of the friends of Israel throughout Europe to these poor people and their cause; it is truly that of the captive and the bondsman.

December 12, 1846.

—*The Final Reliques of Father Prout.*

THE ROMAN WEATHER

ꙮ WE WENT ON SUNDAY to see the Pope take possession of the Lateran,—a ceremony of particular interest, from all the peculiar circumstances connected with the new reign. The church of the Lateran is held in even higher veneration than that of St. Peter's, being built upon the site of the first Christian church founded by Constantine the Great. From the windows of the Palazetto Torlonia, the lodgings of the ———, who most kindly invited us to them, we saw to perfection the procession debouch from the Via San Romualdo, on its descent from the Quirinal into the Piazza del Gesù. The Pope alone being in his carriage, and everybody else on horseback, the reverend body (or bodies) of cardinals were exempted from this part of the day's duty, which would have been, to many of them, all but impossible. The thronged and tapestried streets, the crowded windows and balconies, the wreaths and branches of flowers and evergreens, the universal enthusiasm and "allegria," recalled the days of the Carnival. A very different procession, however, presently filled the many-colored avenue, and suggested memories of a far more serious nature; the Crucifero, in his splendid purple robes, bare-headed, his black hair falling on his shoulders, and his grave and handsome countenance, admirably becoming the solemnity of his costume and office, riding on a snow-white mule, and bearing a huge golden crucifix; then the Guardia Nobile, surrounding the Pope; the Captain of the Swiss Guard, clad in com-

plete sheath armor; the secretaries in middle-age costumes, of
the richest and most picturesque black velvet and gold; and then
the numerous train of Prelati, some in scarlet and point lace,—
others attired in purple robes, with short over-skirts of fine lawn
and lace, with a hood or wimple of the same surmounted by a
round black hat, precisely the costume with which all Petrarch's
representations have rendered us so familiar; all of them mounted,
their horses led at a foot's-pace by serving men on foot.

It is impossible to conceive anything more beautiful in point
of color, or more picturesque in every respect, than this fine procession passing along by the Doria and Alfieri palaces, and all
that noble range of buildings which fronts the Piazza di
Venezia and the Piazza del Gesù. At one moment particularly
the *coup d'oeil* was splendid; a few drops of rain fell, and all the
prelates in scarlet dresses drew over their heads the scarlet silk
hoods, which were hanging on their shoulders, a measure of
prudence for which a painter would have offered up infinite
thanks to the weather. We have had tickets of admission given
us for the Coliseum, but, fearful of losing the benediction, we
omitted going there, and proceeded straight to the Lateran. We
might have done both very well, and I regret extremely that we
did not, for I am sure, from ———'s account, nothing could have
been finer than the view obtained by those (and they were
thousands) who, filling once more with eager expectation the
arches and galleries of the Coliseum, and looking towards the
Capitol, beheld the scarlet and purple procession wind down
from it, traverse the forum, and, passing underneath the arch of
Titus, unroll itself along the Via Sacra. At the time in which we
might have seen this and did not, we were, however, unconscious of our loss, and very happy in the excellent position where
we obtained seats nearly opposite the Church of St. John
Lateran. As the Papal procession approached, the vacant space
before the church, and almost half way to San Pietro in Vincoli,

became thronged with a dense mass of people, through which
the pageant slowly made its way.

We watched the Pope's entrance into the Basilica, by the
movement of the white peacock's fans, and the canopy borne
over him; and after the scarlet priests and purple monsignori had
all disappeared under the sacred portals, we directed our attention to the crowd rolling round us, where the variety and pic-
turesqueness of costume, and the great beauty of the men and
women of the lower classes, and the peasants who had come into
Rome for the celebration, kept our attention perpetually alive
and interested; from time to time we looked to the great window
above the middle portal of the church, but the dark crimson
balcony and alcove were only filled with choristers, and every
now and then a cardinal appeared and looked down on the vast
assembly which was every moment growing more numerous. At
length the clerical subalterns were seen to arrange themselves
in ceremonious order; huge wax tapers, carried by white-robed
priests, came slanting forwards in the dark recess; presently the
white peacock fans were seen, and the Pope was borne to the
front of the balcony: immediately profound silence filled the
whole wide expanse; the crowd suddenly ceased to move, to
speak, it almost seemed, to breathe; and the choristers began
chanting a few bars, during which the stillness became absolutely
perfect; then the Pope rose up, robed all in white, under that
crimson dome, and thus lifted above all heads, looking like some
colossal statue, he chanted with a loud sonorous voice, that resounded over the kneeling crowd, his invocation of the Trinity,
and spreading wide his arms showered down his benediction
upon the city and the world, to which the people responded with
an amen of acclamations, amid which their sovereign was borne
back from their sight. I am persuaded that this must be a finer
thing than even the benediction from St. Peter's; for St. John
Lateran is a beautiful church, and standing close to the walls of

Rome—looks over them, the broken arches of the aqueducts, the campagna, and the Sabine and Alban mountains.

Saturday, 14th February.—St. Valentine's day, the first day of the Carnival, soon after breakfast, ——— and my sister and I walked down and up, for it is both, several times to the Villa Massimo, formerly the Villa Negroni. We sauntered through the vineyards and gardens, under the intense warmth of the unclouded sun; the delicate blossoms of the almond trees stood like silver branches against the deep azure ground of the sky, the laurustinus bushes were in full bloom, the little green and gold lizards glided, and darted, and rustled along the hot stone walls, and among the spiked leaves of the cardoni. We sat ourselves down, with our faces towards the purple hazy hills, and listening to the jangling bells that came through the warm air, across the vineyard, an hour of Italian enjoyment of mere being. At about two o'clock, with our carriage duly lined with white calico, and my green velvet bonnet covered with the same, we set forth to observe the solemnities of the Carnival. On the seat opposite to us was a large tray, heaped with small bunches of fresh flowers and violets; under the seat were two baskets filled with sugar plums of every variety, some of them the size of very large bullets,—formidable missiles, as we found when we received a volley of them. At our feet was a deep large basket, filled with the *confetti* as they are called; a species of small shot, made of dried peas covered with flour, and in throwing handfuls of which consists the chief warfare of the Corso. A couple of wire masks, rounded to fit the face, colored pink to become it, and furnished, screen fashion, with a handle, completed our equipment; and thus we descended to the field of battle, our dresses being as nearly white as possible, and my sister having a large white bournous, and I a large white shawl on, the policy of which miller-like equipment we very soon discovered.

Passing through the Piazza di Spagna, we found it filled with soldiers on horseback, and every street was sending up to the great rout its string of carriages and stream of eager hurrying pedestrians; groups of masks went dancing and laughing by; Harlequins and Pantaloons, Turks, Albanians, Spanish Dons, and girls in short white skirts and colored bodies, with blue or pink silk boots, and very freely-shown legs. Most of these groups had their faces covered either with grotesque masks or the classical black silk visor: in passing the carriage, they threw us confetti or nosegays, or merry words. We were deposited at a house in the Corso, where we had the privilege of occupying Mrs. ———'s balcony. We had hardly taken our stations here, when, from a neighboring balcony, a shower of sweetmeats and flowers assailed us, and we found ourselves the mark of a little man, who, with a most bright and delighted countenance, kept exercising his skill upon us, and enjoying apparently equally our awkwardness in missing him, and his own dexterity in hitting us. While busily engaged with him, sundry treacherous shots reached us from another direction; and we found that we were commanded by a balcony opposite to us, and higher than ours, from which sundry demure gentlefolk—our own countrymen I suspect—were pelting us *sans faire semblant de rien,* and with certain peculiarly convenient tin horns overwhelmed the luckless passengers in the street with perfect hail-storms of confetti, which rattled upon the men's hats and masks, and were received with shouts of laughter both by the sufferers and the lookers-on.

The long irregular street presented the most singular and animated scene; every window was filled with spectators, every balcony or jutting window from which a convenient view could be obtained was adorned with hangings either of crimson and gold, or gay rose color and white; the little balcony in which we stood was all festooned with the latter colors, and tapestry and curtains and carpets were put in requisition to render commodious and gay every point where a station could be obtained. The entrances to many of the shops were turned, by dint of screens and partitions and temporary wooden erections, into small apartments, open to the street, and filled with women of the middle class in gay and bright fancy dresses, where scarlet and gold, and ribbons and flowers, and neck-chains and ear-rings, together with their own beautiful faces and magnificent braided hair, formed a most attractive and curious part of the show. The beauty of the women of the middle and lower class of Rome is something really wonderful; the richest coloring, great purity of features and nobility of form, particularly in the outline of the head, and its position on the shoulders. Their persons are generally clumsy, however, and their feet and ankles extremely ugly, thick, and ill-shaped: their divinity comes no lower than their shoulders.

While we were gazing up and down the Corso, with its lining of bright human countenances, the military suddenly appeared in the Piazza del Popolo, and came slowly down the street; a large body of cavalry and infantry, with trumpets blowing, and drums beating, and alternate snatches of music from the shrill fifes, and the fuller harmony of the brass band. During their passage through the Corso, which every day opens the Carnival, the irregular warfare which had preceded their arrival was suspended. We remained with our hands full of menacing confetti, ready for the next occasion of returning to somebody the pelting somebody else had given us. As we looked down in this threatening attitude, the old general who rode at the head of the troops looked up towards us, and, seeing our malicious purpose, shook his sword smilingly at us, which warning we received with infinite amusement.

The soldiers had no sooner stationed themselves at the various posts, where they were to maintain order, and left the street again empty, than from every cross street and alley debouched the pent-up stream of folly; carriages rushed from every direction into the Corso, and forming themselves into two compact lines, drove slowly up and down, with their cargoes of pelting, screaming, laughing human beings; the carriages skirmished with each

other, and with the lower balconies, and with the foot-passengers;
the lower balconies sent confetti, nosegays, bonbons, and funny
speeches into the carriages, and through the stream of pedestrians,
who divided their attention, equally above, below, and around;
while from the higher balconies the masqueraders fought with
their opposite neighbors across the street, their right- and left-
hand neighbors in the adjoining balconies, and every now and
then showered down on the devoted heads of the walkers and
drivers, whole baskets full of that hateful little hail; with occasional gallantries to objects of special admiration, in the shape
of huge hard bonbons, that struck one like so many small cricket-
balls, leaving bruises to attest their arrival,—nosegays so thick
and heavy, that they stove in one's bonnet,—or, finally, as the
very climax of good will and civility, lemons and oranges, which,
being in a state of unripeness, which protected one's clothes
from injury, were also so hard, that the compliment of receiving
one was as much as one's life was worth. The bright air resounded with the acclamations of joyful human voices, and was
misty with the fine flour, hail, and nosegays flying in all directions.

We soon left our balcony, and finding our carriage waiting in
an adjoining street, got into it, and joined the stream of busy
absurdity in the Corso. It is well to see the *coup d'oeil* from the
shelter and security of a window or balcony, but it is infinitely
more amusing to be among the people themselves, whose good
humor, fantastic and grotesque gaiety, droll fancies, and withal
decent deportment, no foreigner can form the least idea of
without having seen it; whereas, in England, drunkenness, riot,
and violence, would have been the inevitable result of this universal license. The only intoxication to be seen was the ludicrous
assumption of it by pantaloons reeling between the carriages,
bottle in hand, and with whitened faces; and the only angry
and disputatious voices were those of pretended poets, lawyers,
and improvisatori, who, in full court costume, swords, powder and
bag-wigs, harangued at the full blast of their lungs, to the

infinite ecstasy of the crowd which gathered densely round them. The whole day passed in this curious succession of picturesque and ludicrous scenes; our carriage was loaded with elegant and pretty bonbons, which were generally deposited on our knees, or in our hands, by masked pedestrians, with sundry sweet words thereto; and, as the daylight thickened in the deep defile of the Corso, we regained our balcony to see the race of the Barberi. A cannon fired gave the signal for clearing the Corso; after which, the guard on horseback dashed at full gallop down the street, and sentinels were posted at a few yards' distance from each other to keep back the impatient crowd, who, in spite of these precautions, kept breaking bounds and overflowing beyond this military cordon, in their extreme anxiety to catch the first glimpse of the horses.

At length the shout of a thousand voices, rolling towards us like a great wave of the sea, announced their having started, and presently, full tear down the crowded, gaping street, rushed eleven or twelve horses, covered with ribbons, knots, artificial flowers, streaks of bright red paint, and various other intended decorations; to which were added appendages of a less harmless and benevolent character:—plates of brass and wood, acting as flappers by the rapid motion of the horses; crackers and squibs, igniting and going off as they ran; and onions stuck full of pins and needles, which, hanging by cords to their manes and upon their flanks, performed the part of spurs, whose impulse became more sharp and constant in proportion as the terrified creatures increased their speed. This part of the ceremonies of the Carnival may be an improvement upon the former custom of making the unfortunate Jews race through the Corso, for the edification of their Christian fellow-creatures; but it is still, in its present less offensive form, the least agreeable part of the Carnival to me. The terror and agony of the poor horses is most distressing, as is also the risk incurred by the spectators, whose uncontrollable excitement renders it almost impossible for them to repress it within safe bounds.

By some curious old privilege, dating many years back, the head of the noble house of Piccolomini receives a small sum upon every horse admitted to run. They start from an inclosure in the Piazza del Popolo, and are caught between two large cloths like sails let down before and behind them in the narrow street at the end of the Piazza di Venezia, called, from that circumstance, Via della Ripresa dei Barberi. I did not see their start on any day, but was assured by ———— that it was a very curious thing to see them brought to the bar, each held only by a single man, who, together with the plunging, rearing, eager, terrified horse, realized and repeated to the life some of the fine antique statues. After the horse race, the tide of biped life again poured into the Corso, and the universal pelting went on till evening sent the carnivalisti home to dinner or to supper, according as they were English or Italians. Nothing amused me more than the perfect Babel of languages resounding on all sides; as for us, we held our laughing colloquies with the passengers, who challenged us in a leash of tongues—English, French, and Italian; and we were even called upon to respond to Russian and Spanish, which, however, we were forced to decline. Our return home was anything but as triumphant as our going forth; and I am sure would have furnished an admirable subject for a carica- ture. The white lining of the carriage half torn off; the floor of it ankle-deep in confetti, sugar-plums, and nosegays, which had been thrown to and fro till they formed one brown agglomeration of dirty rubbish; the seats under us heaped with the same per- vading trash. Heaven knows how it got there. Hoarse with laugh- ing; our arms aching with hurling things at our fellow-creatures; our shawls awry; our faces all smeared with flour; our bonnets battered and dented into cocked hats with the thumps from nose- gays thrown at us; our very stays filled with the horrid little confetti, that had fallen into our bosoms, and down our backs, and all over us. A more complete sample of "After the Battle" I never saw. To be sure, we brought home *spolia opima,* in the shape of sundry most elegant and fanciful little boxes and baskets full of bonbons, that had been thrown or given to us, and which we piled like a trophy before ————, who, having done his Carnival thoroughly some years ago, looks with eyes of superior wisdom upon our folly in doing ours now.

Easter Sunday.—I was not well, and missed the great climax of the holy ceremonies—the Pope's blessing of the people. From the terrace of the Villa Medici, I watched the sudden gleams and slow curling clouds from the cannons of the castle of St. Angelo, which proclaimed the universal benediction. To be blessed by sound of cannon, seemed to me strange, especially by Christ's Vicar, and in Christ's name; but to be blessed, at any rate, is something, and that the city and the world have been by word of Pope this day. In the evening we drove to St. Peter's, to see the illumination, the stream of human life setting in from every avenue, and street, and alley, and gathering as it rolled towards one common point, the multitudinous voices of all these living rills, as they poured down beside our carriage,—the flaring lights of the windows, which were filled with people, whose bodies were eagerly stretched towards the quarter of St. Peter's, and whose faces, as we drew near the great illumination, were shining as with the light of day; all presented a most curious and exciting spectacle.

At length we reached the end of the street of the Borgo di San Spirito, and debouched together with the crowds of pedestrians abreast of us in the great place of St. Peter's; the vast and noble church, and graceful colonnades, with their outline defined in pale white fire; the springing spray of the beautiful fountains turned into showers of yellow light; the huge mass of compact blackness formed by the thousands of spectators; the confused jarring and rattling and hurtling of the crowded carriages; the rearing and backing of the horses; the outcries and violent movements of the mounted police, whose drawn sabres and accoutrements glittered in the pervading light; above all, the

sea of upturned wondering human faces all flooded with it, and
the hoarse murmur, like the great voice of the ocean, rising from
this mass of people, that rolled its black billows to and fro, as
the sudden breaking of some carriage from the ranks, or darting
forward of some trooper to intercept it, caused them to recede or
advance, was all indescribably strange and striking.

We sat for some time gazing with undiminished wonder and
admiration, when the great bell of St. Peter's tolled the hour.
Suddenly the cornices, the friezes, the pediment, the dome, the
lantern, the very ball and cross, high up in the dizzy neighborhood of the stars, became alive with human figures; men, reduced by their fearful height above us to the size of black
pigmies, ran like so many glow-worms, each carrying a light, all
over the huge fabric, and the hitherto pale illumination became
fiery red in the twinkling of an eye—it was marvellous! Five
hundred men are thus employed twice every year, Easter-day
and on the Feast of St. Peter's: for three days previous they are
not permitted to touch wine, and they all confess and receive
absolution before ascending to their perilous task.

After blunting the edge of our amazement with gazing,—to
have exhausted it would have been impossible—we turned homewards. Our carriage rolled slowly, or rather waded, through the
crowded streets at a foot-pace, and when we came to the Ponte
Sisto we beheld another illumination, which turned the pageant
we had just seen into a splendid tawdry toy. The full moon hung
above the river in a sea of mellow light, indescribably soft and
powerful; the purple line of the Alban hills was distinctly visible
against the pearly horizon, while the roses in the gardens, near
the bridge, showed their colors as though by day, so potent was
the moonlight,—with us, so wan and colorless. Opposite this
great and lovely glory, St. Peter's flamed in the distance like
a huge gold filigree thimble. The pageant vouchsafed to us
nightly is a fine thing; it is well to see it confronting the yearly
pageant of the great church of Rome, to be reminded how fine,

—what an insensible, brutish, dull, irreverend thing is custom.

Coming home we found a perfect opera congregation of carriages on the Pincio, a sort of Haymarket and King Street row. The view of St. Peter's is very fine from here, and many people had driven up to enjoy it. I went to my stand on the terrace of our charming little garden, and here looked up at the moon and down at St. Peter's, till the rolling wheels had all rattled away, and the shuffling feet all departed, and the sound of the fountain in the Piazza di Spagna came up to answer the tiny tinkle of the fountain in the garden, whose roses and orange blossoms and thousand cups of incense were sending up fragrance into the night air like prayer.

—*A Year of Consolation.*

CITY OF JOY

❦ MY LIFE HAD BEEN one of constant hardship; poverty, hard study, and only a scant vacation once a year in Switzerland. It was in Rome that I discovered that happiness is not a dream, that there can be such a thing as happiness in this world. And beauty! In Rome you see a beautiful hill, and on that hill will be a beautiful building, and in that building will be beautiful works of art. Beauty and happiness. In Rome I found both, and it was with a surprise. I had been so starved for them that sometimes, especially at sunset, looking over the city from one of its hills, I would find myself in tears.

—Lucien Price, *Winged Sandals.*

THE SERIO-COMIC IN THE VATICAN ARCHIVES

❧ MUCH HAS BEEN WRITTEN on the private archives of the Vatican. There have appeared ample accounts of what these ancient repertories, with their thirty thousand manuscript tomes, offer to the historical students of the nineteenth and twentieth centuries. Perhaps enough has been said for the present about the outside of these volumes, but a few points taken from the inside of them might interest readers. I will note here some features which have struck my eye or caught my fancy in the study of the folios. I will disown at once all intention of describing the inexhaustible fund of historical treasures. The things I will select are rather of the singular and exceptional sort, and such as I was not looking for.

In the first place, all the great affairs of the times, even in the heart of Protestant countries, form the subject, if not of direct narration, at least of incidental commentary. Where there were no Papal Nuncios, nor formal representatives of any kind, there were always other persons, either on the ground or on the borders of it, who were sending in to the authorities at Rome their accounts of interesting events. One prolific class is not easy to describe, for, I must confess, it is not easy to identify. These are the persons whose correspondence bears no official stamp, and yet is comparatively regular. Whether it is by personal inclination merely, or by some sort of invitation, that they have become correspondents of the Cardinal Secretary of State, they are evidently acceptable to him, and from time to time he answers them. They almost enjoy the privilege of a postal commissary who, when forwarding to Rome the letters which arrive at Lyons from Paris, or at Genoa from Spain, not infrequently uses the occasion to say something on his own account. But the class we speak of, which has nothing whatever to say except on its own account, has a privilege of its own; it is totally disembarrassed, unrestricted by official mechanism and forms. There is no doubt of it, a personal forwardness, if it has not already pushed them into this position of confidence, serves to keep them in it. And evidently they enjoy it. In the suaveness of their French style, in the seeming adulation of their Italian superlatives, in the overflowing gratitude they express at being allowed to address the eminent Cardinal, and the delighted self-abandonment with which they profess themselves his servants, his creatures, his slaves, their ardent affection at times seems to swoon away in the effusiveness of love, of desire, of burning zeal to minister, to expend itself, to lay down life itself in giving the slightest gratification to such an ecclesiastical potentate.

Language seems to fail them in attempting to breathe forth the soul of such sublime conceptions that just struggle for utterance. Generally, a parenthesis comes in sooner or later—a certain abbacy or bishopric for the writer, or some worthy third person, would be thankfully received. And at times it would appear that the failure of the parenthesis seals the fate of the correspondence, which then begins to languish. But the class is not thereby extinguished. When some go others come; and the race, like Tennyson's brook, itself goes on for ever. This is probably the class which supplies the largest income of the gossipy, the spicy, the satirical, the scandalous.

Here I am reminded of an instance in point, which shows the nonsensical trifles or quarrels of which so much court-life was made up. A certain Becatti writes from Venice, at a date near the close of the seventeenth century. He is rich in accounts about the newsmongers there (*i novellisti*), who are tearing the Papacy and the Jesuits to pieces. A new Jesuit preacher had just opened his course, taking for his text: "Generation cometh and generation goeth." Whereat the sensitive aristocrats wax wroth; for they fill up the text, as they saw by the eye and intonation of the preacher that he meant it to be filled up; and so constructed it ran thus: "Generations come and generations go, but the Jesuits go on for ever!"

The ordinary avenues of official information are being trodden every day by the regular couriers. The style of information is very uniform, however varied in matter. Still, it is rather dry. It is that kind which answers to the green books and blue books of Parliament and Congress, wherein statesmen find their natural pabulum; and, while other people would die of melancholy, they somehow seem to thrive and keep cheerful. In such an official series, an historian can follow out his thread with considerable accuracy; for, when a Nuncio touches a chord in some one of his many paragraphs, he will naturally return to it in subsequent letters. And there the investigator will pick his footsteps amid the tangle of other matters until the issue closes; or until he enters into the land of his chosen investigation. Thus, from the first warning notes on Gallicanism or Jansenism, and then remarks about dubious tenets propounded in one university or other, he moves on into a babel of sounds, into a war of cries, complications which fill tomes upon tomes with correspondence about suspected dignitaries, infected institutions, dubious candidates for the episcopacy and the tortuous ways of crowned heads. Here emperors and kings and queens, saints and sinners alike, come forward to have their say; but nothing is to be learnt from their diplomatic phrases, except, perhaps, the transcendent power and dignity of the Court of Rome.

It is notorious in the administration of human affairs, and in the accounts which go under the name of history, that what predominates there is not the even course of events, the normal current of national life. In secular history it is not the life of the towns or of the peasantry, not the smooth development of internal resources, nor the features of domestic simplicity and happiness, that fill the pages of histories, and pretend to be the story of nations. Instead of that we have usurpations, and violence, and wars, and insurrections; we have the flashing of swords and the sacking of cities; we read of earthquakes, inundations, of the errors that have ravaged minds, of the vice that has seized weak imaginations. All this fills up pages, and chapters, and books. And it is very much the same with the administration of all human affairs, and especially with high administration. Here, too, the feature predominates of dealing with the abnormal, with the diseased, with all the woes, intellectual, moral and social, which afflict humanity. That it should be so is of the very heart of the position. Administration, or the exercise of legitimate authority in society, is not for the purpose of interfering in life, but of merely helping it from without, and remedying the evils which afflict the social body. And, in fact, no judicious person ever recurs to a high authority above the level of his ordinary life, except to receive help there, when elsewhere other means have failed.

From this consideration we might divine beforehand a certain trait very conspicuous in the archives of the Vatican. It is that a dominant tone running through them is not that of the even course of the Church's life, the administration of the Sacraments, the growth in virtue of Christian peoples, or of the clergy, or of religious Orders; it is not the progress of Christian education, or of civilization in general. All these things appear and they are refreshing. But they appear only incidentally. Whatever is strange and abnormal—that abounds. Strange and peculiar persons—they come to the front. The correspondence is as wide-reaching as humanity itself; but, as a general rule, the unofficial representatives of humanity, who rush forward and insist on having a word with Peter on his rock, either have singular things to say, or pitch their voices on a singular key to make themselves heard.

We may reasonably suppose that no one meant to be comic. But for the refined sense of humor there is plenty of comedy, and to spare. The subject matter is furnished by the ambition to get deaneries, canonries, abbacies, bishoprics. One would imagine that not only the interested candidates were wide awake early every morning to take a survey of the situation, but that their fathers, their mothers (especially the fathers and mothers of baby candidates), all their brothers and all their sisters were taking in bulletins every day of the likely demise, the imminent death, the unhappy convalescence, the lucky departure at last, of bishop, canon, abbot, of all the enviable prebendaries visible betwixt the rising and the setting sun. Now it is not the post, the place, the duty, the vocation, that are thought of in the least. It is only the revenues. Sometimes there is a miscalculation, and the petition of the candidate or his supporter has arrived in Rome before the incumbent is actually dead. And stationery, ink, and patronage are lost.

Candidates for the episcopacy who write for themselves are not a rarity. One Englishman, Barclay, resident in France, represents how important it is that an Englishman, who has made such sacrifices for the cause of religion in his native land—or rather whose father has done so—should now be appointed to the bishopric of Toul. Incidentally it transpires that he himself is the person thought of in that connection. But he wishes to say that he is not going to curry favor with the French court by buying up the court-ladies all round. Not he! He wishes that "all the glory of his elevation shall redound to the honor of the Holy Father exclusively." (This, of course, would be a less expensive proceeding than buying up the ladies.) Meanwhile, others come in, or they are covered by those (presumably the lady-courtiers) who come in for them. The assiduity of the Englishman is charming. His letters lie through the tomes, like a line of advance pickets—until there is silence. Somebody else has got it. Other bishoprics heave in sight; but the sprightliness of his ingenuity is gone. The last time when he appears over the horizon is when he announces in a letter, somewhat alarming for its tone of stern energy, that he is on his way to Rome to recover enormous damages from a certain bishop, and from "a powerful religious Order," whichever that may be.

With such a system of court-patronage prevailing, the embarrassment in Rome is naturally extreme. When there is such a clamor all round, and all notoriously are interested, who is the man to appoint? Then a queen intervenes, or a king signifies his likings, and political relations are not to be despised. There are not wanting grave admonitions, which the supreme authority of the Church directs shall be given, but in diplomatic style, to some crowned head or other; conveying what in plain terms means that it is none of his or her business, why such or such a person was appointed rather than some favorite, and that the *momenta rationum* belong to the secrets of the Pope's conscience. These royal people may ask for preachers; they may ask for confessors; even the horrors of abbacies given *in commendam* may pass, because in its origin that was a salutary institution. But to manoeuvre the bishoprics in behalf of men who only mind court levees or political concerns, and are first and last gallant gentlemen, that is just a little way beyond the reach of the royal prerogative.

An individual cries out to the Cardinal Secretary of State: "The abbacy of Santon is vacant! I am not known to your Eminence." And he soon after confesses that he does not know the abbey either, never having had anything special to do with it. But he continues: "The abbacy is due to me *ex justitia.*" And he excogitates the title of justice. Then he urges all haste, for "others are now working through their *fattori [agents]* to get it

for themselves." Another, who describes himself as a very great
lector, demands an abbacy for his pains, past, present and future
—the future being especially in the service of His Eminence. It
is noteworthy, how the adulation of this and other classes of
men plays upon the chord, "the exaltation of Your Eminence,"
hoping that there is a response in his inner heart to so delicate
a suggestion of his becoming Pope some day.

But why talk about abbacies, or bishoprics, deaneries, canonries, or the post of preacher during Lent in some cathedral of
distinction? It is within the range of some folk to pick off the
cardinalate itself. An amiable fool of a lay-brother writes to the
Pope, recommending the unnamed bearer of his letter. This
bearer is a man engaged in profound researches for the philosopher's stone. His Holiness has only now to advance him to the
dignity of Cardinal, and then the said investigator for the
philosopher's stone, having become a Cardinal, will render unnamed services to the Holy See—when he has found the stone.
Besides that, he will also do the pleasant writer himself a service
by saving him from the tyranny of his superiors, who at present
make his life very hard!

Here is the field for the attempted exploiting of cabals and
their programs; on the principle, doubtless, so familiar to agita-
tors, that if they can only get the right ear from the beginning
and keep it, they possess the key to the situation. If these restless
people had ever conceived in their wildest flight of thought, that
their papers would stand exposed on the table of students in a
public hall, under the light of the nineteenth and twentieth
centuries, how many a cabal would have been still-born! A
clique in Tuscany, laying its train, wants Cardinal Panzirolo to
illuminate it with the smile of his favor, by pushing in their
candidate at the impending election for a General, and then
they say with a gush of abject devotion: "Your Eminence will
be absolute *padrone* of him." The generalate of Religious Orders
was quite a favorite object of ambition with the noble cousins,

brothers, uncles and perhaps aunts, of likely subjects; and, in this as in other equally worthy causes, a stereotyped argument was that of the Cardinal's commanding the future services of the fortunate creature, and being henceforth "absolute *padrone*" of the same.

It is altogether certain that some men had missed their vocation. Here is one who should have been a Yankee traveling agent on an American railroad. He is about to dedicate a book to His Holiness. He narrates how, being a man now of forty-five years' standing in his profession, he has come to understand St. Thomas. No one else in creation has ever yet understood him. He knows it all now; there is no mistake about it. And he just tantalizes the Pope by sketching the title-page, in which the inspiring idea is grovelling flattery of His Holiness. It would be passable, if the attempted sketch were, I do not say pretty, but barely decent. As it stands, it would not do credit to a schoolboy of only ten years' standing in the world of breathing things.

There is many a document of the style called memorials; many a narrative told of current events, of wars and intrigues; many a practical question expounded in theology or canon law. It sounds like an echo of our time, when a memorialist, writing from Germany in 1655, speaks at some length on behalf of Protestant pastors and preachers who wish to become Catholics, but whose conscience is checked by the insuperable objection of having a wife and children, and no prospective means of living, if they submit to the Church. The memorialist suggests a kindly remedy, that of providing a relief fund for the maintenance of the newly converted. Probably the question was left just where it stands today, and where God placed it; that He has a right to demand the sacrifice of all and of everything on the part of those who want Him. Another memorialist offers an ample scheme, which he begs the Pope to keep strictly to himself. It is a political program, which might be described as feudal-democratic-paternal-universal, subjugating the whole civil-

ized world to the Holy See by a system very like the modern
"armed peace" of Europe, but with several important variations.
The Pope is to be the center; he will have Cardinals placed in
each of the great cities of the world; all kingdoms will be held
by some kind of feudal tenure. But there is a democratic cast
somehow on the affair; and the powerful government at Rome,
while being of the paternal kind, will have at command the
armed force of all against each, if any part thinks of rebelling
against the central authority. The memorialist naively observes
that hereby the principle of authority will be preserved along
with that of force.

As interesting a circumstance as any, in the history of documents, is the fate which awaits them. There they lie. And there
they have lain, so many of them, since the day they were received.
To be sure, the greater number were acknowledged. Many
among them have not only the endorsement, including a sum-
mary of their contents, but likewise a note of the answer to be
given. Many others must have been simply ignored. For instance,
the summarist writes: "N. N. to His Holiness about Padre N. N.
He says that the Padre is a saint; that he always knew that the
Padre was a saint; *ed altre semplicità*." Many are endorsed:
"Postpone answering." Others of greater consequence: "Keep the
letter till further instance be made." When a note like this appears on an important epistle from the faculty of Louvain, containing an urgent appeal for the defence of their privileges, one
feels in the light of other correspondence which is going on at
the same time, that the Pope will use their claim for defence as a
lever against themselves, against the Baianism, Erasmianism and
other little peccadilloes which are giving him concern in the
management of that great institution.

A Greek letter comes from a schismatic Bishop, recommending a certain missionary for a bishopric in Tartary. The Pope
refers the matter to a Monsignore, who answers that he will
examine the antecedents of the affair. Then comes a pretty

exposure. It appears that the gentleman proposed had been involved in political intrigues in Tartary, and had made the place somewhat hot for himself; that recently, when he was back in Europe, and stayed awhile in Rome, he had been noticed here as going about with all the airs and ways of rather a fast secular, with little or nothing of the ecclesiastic about him; that formerly he had worked other wires to get himself appointed bishop; finally, concludes the secretary, this would seem to be only the old plan under a new guise.

The smooth Jansenist, Antoine Arnauld, comes forward from time to time, smooth and sleek, with all the humble and sweet devotion of a devout Catholic. He presents to the Pontiff his *Perpétuité de la Foi*. But never a word about Jansenism; though the tomes are just teeming with collateral accounts of what is going on in France, thanks to Antoine Arnauld and his clever little clique.

The gist of many an important principle is given in a note, either endorsed as the immediate answer of the Holy Father, or reported from some quarter to which he has referred it: "To Salamanca. The favor asked for by the Chapter cannot be granted, since the case expounded does not concern the necessities or utility of the Church, as is necessary, but only the interest of a private family." To a petition from France, that the King's gift of a certain abbey *in commendam* may be confirmed in favor of a secular abbé, this principle is laid down as the basis of the reply: "The said abbey could be committed *in commendam* only in case the buildings were in a state of ruin, and then only for the purpose of restoring them; or in case the goods had been alienated, and then for the purpose of recovering them; and, even so, it could not be done without the consent of the Abbot General, along with an authentic attestation of the state of ruin into which the property had lapsed." Soon after appears a forcible remonstrance from the Abbot General of the Cistercians, detailing the untold evils into which the abuse of the *commendam* had sunk the monasteries of his Order. Since those times Divine Providence has so arranged that the titles and revenues of abbeys and monasteries go no longer into the pockets of courtiers, who sucked out the very life-blood of the Orders, and bloated themselves in luxury and dissipation.

However, we must not rest under the impression that there is nothing pleasant and edifying among so much that is weighty and distressing.

Sister Gonzaga writes from time to time about the beatification and canonization of her dear uncle, Luigi (Aloysius). The whole line of Visitation convents comes forth, on special invitation from Rome, asking for the canonization of St. Francis de Sales, and then thanking the Holy Father afterwards. The relations previously existing between the former Nuncio, now elected Pope, and his friends, are far from being broken off by his elevation. The physician asks about his health. Some maternal duchess or queen loves to say a word to her old friend. Two seasons are specially prolific in this respectful or affectionate correspondence, which shows the great figure of the Vicar of Christ on his human side; the first, just after his election; and, secondly, every year at Christmas time. And no one seems beneath his kindly regard. He answers the humble nun in her convent; his old confessor, who has scarcely ventured to write; or a devout friend, who is suffering under some affliction. He is the father of all, and his supernatural dignity is thrown out into splendid relief in the reverence, devotion, affection, without flattery, that rises towards his throne from the Christian hearts of the faithful all over the world.

But perhaps these are specimens enough of the by-play in the great historical drama that unfolds amid the archives of the Vatican Palace.

—*The Plurality of Worlds and Other Essays.*

MY FRIEND CIPOLLA

❧ ONE MORNING in the great piazza of Saint Peter's I found that one may cross the chasm with a glance. I have thought of writing a story about that glance. It would be based on a chance encounter with a little humped man who caught my eye as I lowered it from what I took to be the outline of the roof of the Appartamento Borgia: a passing revival of my old interest in Savonarola, who, as we all know, was the Borgia's greatest enemy in Florence. I might easily have snubbed this strange-looking figure, but God had sent him, and it was not to be. I answered his polite query truthfully. He said, throwing out his fly on my stream of consciousness: "You know Michelangelo's portrait of Savonarola?" In surprise I said that I did not. When he offered to show it to me, saying it was in the Sistine Chapel, I knew he was an unofficial guide, and unjustly decided that he was a fraud as well, for I knew, or I thought I did, that there was no portrait in the Sistine Chapel. It turned out that he was quite right. There is a little *ritratto* of Savonarola tucked away in the bottom left-hand corner of the Last Judgment.

Having nothing better to do, and glad to talk to somebody, and willing to look at the Sistine ceiling again, I let him lead me away around the streets, as one must now do, to the Vatican Museum. In two minutes I realized that he was as mad as a March hare. His name was Cipolla. He was not in the least interested in the Sistine Chapel nor did he afterwards once mention it. I think now it must have been he who put into my head the fancy, which I have already thrown out, of the scholar who visits Rome for a holiday and is lost for ever down its catacombs of history and archaeology. (Have I mentioned that if all the passages of the catacombs were put end to end they would reach from Venice to Sicily? Cipolla had reached about as far as Calabria.) His pet theory was that the cradle of Aryan Adam is not where men usually place it, somewhere about buried Samarkand, north of the Hindu Kush, but in Asia Minor among the Galatians; a theory much to my taste, since the Galatians were Celts. On this he talked volubly. Of the Sistine Chapel he talked not at all. The result was that our perambulation paused three times at pubs, where he traced with a dirty finger in spilt beer the vagrant growth of Western civilization. In my fiction we should have gone arguing from pub to pub until nightfall—I would call the story "Why I never saw the Sistine Chapel"—and under the moon put an end to all wars in the Common Fatherhood of Man: his phrase. Or was it his? For, though I shall not be believed, I had earlier met another Italian who believed that all Europe sprang from a common Ligurian source. I can give this man's name also, Tombolini; he has written a large book on our Ligurian origins, and been decorated for it by King Umberto. And only last week I read a learned article about the secret sales of pottery made to archaeologists in Pisa by peasants from Monte-pulciano. The theme of that writer was the Etruscan origin of all Western civilization.

Now and again, in between the Galatians and Civilization, my dear lunatic talked also of the vast wealth of the Vatican with the inevitable cynicism of all Italians no matter what the subject, and most of all inevitable when the Church is in question.

"But," I said, "surely the Church must be poor nowadays? With all those countries that have been overrun by war or absorbed by Communism?"

He spread his hands, and gazed at me as if it were I who was mad.

"Consider," he reminded me, "the amount of food and money the Church is distributing in relief. Relief sent from all over the world. It is largesse. The poor have become more than ever dependent on the Church."

"Yes," I remembered with pride. "We in Ireland sent what we could. Sugar, I believe. And wheat."

"The Vatican makes a good profit on all that," he smiled, making the curious Italian gesture of placing the left of the thumb of the right hand to the right side of his temple and drawing it slowly downward with a cunning smile.

"Profit!" I cried. "But it was sent gratis!"

"Aha! Gratis! Yes! But there are certain *expenses* attach to distribution!"

I shrugged. He enlarged, annoyed by my incredulity.

"But I assure you that the Vatican is *very* rich. It has investments in businesses all over the world. Religious Orders and the faithful all over the world invest in the Vatican Bank—which pays a fine dividend—indirectly, through these businesses. Oh!" he forestalled my objections, "the Church does not go into business directly, you may be sure! It gets wealthy business-men in Belgium or America to work for it. It never takes on a whole business. Perhaps half, perhaps a quarter. These people"—waving his hands madly towards the Vatican, and evoking a picture of rows and rows of cardinals bent over ancient ledgers, large as the Domesday Book, fat as the Borgias—"are *splendid* business-men! They are at it *all day long!* They are *excellent* men of affairs. What would you expect? They've been at it for nearly two thousand years! Ah!" he groaned, back to his Galatians, "if I only had a few thousand lire to complete my studies! I need so little! A few hundred thousand lire! But would *they* give it to me? If I could undertake a *scavazione* in Hierapolis. . . ."

For a while I listened, deeply puzzled. Then I interrupted him.

He was at the moment in the middle of an attack on Communism.

"You *are* a Catholic?" I asked.

He looked at me, a little coldly.

"Naturalmente!" He resumed: "These *scum,* who are destroying Christianity. . . ."

As I listened to him a great glow of joy spread through me. It was as if the heavens had parted and a voice had come from a soft heart of light, rosy-colored and mothering, to explain to me something whose obduracy had troubled me all my life, without my knowing, indeed, what it was that so long oppressed me. The Voice said: "Now thou knowest why so many Catholics are such tiresome people." This man was a Catholic, and he was not at all tiresome. He was most engaging. But he was a sort of Catholic I had never met before. He was the first Catholic I had ever talked to about religion who eluded Gibbon's theory for the Roman toleration of the Jews as contrasted with their prosecution of the Christians: namely, that the Jews were a *nation* and therefore entitled to their own odd religious beliefs, but the Christians, being Romans, could only be regarded as a *sect.* Signor Cipolla escaped the impeachment completely. So, I realized, do most Italians. The discovery was to alter my whole life.

Elsewhere—I will qualify this presently for Ireland—it is the misery of Catholics to be still regarded as the ancient Romans regarded the early Christians, a body of people who can never be entirely trusted, since their higher loyalties, as with Communists, pass the bounds of country; as, indeed, they do and should do. This breeds in Catholics outside Italy a defensive or "on guard" mentality which prevents their religion from being as unselfconscious as their nationality. Whereas, in Italy, if faith and fatherland are not absolutely identical they come as close to it as is humanly possible. This dear dotty Signor Cipolla was the first Catholic I had talked to who had not the outlook of a sectarian. That he was a little dotty added to the wonder of the discovery in the amazement of his liberty: a man whose intellect (such as it was) had sold itself neither to his race nor to his religion, as his Asiatic theory on the one hand and his anticlericalism on the other showed. He was an Italian and a Roman and a Catholic and a sceptic and a citizen of the world, and yet he was unaware of any of these things, being all of them simultaneously and instinctively. In no other one of the three countries in which I have lived for any length of time, Ireland, England or America, have I found religion so limber and so light-hearted. I had never conceived that it could be so. I fell in love with it on the spot. I desired to possess it immediately; so much so that had Signor Cipolla been a handsome young woman instead of a crochety old man of seventy my desires might have wandered somewhat from their true object.

One might imagine that I would have met many Signor Cipollas in Ireland; and Ireland should, one might also think, being a nation mainly composed of Catholics, be as free of sectarianism as Italy, and one day I trust she will be. Unhappily the hang-over from the centuries when Catholicism was a persecuted sect—something as alien to the British Empire as Christianity was to the Roman Empire—keeps the defensive sectarian mind alive amongst us long after what bred it has passed; just as the oppression of our nationalism has made that, too, nervy and sensitive. The result is that intellectual liberty is still almost unknown in Ireland. In England things are a little better. There Catholics are in a minority, and that minority has been politically suspect since the days of Queen Elizabeth, but they are given every liberty by the majority, if only for the same reason that Christians in the provinces of the Roman empire often had an easy time under some tolerant proconsul like Gallio: they might kick nobody in the belly, but nobody might kick them in the belly either. Gallio was tolerant to Saint Paul because he did not care. But minorities naturally form cliques, and cliques, inevitably, lay tremendous stress on loyalties, and loyalties are inevitably touchy about criticism. There are no Catholic anti-clericals in Britain. And nobody can be a sound Catholic who cannot be, if he wants to be, a sound anti-clerical. It is his self-assurance of an inmost and unassailable core of Faith. All the Catholics I had hitherto known or known of in Ireland or England had either had a chip on the shoulder (Mr. Evelyn Waugh), developed complexes (Mr. Graham Greene), been controversialists (Mr. Arnold Lunn), been terrified rigorists (the type illlustrated by our Irish Censorship), or lived in a hallucinatory blue funk (anti-Communists in Connemara). The one type I had not met in these Saxon or Celtic countries was the type who, like old Cipolla, took his Catholicism as mildly and naturally as breathing.

Dear Signor Cipolla, I salute you. You are as legion as your race. And yet, I had never known you existed until we sat in that pub under the Vatican walls, which you both defended and assailed with so much gusto, and with your finger wandering in the beer-stains all unknowingly drew my line of fate.

He was still talking when we sat in the benches of the Sistine Chapel. But, gradually, the old man's voice became drowsy, and when he said, "Lean back and look up" (as all the other tourists were doing) he leaned back and fell sound asleep. I saw, then, not so much Michelangelo's God the Father sending the electricity of life along his finger into Adam as a vast procession of men, not all Italians, for whom Christianity was less a creed than the color of life itself, inconceivable in any other coloring, and as completely unlimited, untrammelled and unaware as a wave, or the wind, or a tree.

Cipolla slept on. I pushed a thousand-lire note into his pocket and stole away. It was still not noon; one begins one's sightseeing early in Rome to avoid the great heat of the zenith. I motored back to Saint Peter's, for I was by now in a fever of haste. That great village, for it is more like a village or a small town than a church, was conducting its usual variety of affairs in its various

market-places. A long file of Calabrian pilgrims were entering
its hollow halls, their wailing voices rising and falling in a
strange, unearthly, flesh-creeping hymn that went echoing about
the dome like a banshee. A stout cardinal led them to a side-altar
to pray, stoutly, in shouting unison. Tourists wandered to and
fro. The usual guides ushered the usual groups in the aisles.
Americans looked up from the Baedekers or Murrays in secular
curiosity or clicked cameras behind pillars. Friends chatted. A
mass was being said in one of the transepts. In the same transept
a dozen confessionals were busy, each indicating, on a plaque outside, the language in which one could confess—French, English,
Polish, Hungarian, German, Italian, Czechoslovakian, all the
tongues of Babel. Outside each confessional a slim wand is fixed
like a little fishing-rod, and as each penitent emerges he, or she,
kneels outside the priest's compartment, a hand comes out, lifts
the rod from its fixture and taps the forgiven sinner on the
shoulder.

   I thought with emotion of my dear anti-clerical friend, now
sleeping softly in the Sistine. My one wish was to become one
with him in Christ. But it was more years than I cared to count
since I had been to confession, and how could I ever explain to
a confessor the reason why. A French priest, an Italian, indeed
any priest of these hidden confessors, with conched hand to ear,
would understand all the usual stories, be bored to yawning by
them. Women? That would cause no trouble to either of us.
It would be so normal as to be almost a relief. Theft? I would
be asked how much and bade to make restitution. The sin of
Simon Magus? Since the sinner was returned that would thereby
be all over. These things would pass lightly. They were the
worn coins of sin. But mine? I looked longingly at the Czechoslovakian confessional and wished I knew the language. He
would understand. A Hungarian priest would understand. Best
of all a Spaniard; even an Italian would do, and under pretence
of reading a prayer-book I covertly consulted my dictionary.

Ragione politica? But he might think I was an anarchist or a communist. . . . Regretfully I decided that my Italian was not good enough. An English priest?

"You see—" I rehearsed, while the Calabrians howled the responses a quarter of a mile away, and the bell tinkled on the altar, a band of sun crept down from miles high, and the penitents came and went, a girl grinning back at her lover, a boy coming out with a smile of contentment—"you see Father, when we took up arms to defend the Republic the Church pronounced us virtually excommunicate."

The good priest, possibly from Bury-Saint-Edmunds, perhaps a convert Wykehamist, probably a mild paleographer, would peer at me in astonishment. He might think hastily of the Spanish Civil War; or it might occur to him that I am a Mosleyite. For what could he possibly know about the intricacies of Irish revolutionary politics? The whole thing suddenly seemed silly and embarrassing. Suppose he said, "What Republic?" How could I explain that there wasn't really any Republic at all; it was something Mr. de Valera had thought up with a lot of distinctions with *de jure* and *de facto*. No Englishman could sympathize with nonsense like that. And yet, if only in sheer courtesy, I must give some explanation. I wondered had he ever heard of the Fenians? I wished that even my grandfather had been a Fenian, but all I knew about him was that he drank himself out of a farm in County Limerick. Impulsively, I shoved myself by main force into the empty compartment, deciding to talk in broken English like a foreigner.

He drew the slide. As soon as his voice whispered to me I knew I was sunk. It was rich with the buttermilk of County Limerick. The sweat broke out on me. This man would know *all* about the Republic. He would take the side of the Bishops, as in duty bound. Or else he would say something like:

"Yerrah, for goodness' sake? And what Brigade was that now? The First Cork? Sure, don't I know Tommy Barry as well as I know my own hand?"

And we would become so pally that I would sweat again with shame to have to tell him my tale. When he actually said, in a rapid, soft and gentle voice, was this:

"Well, now, I suppose all the usual sins since then? Women and drink and no mass and bad language and dirty stories and all the rest of it? Ah, well! My poor child! God has been very patient with you. Say three Hail Marys now. And God bless you."

And I was hardly through the Contrition before his hand lifted in the Absolvo te . . . and the slide drew. I came out of the confessional trembling with fury. Three miserable, miserly, paltry Hail Marys! After years of defiance! The thing was fantastic! I fumed at the humiliation of it! Under the vast dome, in that great town of Saint Peter's, I felt as minute as a Lilliputian. And then I realized the infinite kindness of the man and I was overcome with emotion.

The bell tinkled. A woman kneeling on the marble beside me fluttered her fan under her face and breathed out a loving "O Vivo pan del Ciel." Out of the corner of my eye I saw the girl whom I had seen grinning back at her lover when she entered the box. She was looking at the altar with dilated eyes. In those seconds I knew that I was caught, and caught for ever. I was lost or saved, according as you happen to look at it. People approached the altar. The Light of the World became flesh of their flesh, I was present at the greatest drama in all the world, in all eternity. *Ecce Agnus Dei.* . . .

As I stood in the too-great heat and brilliance of noon on the steps before the portico I looked about me for Signor Cipolla— it was he who had done this to me—with a simultaneous desire to embrace him and to put my toe under his behind. The little dark figures made the piazza into a plain. He was a grain of sand. He was a drop of rain. I would never see him again. I shall always remember him with affection. The obelisk cast no shadow. From a pedlar I bought a rosary. A carozza was un-burthening itself of three American soldiers. I took it and bade the cabby drive to the Janiculum. As we passed the Garibaldi monument he lifted his whip.

"See," he grinned, "he looks always defiantly towards the Vatican!"

I looked up at the old bearded guerrilla in his roundy hat glaring sideways at Saint Peter's. Then I looked at the cabby.

"You are a Catholic?" I asked him.

He seemed aggrieved at the question.

"Naturalmente!"

We climbed out and leaned over the balustrade and surveyed the roofs of Rome over which the heated air formed a quivering mirage like steam or water. The cabby started to talk. I did not listen. As I looked I was murmuring under my breath the words "Civis Romanus sum." By degrees I gathered that the voice beside me was simultaneously glorifying Garibaldi, talking of the wealth of the Vatican and denouncing the Communists. Below us in the valley a bell tolled softly. Then another. The deep notes and the little notes tolled out the Angelus. The cabby paused in his flow. I glanced sideways at him. A far-off look passed over his eyes like a cloud and I knew that he was murmuring a prayer.

"But," he resumed like a torrent, "they make *millions* of lire! I, myself, I have a cousin who knows, for a fact, that. . . ."

I threw in an occasional "Si! Si!" for politeness' sake. The scene spread far beyond the pallid hills; far over Italy and far beyond it; as far as thought can reach. To myself I said: "I have left a nation and joined an empire." As to what kind of empire . . . I thought of John Henry Newman's—"a vast and ever-growing imperial Church great enough to make flaws and imperfections of no account." A bit strong, that; a bit too off-the-earth; a little bit too philosophical. Poor old Savonarola would have frothed at this bland reference to "flaws and imperfections." Yet, Newman was essentially right. Imperfect in an imperfect world. Should it not be said honestly, though, when the imperfections

showed? Bloy, Péguy and Bernanos would say so. J. H. N. could
not: the convert with his back to the wall. I spread my hands.
The cabby thought I was being sceptical.

"But my own cousin told me," he cried. . . .

"I once met a bishop in a railway train," I said, "who believed
that the three marks of the Church should be that she be poor,
unprivileged and free. I disagree. She should be immune; an
immunitas—Lord Acton's word; privileged on every count and
exempt on every count; an enclave recognized by all men as
something separated from this fleshly world. She should therefore be celestial; that is she should have to do only with the
heavenly order, and though she must, since this is the world
and not the otherworld, have to do with temporal things she
should employ no temporal weapons. Whenever she does she
is in danger of becoming a tyrant and a bully. She should be
rich, the richest of all mortal institutions, so that she should be
able to influence the thoughts of men by all these same things,
and more, with which the universities of the world influence
civilized men. In fact, as universities should be immune, rich
and profane she should differ only by being immune, rich and
sacred, so that the world should be content to judge her by
two worldly tests—that she did not meddle with temporal things
and was never vulgar. As to her celestial work nobody could
judge that but herself and heaven. People would say to that,
of course, that her wealth would corrupt her. Wealth is less
corrupting, by far, than poverty, and less, too, than power; and
what has ever corrupted the Church but power? Make her
celestial, immune and rich and she will have no power but the
power of heaven and of the intelligence."

The cabby looked at me miserably. He naturally did not know
what I was talking about. I said:

"Let's have a beer."

He understood that.

—A Summer in Italy.

II

Painters and Pilgrims

NEWS of the Vatican has always been of prime interest, whether it was conveyed in the Fugger Newsletters, or in the dispatches of the Venetian Ambassador, or sent around the world in thirty languages by Vatican Radio. Ellery Sedgwick recalls the incident (though he would not tell it on oath) that Frank Munsey, in the most saffron era of yellow journalism, "cabled the Pope direct, setting forth the influence of Munsey's Magazine and inviting the Holy Father to contribute a paper on 'Home Life in the Vatican' and to put snap into it."

This section of the book plays back voices from many centuries: some friendly, some self-seeking, some content to find the Papacy named in the bizzare metaphors of the Apocalypse. Here are the Renaissance men who helped build the City, the painters who spread their empery of color through its buildings, the historians and novelists who wrote under the Roman proscenium. Here are Romantics of the Grand Tour, whose thronging coaches and levees made the Piazza di Spagna as English as Mayfair. Finally there are the Americans, who might be raucous backwoodsmen out of Chuzzlewit or as devout as any medieval penitent.

BENVENUTO DEFENDS THE CITY

THE WHOLE WORLD was now in warfare. Pope Clement had sent to get some troops from Giovanni de' Medici, and when they came, they made such disturbances in Rome, that it was ill living in open shops. On this account I retired to a good snug house behind the Banchi, where I worked for all the friends I had acquired. Since I produced few things of much importance at that period, I need not waste time talking about them. I took much pleasure in music and amusements of the kind. On the death of Giovanni de' Medici in Lombardy, the Pope, at the advice of Messer Jacopo Salviati, dismissed the five bands he had engaged; and when the Constable of Bourbon knew there were no troops in Rome, he pushed his army with the utmost energy up to the city. The whole of Rome upon this flew to arms. I happened to be intimate with Alessandro, the son of Piero del Bene, who, at the time when the Colonnesi entered Rome, had requested me to guard his palace. On this more serious occasion, therefore, he prayed me to enlist fifty comrades for the protection of the said house, appointing me their captain, as I had been when the Colonnesi came. So I collected fifty young men of the highest courage, and we took up our quarters in his palace, with good pay and excellent appointments.

Bourbon's army had now arrived before the walls of Rome, and Alessandro begged me to go with him to reconnoitre. So we went with one of the stoutest fellows in our Company; and on the way a youth called Cecchino della Casa joined himself to us. On reaching the walls by the Campo Santo, we could see that famous army, which was making every effort to enter the town. Upon the ramparts where we took our station several young men were lying killed by the besiegers; the battle raged there desperately, and there was the densest fog imaginable. I turned to Alessandro and said: "Let us go home as soon as we can, for there is nothing to be done here; you see the enemies are mounting, and our men are in flight." Alessandro, in a panic, cried: "Would God that we had never come here!" and turned in maddest haste to fly. I took him up somewhat sharply with these words: "Since you have brought me here, I must perform some action worthy of a man"; and directing my arquebuse where I saw the thickest and most serried troop of fighting men, I aimed exactly at one whom I remarked to be higher than the rest; the fog prevented me from being certain whether he was on horseback or on foot. Then I turned to Alessandro and Cecchino, and bade them discharge their arquebuses, showing them how to avoid being hit by the besiegers. When we had fired two rounds apiece, I crept cautiously up to the wall, and observing among the enemy a most extraordinary confusion, I discovered afterwards that one of our shots had killed the Constable of Bourbon; and from what I subsequently learned, he was the man whom I had first noticed above the heads of the rest.

Quitting our position on the ramparts, we crossed the Campo Santo, and entered the city by St. Peter's; then coming out exactly at the church of Santo Angelo, we got with the greatest difficulty to the great castle; for the generals Renzo di Cier and Orazio Baglioni were wounding and slaughtering everybody who abandoned the defence of the walls. By the time we had reached the great gate, part of the foemen had already entered Rome, and we had them in our rear. The castellan had ordered the portcullis to be lowered, in order to do which they cleared a little space, and this enabled us four to get inside. On the instant that I entered, the captain Pallone de' Medici claimed me as being of the Papal household, and forced me to abandon Alessandro, which I had to do, much against my will. I ascended to the keep, and at the same instant Pope Clement came in through the corridors into the castle; he had refused to leave the palace of St. Peter earlier, being unable to believe that his enemies would effect their entrance into Rome.

Having got into the castle in this way, I attached myself to certain pieces of artillery, which were under the command of a bombardier called Giuliano Fiorentino. Leaning there against the battlements, the unhappy man could see his poor house being sacked, and his wife and children outraged; fearing to strike his own folk, he dared not discharge the cannon, and flinging the burning fuse upon the ground, he wept as though his heart would break, and tore his cheeks with both his hands. Some of the other bombardiers were behaving in like manner; seeing which, I took one of the matches, and got the assistance of a few men who were not overcome by their emotions. I aimed some swivels and falconets at points where I saw it would be useful, and killed with them a good number of the enemy. Had it not been for this, the troops who poured into Rome that morning, and were marching straight upon the castle, might possibly have entered it with ease, because the artillery was doing them no damage. I went on firing under the eyes of several cardinals and lords, who kept blessing me and giving me the heartiest encouragement. In my enthusiasm I strove to achieve the impossible; let it suffice that it was I who saved the castle that morning, and brought the other bombardiers back to their duty. I worked hard the whole of that day; and when the evening came, while the army was marching into Rome through the Trastevere, Pope Clement appointed a great Roman nobleman named Antonio Santacroce to be captain of all the gunners.

The first thing this man did was to come to me, and having greeted me with the utmost kindness, he stationed me with five

fine pieces of artillery on the highest point of the castle, to which
the name of the Angel specially belongs. This circular eminence
goes round the castle, and surveys both Prati and the town of
Rome. The captain put under my orders enough men to help in
managing my guns, and having seen me paid in advance, he gave
me rations of bread and a little wine, and begged me to go forward
as I had begun. I was perhaps more inclined by nature to the
profession of arms than to the one I had adopted, and I took
such pleasure in its duties that I discharged them better than
those of my own art. Night came, the enemy had entered Rome,
and we who were in the castle (especially myself, who have
always taken pleasure in extraordinary sights) stayed gazing on
the indescribable scene of tumult and conflagration in the
streets below. People who were anywhere else but where we were,
could not have formed the least imagination of what it was. I
will not, however, set myself to describe that tragedy, but will
content myself with continuing the history of my own life and
the circumstances which properly belong to it.

During the course of my artillery practice, which I never
intermitted though the whole month passed by us beleaguered
in the castle, I met with a great many very striking accidents,
all of them worthy to be related. But since I do not care to be
too prolix, or to exhibit myself outside the sphere of my profession, I will omit the larger part of them, only touching upon
those I cannot well neglect, which shall be the fewest in number
and the most remarkable. The first which comes to hand is this:
Messer Antonio Santacroce had made me come down from the
Angel, in order to fire on some houses in the neighborhood, where
certain of our besiegers had been seen to enter. While I was
firing, a cannon shot reached me, which hit the angle of a
battlement, and carried off enough of it to be the cause why I
sustained no injury. The whole mass struck me in the chest and
took my breath away. I lay stretched upon the ground like a
dead man, and could hear what the bystanders were saying.

Among them all, Messer Antonio Santacroce lamented greatly, exclaiming: "Alas, alas! we have lost the best defender that we had!" Attracted by the uproar, one of my comrades ran up; he was called Gianfrancesco, and was a bandsman, but was far more naturally given to medicine than to music. On the spot he flew off, crying for a stoop of the very best Greek wine. Then he made a tile red-hot, and cast upon it a good handful of wormwood; after which he sprinkled the Greek wine, and when the wormwood was well soaked, he laid it on my breast, just where the bruise was visible to all. Such was the virtue of the wormwood that I immediately regained my scattered faculties. I wanted to begin to speak, but could not; for some stupid soldiers had filled my mouth with earth, imagining that by so doing they were giving me the sacrament; and indeed they were more like to have excommunicated me, since I could with difficulty come to myself again, the earth doing me more mischief than the blow. However, I escaped that danger, and returned to the rage and fury of the guns, pursuing my work there with all the ability and eagerness that I could summon.

Pope Clement, by this, had sent to demand assistance from the Duke of Urbino, who was with the troops of Venice; he commissioned the envoy to tell his Excellency that the Castle of S. Angelo would send up every evening three beacons from its summit accompanied by three discharges of the cannon thrice repeated, and that so long as this signal was continued, he might take for granted that the castle had not yielded. I was charged with lighting the beacons and firing the guns for this purpose; and all this while I pointed my artillery by day upon the places where mischief could be done. The Pope, in consequence, began to regard me with still greater favor, because he saw that I discharged my functions as intelligently as the task demanded. Aid from the Duke of Urbino never came; on which, as it is not my business, I will make no further comment.

While I was at work upon that diabolical task of mine, there came from time to time to watch me some of the cardinals who were invested in the castle; and most frequently the Cardinal of Ravenna and the Cardinal de' Gaddi. I often told them not to show themselves, since their nasty red caps gave a fair mark to our enemies. From neighboring buildings, such as the Torre de' Bini, we ran great peril when they were there; and at last I had them locked off, and gained thereby their deep ill-will. I frequently received visits also from the general, Orazio Baglioni, who was very well affected toward me. One day while he was talking with me, he noticed something going forward in a drinking-place outside the Porta di Castello, which bore the name of Baccanello. This tavern had for sign a sun painted between two windows, of a bright red color. The windows being closed, Signor Orazio concluded that a band of soldiers were carousing at table just between them and behind the sun. So he said to me, "Benvenuto, if you think you could hit that wall an ell's breadth from the sun with your demi-cannon here, I believe you would be doing a good stroke of business, for there is a great commotion there, and men of much importance must probably be inside the house." I answered that I felt quite capable of hitting the sun in its center, but that a barrel full of stones, which was standing close to the muzzle of the gun, might be knocked down by the shock of the discharge and the blast of the artillery. He rejoined: "Don't waste time, Benvenuto. In the first place, it is not possible, where it is standing, that the cannon's blast should bring it down; and even if it were to fall, and the Pope himself was underneath, the mischief would not be so great as you imagine. Fire, then, only fire!" Taking no more thought about it, I struck the sun in the center, exactly as I said I should. The cask was dislodged, as I predicted, and fell precisely between Cardinal Farnese and Messer Jacopo Salviati. It might very well have dashed out the brains of both of them, except that just at that very moment Farnese was reproaching Salviati with having caused the sack of Rome, and while they stood apart from one another to exchange opprobrious remarks, my gabion fell without destroying them.

When he heard the uproar in the court below, good Signor Orazio dashed off in a hurry; and I, thrusting my neck forward where the cask had fallen, heard some people saying: "It would not be a bad job to kill that gunner!" Upon this I turned two falconets toward the staircase, with mind resolved to let blaze on the first man who attempted to come up. The household of Cardinal Farnese must have received orders to go and do me some injury; accordingly I prepared to receive them, with a lighted match in hand. Recognizing some who were approaching, I called out: "You lazy lubbers, if you don't pack off from there, and if but a man's child among you dares to touch the staircase, I have got two cannon loaded, which will blow you into powder. Go and tell the Cardinal that I was acting at the order of superior officers, and that what we have done and are doing is in defence of them priests,[1] and not to hurt them." They made away; and then came Signor Orazio Baglioni, running. I bade him stand back, else I'd murder him; for I knew very well who he was. He drew back a little, not without a certain show of fear, and called out: "Benvenuto, I am your friend!" To this I answered: "Sir, come up, but come alone, and then come as you like." The general, who was a man of mighty pride, stood still a moment, and then said angrily: "I have a good mind not to come up again, and to do quite the opposite of that which I intended toward you." I replied that just as I was put there to defend my neighbors, I was equally well able to defend myself too. He said that he was coming alone; and when he arrived at the top of the stairs, his features were more discomposed than I thought reasonable. So I kept my hand upon my sword, and stood eyeing him askance. Upon this he began to laugh, and the color coming back into his face, he said to me with the most pleasant manner: "Friend Benvenuto, I bear you as great love as I have it in my

[1] *Loro preti.* Perhaps *their priests.*

heart to give; and in God's good time I will render you proof
of this. Would to God you had killed those two rascals; for
one of them is the cause of all this trouble, and the day perchance
will come when the other will be found the cause of something
even worse." He then begged me, if I should be asked, not to
say that he was with me when I fired the gun; and for the rest
bade me be of good cheer. The commotion which the affair
made was enormous, and lasted a long while. However, I will
not enlarge upon it further, only adding that I was within an
inch of revenging my father on Messer Jacopo Salviati, who
had grievously injured him, according to my father's complaints.
As it was, unwittingly I gave the fellow a great fright. Of Farnese
I shall say nothing here, because it will appear in its proper
place how well it would have been if I had killed him.

I pursued my business of artilleryman, and every day performed
some extraordinary feat, whereby the credit and the favor I
acquired with the Pope was something indescribable. There never
passed a day but what I killed one or another of our enemies in
the besieging army. On one occasion the Pope was walking
round the circular keep, when he observed a Spanish Colonel in
the Prati; he recognized the man by certain indications, seeing
that this officer had formerly been in his service; and while he
fixed his eyes on him, he kept talking about him. I, above by the
Angel, knew nothing of all this, but spied a fellow down there,
busying himself about the trenches with a javelin in his hand;
he was dressed entirely in rose-color; and so, studying the worst
that I could do against him, I selected a gerfalcon which I had
at hand; it is a piece of ordnance larger and longer than a swivel,
and about the size of a demi-culverin. This I emptied, and loaded
it again with a good charge of fine powder mixed with the coarser
sort; then I aimed it exactly at the man in red, elevating prodi-
giously, because a piece of that caliber could hardly be expected
to carry true at such a distance. I fired, and hit my man exactly
in the middle. He had trussed his sword in front for swagger,

after a way those Spaniards have, and my ball, when it struck
him, broke upon the blade, and one could see the fellow cut in
two fair halves. The Pope, who was expecting nothing of this
kind, derived great pleasure and amazement from the sight,
both because it seemed to him impossible that one should aim
and hit the mark at such a distance, and also because the man
was cut in two, and he could not comprehend how this should
happen. He sent for me, and asked about it. I explained all the
devices I had used in firing; but told him that why the man was
cut in halves, neither he nor I could know.

—*The Autobiography of Benvenuto Cellini.*

PAINTER TO THE POPE

❧ AT A WORD, the Pontiff was persuaded to employ Michelagnolo [Michael Angelo] on his return in the painting of that Chapel, which had been constructed in the Palace and at the Vatican, in memory of his uncle Pope Sixtus. Bramante and the other rivals of Michelagnolo, thinking they should thus detach him from his Sculpture, in which they saw that he was perfect, and throw him into despair, they being convinced that by compelling him to paint in fresco they should also bring him to exhibit works of less perfection (he having but little experience in that branch of art), and thus prove himself inferior to Raphael. Or even supposing him to succeed in the work, it was almost certain that he would be so much enraged against the Pope as to secure the success of their purpose, which was to rid themselves of his presence.

When Michelagnolo returned to Rome, therefore, he found Julius no longer disposed to have the Tomb finished, but desiring that Michelagnolo should paint the ceiling of the Chapel. This was a great and difficult labor, and our artist, aware of his own inexperience, did all he could to excuse himself from undertaking the work, proposing at the same time that it should be confided to Raphael. But the more he refused the more Pope Julius insisted, impetuous in all his desires, and stimulated by the competitors of Michelagnolo, more especially by Bramante, he was on the point of making a quarrel with our artist, when the latter, finding His Holiness determined, resolved to accept the task. The Pope then ordered Bramante to prepare the scaffolding, which the latter suspended by ropes, perforating the ceiling for that purpose. Seeing this, Michelagnolo inquired of the architect how the holes thus made were to be filled in when the painting should be completed; to which Bramante replied that they would think of that when the time came, and that it could not be done otherwise. But Michelagnolo, perceiving that the architect was either incapable or unfriendly towards himself, went at once to the Pope, whom he assured that such a scaffolding was not the proper one, adding that Bramante did not know how to construct it; and Julius, in the presence of Bramante, replied, that Michelagnolo might construct it himself after his own fashion. The latter then erected his scaffolding on props in such a manner that the walls were not injured, and this method has since been pursued by Bramante and others, who were hereby taught the best way in which preparations for the execution of pictures on ceilings, and other works of the kind could be made. The ropes used by Bramante and which Michelagnolo's construction had rendered needless, the latter gave to the poor carpenter, by whom the scaffolding was rebuilt, and who sold them for a sum which enabled him to make up the dowry of his daughter.

Michelagnolo now began to prepare the cartoons, for the ceilings, His Holiness giving orders to the effect that all the paintings executed on the walls by older masters in the time of Pope Sixtus, should be destroyed, it was furthermore decided that Michelagnolo should receive fifteen thousand ducats for the work, an estimation of its value which was made by Giuliano da Sangallo. But the extent of the work now compelled Michelagnolo to seek assistance; he therefore sent for men to Florence, resolving to prove himself the conqueror of all who had preceded him, and to show modern artists how drawing and painting ought to be done. The circumstances of the case became a stimulus to his exertions, and impelled him forward, not for his own fame

only, but for the welfare of Art also. He had finished the cartoons, but deferred commencing the frescoes until certain of
the Florentine painters who were his friends should arrive in
Rome, partly to decrease his labor by assisting in the execution of
the work, but also in part to show him the processes of fresco-
painting, wherein some of them were well-experienced. Among
these artists were Granacci, Giuliano Bugiardini, Jacopo di
Sandro and the elder Indaco, with Agnolo da Donnino, and
Aristotile da Sangallo.

These masters having reached the city, the work was begun,
and Michelagnolo caused them to paint a portion by way of
specimen, but what they had done was far from approaching his
expectations or fulfilling his purpose, and one morning he determined to destroy the whole of it. He then shut himself up in
the chapel, and not only would he never again permit the building to be opened to them, but he likewise refused to see any one
of them at his house. Finally therefore, and when the jest
appeared to them to be carried too far, they returned, ashamed
and mortified, to Florence. Michelagnolo then made arrangements for performing the whole work himself, sparing no care
nor labor, in the hope of bringing the same to a satisfactory
termination, nor would he ever permit himself to be seen, lest
he should give occasion for a request to show the work; wherefore
there daily arose, in the minds of all around him, a more and more
earnest desire to behold it. Now Pope Julius always greatly
enjoyed watching the progress of the works he had undertaken,
and more than ever desired to inspect anything that was purposely
concealed from him: thus it happened that he one day went to
see the chapel, as we have related, when the refusal of Michelagnolo to admit him occasioned that dispute which caused the
master to leave Rome, as before described.

[But there are some who ascribe Michelagnolo's departure
from Rome, and his disputes with the Pope, to the following
cause. The artist would never suffer anyone to see his works

while in progress, but he suspected that his people sometimes permitted strangers to inspect them in his absence,
and one day when the Pope, having bribed Michelagnolo's
assistants, was entering the Chapel of his uncle Pope Sixtus,
which he was causing our artist to paint, as will be related
hereafter, the latter, who had that day hidden himself,
because suspicious of his young men as we have said,
rushed upon him with a plank of the scaffolding, and not
perceiving who it was that he was turning out, drove His
Holiness forth in a fury. Let it suffice, however, that for one
cause or another, Michelagnolo fell into discord with the
Pope, and then, beginning to fear for his safety, departed
from Rome as we have said.

Arrived at Bologna, his feet were scarcely out of the
stirrups before he was conducted by the servants of the
Pontiff to the presence of His Holiness, who was at the
Palace of the Sixteen. He was accompanied by a Bishop,
sent by Cardinal Soderini, who was himself too ill to fulfill
that office. Having reached the presence, Michelagnolo
knelt down before His Holiness, who looked askance at
him with an angry countenance, and said, "Instead of
coming to us, it appears that thou hast been waiting till
we should come to thee," in allusion to the fact that Bologna
is nearer to Florence than is Rome. But with a clear voice
and hands courteously extended, Michelagnolo excused
himself, having first entreated pardon, admitting that he
had acted in anger, but adding that he could not endure
to be thus ordered away; if he had been in error, His Holiness would doubtless be pleased to forgive him.]
Michelagnolo afterwards told me the cause of this refusal,
which was as follows: When he had completed about one third
of the painting, the prevalence of the north wind during the
winter months had caused a sort of mould to appear on the
pictures; and this happened from the fact that in Rome, the

plaster, made of travertine and puzzolana, does not dry rapidly, and while in a soft state is somewhat dark and very fluent, not to say watery; when the wall is covered with this mixture, therefore, it throws out an efflorescence arising from the humid saltness which bursts forth; but this is in time evaporated and corrected by the air. Michelagnolo was, indeed, in despair at the sight of these spots, and refused to continue the work, declaring to the Pope that he could not succeed therein, but His Holiness sent Giuliano da Sangallo to look at it, and he, telling our artist whence these spots arose, encouraged him to proceed, by teaching him how they might be removed.

When the half was completed, Pope Julius, who had subsequently gone more than once to see the work (mounting ladders for that purpose with Michelagnolo's aid), and whose temper was hasty and impatient, would insist on having the pictures opened to public view, without waiting until the last touches had been given thereto, and the chapel was no sooner thrown open than all Rome hastened thither, the Pope being the first; he had indeed, not patience to wait until the dust caused by removing the scaffold had subsided. Then it was that Raffaelo da Urbino, who was very prompt in imitation, having seen this work, instantly changed his manner, and to give proof of his ability, immediately executed the Prophets and Sibyls in the Church of the Pace. Bramante also then labored to convince Pope Julius that he would do well to confide the second half of the Chapel to Raffaelo. Hearing of this Michelagnolo complained to the Pope of Bramante, enumerating at the same time, without sparing him, many faults in the life, as well as errors in the works, of that architect; of the latter, indeed, he did himself become the corrector at a subsequent period. But Julius, who justly valued the ability of Michelagnolo, commanded that he should continue the work, judging from what he saw of the first half, that our artist would be able to improve the second materially; and the master accordingly finished the whole,

completing it to perfection in twenty months, without having
even the help of a man to grind the colors. It is true that he sometimes complained of the manner in which the Pope hastened
forward the work, seeing that he was thereby prevented from
giving it the finish which he would have desired to bestow; His
Holiness constantly inquiring when it would be completed.
On one occasion, therefore, Michelagnolo replied, "It will be
finished when I shall have done all that I believed required to
satisfy Art." "And we command," rejoined the Pontiff, "that
you satisfy our wish to have it done quickly"; adding finally,
that if it were not at once completed, he would have him,
Michelagnolo, thrown headlong from the scaffolding.

Hearing this, our artist, who feared the fury of the Pope, and
with good cause, desisted instantly, without taking time to add
what was wanting, and took down the remainder of the scaffolding, to the great satisfaction of the whole city, on All Saints'
day, when Pope Julius went into that Chapel to sing mass; but
Michelagnolo had much desired to retouch some portions of
the work *a secco*, as had been done by the older master who had
painted the stories on the walls; he would also gladly have added a
little ultramarine to some of the draperies, and gilded other parts,
to the end that the whole might have a richer and more striking
effect. The Pope, too, hearing that all who beheld the Chapel
praised it highly, would now fain have had the additions made,
but as Michelagnolo thought reconstructing the scaffold too long
an affair, the pictures remained as they were, although the Pope,
who often saw Michelagnolo, would sometimes say, "Let the
Chapel be enriched with bright colors and gold; it looks poor."
When Michelagnolo would reply familiarly, "Holy Father, the
men of those days did not adorn themselves with gold; those
who are painted here less than any, for they were none too rich;
besides which, they were holy men, and must have despised
riches and ornaments. . . ."

When this work was completed, all the world hastened from

every part to behold it, and having done so, they remained astonished and speechless. The Pope rewarded Michelagnolo with rich gifts, and was encouraged by the success of this undertaking to project still greater works; wherefore, the artist would sometimes remark, in respect to the extraordinary favors conferred on him, that he saw well the Pope did esteem his abilities, and if he should now and then inflict some rudeness by a peculiar way of proving his amicable feeling towards him, yet he always cured the wound by gifts and distinguished favors. On one occasion, for example, when Michelagnolo requested leave from His Holiness to pass the festival of San Giovanni in Florence, and begged also to have some money for that purpose, Pope Julius said, "Well, but when will this chapel be finished?" "When I can, Holy Father," replied our artist, and the Pope, who had a staff in his hand, struck Michelagnolo therewith, exclaiming, "When I can—when I can! I'll make thee finish it, and quickly, as thou shalt see." But the master had scarcely returned to his house, to prepare for his journey to Florence, before the Pontiff sent Cursio, his chamberlain, with five hundred crowns to pacify him, having some fear lest Michelagnolo should play him a prank, as he did before. The chamberlain excused Pope Julius moreover, declaring that these things must all be considered favors and marks of kindness; and as Michelagnolo knew the disposition of the Pontiff, and was, after all, much attached to His Holiness, he laughed at what had happened, the more readily as things of this kind always turned to his profit, and he saw well that the Pope did his utmost to retain him as his friend.

—*The Lives of the Painters.*

GREGORY XIII RECEIVES MONTAIGNE

❧ ON DECEMBER 29TH M. d'Abein,[1] our ambassador, a learned
gentleman and a long-standing friend of M. de Montaigne, ad-
vised him to go and kiss the feet of the Pope. M. de Montaigne
and M. d'Estissac went in the coach of the ambassador, who, after
he had been granted an audience, caused them to be called by
the Pope's chamberlain. According to custom, only the ambassador was with the Pope, who had by his side a bell which he
would ring when he might wish anyone to be introduced. The
ambassador was seated, uncovered, at his left hand; the Pope
himself never uncovers before anyone, nor can any ambassador
remain covered in his presence. M. d'Estissac entered first, then
M. de Montaigne, then M. de Mattecoulon, and last M.
d'Hautoy.

After taking a step or two into the chamber, in a corner of
which sits the Pope, the incomer, whoever he may be, kneels
and waits for the Pope to give him benediction. This done, he
will rise and advance to the middle of the room, but a stranger
rarely approaches the Pope by going direct across the floor,
the more ordinary practice being to turn to the left on entering,

[1] Louis Chasteignier de la Roche Posay, seigneur d'Abain. He went
with Henry III into Poland, and was subsequently sent by Henry as
ambassador to Rome. He was afterwards charged by the Pope to carry
the papal absolution to Henry IV.

and then, after making a detour along the wall, to approach his chair. But when the stranger has gone half the distance he must kneel again on one knee, and, having received a second benediction, next advances as far as the thick carpet spread out some seven or eight feet in front of the Pope. Here he must kneel on both knees, while the ambassador who presents him kneels on one, and moves back the Pope's robe from his right foot, which is shod in a red shoe with a white cross thereupon. The kneeling stranger must keep himself in the same posture until he is close to the Pope's foot, and then bend down to kiss it.

M. de Montaigne declared that the Pope raised the point of his foot a little. They all kissed it one after the other, making room for each other after the ceremony was done. Then the ambassador covered the Pope's foot, and, having risen to his seat, said what seemed necessary on behalf of M. d'Estissac and M. de Montaigne. The Pope, with courteous expression of face, admonished M. d'Estissac to cultivate learning and virtue, and M. de Montaigne to maintain the devotion he had always exhibited towards the Church and the interests of the most Christian King: whatever service he could do them they might depend on, this being an Italian figure of speech. They said nothing, but, having been blessed again before rising as a sign of dismissal, they went back in the same order. Each one retreats as it seems best, but the ordinary custom is to go backward, or at least sideways, so as always to look the Pope in the face. As in entering, each one kneels half-way on one knee for another benediction, and again at the door for the last.

The Pope in speaking Italian betrays his Bolognese descent, the idiom of this city being the worst in Italy; and besides this, his speech is halting by nature. In other respects he is a very fine old man, of medium height, and upright, with a face full of majesty, and a long white beard. His age is over eighty, and for his years he is the most healthy and vigorous man possible, troubled neither with gout nor colic nor stomach complaints nor oppression of any kind. By nature he is kind, caring little

about affairs of state, a great builder, and in the last-named
capacity he will leave a memory highly honored in Rome and
elsewhere.

On January 3rd, 1581, the Pope passed beneath our windows,
and before him went some two hundred horses belonging to
personages of the court, of one robe or another. Close beside him
was the Cardinal dei Medici, who conversed with him covered,
and took him to his house to dinner. The Pope wore a red hat, a
white garment, and a red velvet cowl, as is the habit. He was
mounted on a white hackney, harnessed with red velvet, and
with fringe and lace of gold. Though he was nearly eighty-one,
he mounted without any aid, and every fifteen paces or so he
gave his benediction. After him came three cardinals, and then
some hundred men-at-arms, each with lance on thigh, and fully
armored save the head. They had in readiness also another hackney with like equipment, a mule, a handsome white courser,
and a litter. Also two robe-bearers with valises at their saddlebows.

On the morning of Holy Thursday the Pope, in pontifical garb,
accompanied by the cardinals, repaired to the second platform
of the great portico of Saint Peter's bearing a lighted torch in
his hand. Then a canon of Saint Peter's, who stood on one side
of the balcony, read in a loud voice a bull written in Latin by
which men of an infinite variety of sorts and conditions were
excommunicated; amongst others the Huguenots were specially
named, and all those princes who keep hold on any of the lands
of the Church, an article which caused loud laughter from the
Cardinals Medici and Carafa, who stood close to the Pope. The
reading of this bull lasted a good hour; for when the canon had
finished reading an article in Latin, the Cardinal Gonzaga, who
stood on the opposite side—uncovered like the canon—would
repeat the same in Italian. When the reading was done the
Pope cast the lighted torch down amongst the people; and,
whether out of jest or not, Cardinal Gonzaga threw down another,

three torches having been kindled. This having fallen amongst
the people caused a vast disturbance below, everyone scrambling
to pick up a fragment of the torch, and giving and taking shrewd
blows with fist or cudgel. During the reading of this sentence the
balustrade of the portico in front of the Pope was covered with a
large piece of black taffeta; but, the excommunication having
been pronounced, they folded up this black covering and disclosed one of a different color, whereupon the Pope gave his
public blessing.

On these days they exhibit the handkerchief of Saint Veronica.
This is a countenance wrought in needlework, of a dark and
somber tint, and framed after the fashion of a mirror. It is shown
with great ceremony from a high pulpit, five or six paces in width,
and the priest who holds it wears on his hands red gloves, while
two or three other priests assist him in displaying it. No spectacle
provokes such great show of reverence as this, the people all
prostrate themselves on the ground, the greater part of them
weeping and uttering cries of pity. A woman, whom they declared
to be possessed, made a great uproar at the sight of this effigy,
and began to screech, and twist her arms, and throw them about.
The priests moved round the pulpit and exhibited the effigy,
now from one side and now from another, and at every fresh
display the people who beheld it cried out aloud. On these same
occasions they show to the people likewise with equal ceremonies
a lance head enclosed in a crystal vessel. This display is made
several times during the day, and the crowd which comes to
witness the same is so vast that, as far as the eye can reach from
the pulpit aforesaid outside the church, there is nought to be
seen but an endless crowd of men and women. Here is the true
papal court; the pomp of Rome and its chief grandeur lies in
the outward show of religion: and it is a fine sight in these days,
this unbounded ardor of the people for their faith.

—*Works of Michel de Montaigne.*

ON THE CAPITOLINE

❧ IT WAS AT ROME, on the 15th of October 1764, as I sat musing amidst the ruins of the Capitol, while the bare-footed friars were singing vespers in the temple of Jupiter, that the idea of writing the decline and fall of the city first started to my mind. But my original plan was circumscribed to the decay of the city rather than of the empire; and though my reading and reflections began to point towards that object, some years elapsed and several avocations intervened before I was seriously engaged in the execution of that laborious work.

—Memoirs of Edward Gibbon.

LARS PORSENA AND ALL THAT

❦ NOVEMBER 15.—On arriving this morning, I walked straight from the hotel door to St. Peter's. I was so much excited by the expectation of what I was to see that I could notice nothing else. I was quite nervous. The colonnade in front is noble—very, very noble: yet it disappointed me: and would have done so had it been the portico of Paradise. In I went, and I was for a minute fairly stunned by the magnificence and harmony of the interior. I never in my life saw, and never, I suppose, shall again see, anything so astonishingly beautiful. I really could have cried with pleasure. I rambled about for half an hour or more, paying little or no attention to details, but enjoying the effect of the sublime whole.

In rambling back to the Piazza di Spagna I found myself before the portico of the Pantheon. I was as much struck and affected as if I had not known that there was such a building in Rome. There it was, the work of the age of Augustus; the work of men who lived with Cicero, and Caesar, and Horace, and Virgil. What would they have said if they had seen it stuck all over with "*Invito Sacro,*" and "*Indulgenza perpetua*"?

November 16.—As soon as it cleared up I hastened to St. Peter's again. There was one spot near which an Englishman could not help lingering for a few minutes. In one of the side aisles, a monument by Canova marks the burial-place of the latest princes of the House of Stuart: James the Third; Charles

Edward; and Cardinal York, whom the last of the Jacobites affected to call Henry the Ninth. I then went towards the river, to the spot where the old Pons Sublicius stood, and looked about to see how my Horatius agreed with the topography. Pretty well: but his house must be on Mount Palatine; for he would never see Mount Coelius from the spot where he fought. Thence to the Capitol, and wandered through the gallery of paintings placed there by Benedict the Fourteenth, my favorite Pope.

November 26.—At ten Colyar came, and we set out. The day would furnish matter for a volume. We went to the English College, and walked about the cloisters; interesting cloisters to an Englishman. There lie several of our native dignitaries who died at Rome before the Reformation. There lie, too, the bones of many Jacobites, honest martyrs to a worthless cause. We looked into the refectory, much like the halls of the small colleges at Cambridge in my time,—that of Peterhouse, for example,—and smelling strongly of yesterday's supper, which strengthened the resemblance. We found the principal, Dr. Wiseman, a young ecclesiastic full of health and vigor,—much such a ruddy, strapping divine as I remember Whewell eighteen years ago,—in purple vestments standing in the cloister. With him was Lord Clifford, in the uniform of a Deputy Lieutenant of Devonshire, great from paying his court to Pope Gregory. He was extremely civil, and talked with gratitude of General Macaulay's kindness to him in Italy. Wiseman chimed in. Indeed, I hear my uncle's praises wherever I go.

Lord Clifford is not at all like my notion of a great Catholic Peer of old family. I always imagine such an one proud and stately, with the air of a man of rank, but not of fashion; such a personage as Mrs. Inchbald's Catholic Lord in the Simple Story, or as Sir Walter's Lord Glenallan without the remorse. But Lord Clifford is all quicksilver. He talked about the Pope's reception of him and Lord Shrewsbury. His Holiness is in high health and spirits, and is a little more merry than strict formalists approve.

Lord Shrewsbury says that he seems one moment to be a boy eager for play, and the next to be another Leo arresting the march of Attila. The poor King of Prussia, it seems, is Attila. We went into Dr. Wiseman's apartments, which are snugly furnished in the English style, and altogether are very like the rooms of a senior Fellow of Trinity. After visiting the library, where I had a sight of the identical copy of Foxe's book of Martyrs in which Parsons made notes for his answer, I took leave of my countrymen with great good-will.

We then crossed the river, and turned into the Vatican. I had walked a hundred feet through the library without the faintest notion that I was in it. No books, no shelves were visible. All was light and brilliant; nothing but white, and red, and gold; blazing arabesques, and paintings on ceiling and wall. And this was the Vatican Library; a darker Bodleian! The books and manuscripts are all in low wooden cases ranged round the walls; and, as these cases are painted in light colors, they harmonize with the gay aspect of everything around them, and might be supposed to contain musical instruments, masquerade dresses, or china for the dances and suppers for which the apartments seem to be meant. They bore inscriptions, however, more suited to my notions of the place.

Thence I went through the Museum, quite distracted by the multitude and magnificence of the objects which it contained. The splendor of the ancient marbles, the alabaster, the huge masses of porphyry, the granites of various colors, made the whole seem like a fairy region. I wonder that nobody in this moneyed and luxurious age attempts to open quarries like those which supplied the ancients. The wealth of modern Europe is far greater than that of the Roman Empire; and these things are highly valued, and bought at enormous prices. And yet we content ourselves with digging for them in the ruins of this old city and its suburbs and never think of seeking them in the rocks from which the Romans extracted them. Africa and Greece were the parts of the world which afforded the most costly marbles; and perhaps, now that the French have settled in Africa, and that a Bavarian prince reigns in Greece, some researches may be made.

—*Life and Letters of Macaulay.*

SIGHTSEEING WITH THE
HAWTHORNES

❦ WE MIGHT HAVE GONE to see the pictures in the Palace of the Conservatori, and Sophia, whose receptivity is unlimited and forever fresh, would willingly have done so; but I objected, and we went towards the Forum. I had noticed, two or three times, an inscription over a mean-looking door in this neighborhood, stating that here was the entrance to the prison of the holy Apostles Peter and Paul; and we soon found the spot, not far from the Forum, with two wretched frescoes of the apostles above the inscription. We knocked at the door without effect; but a lame beggar, who sat at another door of the same house (which looked exceedingly like a liquor shop), desired us to follow him, and began to ascend to the Capitol, by the causeway leading from the Forum. A little way upward we met a woman, to whom the beggar delivered us over, and she led us into a church or chapel door, and pointed to a long flight of steps, which descended through twilight into utter darkness. She called to somebody in the lower regions, and then went away, leaving us to get down this mysterious staircase by ourselves.

Down we went, farther and farther from the daylight, and found ourselves, anon, in a dark chamber or cell, the shape or boundaries of which we could not make out, though it seemed to be of stone, and black and dungeon-like. Indistinctly, and from a still farther depth in the earth, we heard voices,—one voice, at least,—apparently not addressing ourselves, but some other persons; and soon, directly beneath our feet, we saw a glimmering of light through a round, iron-grated hole in the bottom of the dungeon. In a few moments the glimmer and the voice came up through this hole, and the light disappeared, and it and the voice came glimmering and babbling up a flight of stone stairs, of which we had not hitherto been aware. It was the custode, with a party of visitors, to whom he had been showing St. Peter's dungeon. Each visitor was provided with a wax taper, and the custode gave one to each of us, bidding us wait a moment while he conducted the other party to the upper air. During his absence we examined the cell, as well as our dim lights would permit, and soon found an indentation in the wall, with an iron grate put over it for protection, and an inscription above informing us that the Apostle Peter had here left the imprint of his visage; and, in truth, there is a profile there,—forehead, nose, mouth, and chin,—plainly to be seen, an intaglio in the solid rock. We touched it with the tips of our fingers, as well as saw it with our eyes.

The custode soon returned, and led us down the darksome steps, chattering in Italian all the time. It is not a very long descent to the lower cell, the roof of which is so low that I believe I could have reached it with my hand. We were now in the deepest and ugliest part of the old Mamertine Prison, one of the few remains of the kingly period of Rome, and which served the Romans as a state prison for hundreds of years before the Christian era. A multitude of criminals or innocent persons, no doubt, have languished here in misery, and perished in darkness. Here Jugurtha starved; here Catiline's adherents were strangled; and, methinks, there cannot be in the world another such an evil den, so haunted with black memories and indistinct surmises of guilt and suffering. In old Rome, I suppose, the citizens never spoke of this dungeon above their breath. It looks just as bad as it is; round, only seven paces across, yet so obscure that our tapers could not illuminate it from side to side,—the stones of which it is constructed being as black as midnight.

The custode showed us a stone post, at the side of the cell, with the hole in the top of it, into which, he said, St. Peter's chain had been fastened; and he uncovered a spring of water, in the middle of the stone floor, which he told us had miraculously gushed up to enable the saint to baptize his jailer. The miracle was perhaps more easily wrought, inasmuch as Jugurtha had found the floor of the dungeon oozy with wet. However, it is best to be as simple and childlike as we can in these matters; and whether St. Peter stamped his visage into the stone, and wrought this other miracle or no, and whether or no he was ever in the prison at all, still the belief of a thousand years and more gives a sort of reality and substance to such traditions. The custode dipped an iron ladle into the miraculous water, and we each of us drank a sip; and, what is very remarkable, to me it seemed hard water and almost brackish, while many persons think it the sweetest in Rome. I suspect that St. Peter still dabbles in this water, and tempers its qualities according to the faith of those who drink it.

February 23, 1858.

—Nathaniel Hawthorne, *Passages from the French and Italian Note-Books.*

After leaving the Museum, we went into the Mamertine prison. This is one of the few remaining structures of the Kingly Period. We went down into the cell where Jugurtha was starved to death, and where St. Peter was chained. Prisoners were let through openings in the ceiling. It is a terrific dungeon, but now very clean, and now also there are stairs for visitors to descend comfortably. But the true way to show it, and give one a due sense of its horror and misery, would be to be lowered into it, as the prisoners were, through the trap-door, with a shuddering sense that hope was left behind, unless, by human aid, deliverance should come. There was very little room there. I really think a man might at least be allowed room enough, if he must be confined in a dungeon. That is enough, without a refinement of cruelty. We drank of the miraculous fountain, which sprang up for St. Peter to baptize his keepers with. We saw the stone column to which he was chained. The prison is of enormous strength, a true Etruscan work, of huge square blocks of stone. On the floor upon which we stood, the Catiline conspirators were strangled. It was astonishing to find myself in the very spot upon which St. Peter's stood! It was a den for State criminals only.

In the apartment above St. Peter's cell, and equally dark and strong, is an altar, and the marble busts of St. Peter and St. Paul, enclosed in an iron grate, carved in the time of Constantine. The guide showed us the walled-up, ancient staircase that led to these cells from the Capitol, by a secret way—the way along which the stranglers came. It made me faint to think how utterly impossible it would be to escape. It would be as easy to tear asunder a mountain as to break through these ponderous stones. I hope St. Peter was allowed a torch. O wonderful revolution! He who was chained and martyred then, now rules Christendom from the throne of the most magnificent Cathedral in the world, and a hundred ever-burning lamps watch round his sacred grave, under the high altar, like so many sleepless eyes of seraphs. He who was in black darkness has light enough now, and having died for his Lord Jesus, he has found his life, which he can never lose again.

—Sophia Hawthorne, *Notes in England and Italy.*

Yesterday afternoon my wife and I went to St. Peter's to see the pope pray at the chapel of the Holy Sacrament. We found a good many people in the church, but not an inconvenient number; indeed, not so many as to make any remarkable show in the great nave, nor even in the front of the chapel. A detachment of the Swiss Guard, in their strange, picturesque, harlequin-like costume, were on duty before the chapel, in which the wax tapers were all lighted, and a *prie-dieu* was arranged near the shrine, and covered with scarlet velvet. On each side, along the breadth of the side-aisle, were placed seats, covered with rich tapestry or carpeting; and some gentlemen and ladies—English, probably, or American—had comfortably deposited themselves here, but were compelled to move by the guards before the pope's entrance. His holiness should have appeared precisely at twelve, but we waited nearly half an hour beyond that time; and it seemed to me particularly ill-mannered in the pope, who owes the courtesy of being punctual to the people, if not to St. Peter. By and by, however, there was a stir; the guard motioned to us to stand away from the benches, against the backs of which we had been leaning; the spectators in the nave looked towards the door, as if they beheld something approaching; and first, there appeared some cardinals, in scarlet skull-caps and purple robes, intermixed with some of the Noble Guard and other attendants.

It was not a very formal and stately procession, but rather straggled onward, with ragged edges, the spectators standing aside to let it pass, and merely bowing, or perhaps slightly bending the knee, as good Catholics are accustomed to do when passing before the shrines of saints. Then, in the midst of the purple cardinals, all of whom were gray-haired men, appeared a stout old man, with a white skull-cap, a scarlet, gold-embroidered cape falling over his shoulders, and a white silk robe, the train of which was borne up by an attendant. He walked slowly, with a sort of dignified movement, stepping out broadly, and planting his feet (on which were red shoes) flat upon the pavement, as if he were not much accustomed to locomotion, and perhaps had known a twinge of the gout. His face was kindly and venerable, but not particularly impressive.

Arriving at the scarlet-covered *prie-dieu*, he kneeled down and took off his white skull-cap; the cardinals also kneeled behind and on either side of him, taking off their scarlet skull-caps; while the Noble guard remained standing, six on one side of his holiness and six on the other. The pope bent his head upon the *prie-dieu,* and seemed to spend three or four minutes in prayer; then rose, and all the purple cardinals, and bishops, and priests of whatever degree, rose behind and beside him. Next, he went to kiss St. Peter's toe; at least I believe he kissed it, but I was not near enough to be certain; and lastly, he knelt down, and directed his devotions towards the high altar. This completed the ceremonies, and his holiness left the church by a side door, making a short passage into the Vatican.

I am very glad I have seen the pope, because he may be crossed out of the lists of sights to be seen. His proximity impressed me kindly and favorably towards him, and I did not see one face among all his cardinals (in whose number, doubtless, is his successor) which I would so soon trust as that of Pio Nono.
March 27, 1858.

—Nathaniel Hawthorne, *Passages from the French and Italian Note-Books.*

We went today to see the Pope pray at St. Peter's. He prays there every Friday during Lent. I thought it would be a good, quiet time to see his face, which I had not yet done. In due time a great many attendants arrived, with various-colored, long-bodied, old-fashioned coats, trimmed richly with pie-colored borders, and three-cornered hats upon their heads. They looked like sudden apparitions out of an old picture-book of ancient costumes. They arranged themselves in lines from the chief entrance, edging the crowd with their finery. Then followed the Swiss Guard, a body of stalwart young men. Their dress is entirely peculiar—trousers full to the knee like a Turk's, with a tunic—in stripes of bright yellow, red, blue, and white. The dress is made of separate strips of cloth of the pure colors, so that a battalion of them looks very gorgeous and harlequiny. These gay tulips lined the way quite to the chapel. The space before the Chapel of the Holy Sacrament, to which the Pope would come first, was left wholly free for his Holiness. Near the gate was placed a *prie-dieu,* covered with crimson velvet and gold, as was the floor beneath—and crimson velvet cushions were arranged for him to kneel upon and to rest his arms.

We patiently waited a long time, and at last a stir announced the entrance of the Pontifex Maximus. He was preceded and followed by Cardinals, dressed today in violet robes, significant of mourning, just as all the pictures are veiled during Lent in violet. The Pope was arrayed in white silk, with red shoes and a red mantle. I do not know why he also was not in violet, unless he is to be presumed beyond penitence and mourning. He was, however, without tiara, and only a white silk skull-cap, and his aspect, and that of all his suite, was grave and sad. I saw him very well as he passed me. His face is benign and comely, and every few seconds he blessed the crowd by a motion of his right hand, and a slight bend of the head, at once majestic and gracious. If one could only believe him a perfect saint and virtually the Head of the Church, this would have been very impressive.

He made a deep obeisance to the Chapel of the Holy Sacrament, where he believed God was present in the wafer, and then he knelt on the crimson-velvet cushion, and the Cardinals knelt behind and on each side of him; and profound silence fell over all while they prayed. Every Catholic was on his knees, with moving lips. As soon as the Pope rose, there was a rush for the next *prie-dieu,* prepared in front of St. Peter's shrine. We stood close by the ever-burning lamps, and the same ceremony was repeated, watched and guarded by a military band. I at first thought these mailed and halberded soldiers symbolized the Church Militant. But they are merely the attendants of the temporal prince, as the Pope claims to be King and Imperator, as well as Pontifex.
March 26, 1858.

—Sophia Hawthorne, *Notes in England and Italy.*

NOT SO WIDE AS THE HUDSON

❧ WE ENTERED ROME by the gate of St. John, and looked about us with reverential awe mingled with an intense curiosity. Little appeared at first besides a few churches, broken aqueducts and gardens. On the left was a deserted-looking palace, with a large church attached, the buildings of St. John in the Lateran. An Egyptian obelisk, of great antiquity, pointed to the skies. These edifices were vast and princely, but they stood almost alone. Farther in advance was a straggling sort of town, a mere suburb, and the line of houses often broken by waste spots. Presently the carriage came under the walls of a huge oval structure of a reddish stone, in which arches rose above arches to the height of an ordinary church tower, a mountain of edifice; and, though not expecting to see it, I recognized the Coliseum at a glance. Objects now crowded on us, such as the arches of Constantine and of Titus, ruined temples, the Forum, and then the town itself. My head became confused, and I sat stupid as a countryman who first visits town, perplexed with the whirl of sensations and the multiplicity of the objects.

We drove to the Hotel de Paris, entirely across the city, near the Porto del Popolo, and took lodgings. I ordered dinner; but, too impatient to restrain my curiosity, as there was still an hour of daylight, I called a *laquais de place,* and, holding little P——— by the hand, sallied forth. "Where will the signore go?" asked the *laquais,* as soon as we were in the street. "To St. Peter's."

In my eagerness to proceed, I looked neither to the right nor to the left. We went through crooked and narrow streets, until we came to a bridge lined with statues. The stream beneath was the Tiber. It was full, turbid, swift, sinuous, and it might be three hundred feet wide, or perhaps not quite so wide as the Seine at Paris at the same season. The difference, however, is not material, and each is about half as wide as the Thames above London Bridge on a full tide, which is again three-fourths of the width of the Hudson at Albany. A large round castellated edifice, with flanking walls and military bastions, faced the bridge: this was the tomb of Adrian, converted into a citadel by the name of the Castle of St. Angelo, an angel in bronze surmounting the tower. Turning to the left, we followed the river until a street led us from its windings, and presently I found myself standing at the foot of a vast square, with colonnades on a gigantic scale sweeping in half circles on each side of me, two of the most beautiful fountains I had ever seen throwing their waters in sheets down their sides between them, and the façade of St. Peter's forming the background. A noble Egyptian obelisk occupied the center of the area.

Everyone had told me I should be disappointed in the apparent magnitude of this church, but I was not. To me it seemed the thing it is, possibly because some pains had been taken to school the eye. Switzerland often misled me in both heights and distances, but a ship or an edifice rarely does so. Previously to seeing Switzerland, I had found nothing to compare with such a nature, and all regions previously known offered no rules to judge by; but I had now seen too many huge structures not to be at once satisfied that this was the largest of them all.

The *laquais* would have me stop to admire some of Michael Angelo's sublime conceptions, but I pressed forward. Ascending the steps, I threw out my arms to embrace one of the huge half columns of the façade, not in a fit of sentimentalism, but to ascertain its diameter, which was gigantic, and helped the previous impression. Pushing aside the door in common use, I found myself in the nave of the noblest temple in which any religious rites were ever celebrated.

I walked about a hundred feet up the nave, and stopped. From a habit of analyzing buildings, I counted the paces as I advanced, and knew how far I was within the pile. Still men, at the farthest extremity, seemed dwindled into boys. One, whose size did not appear disproportioned, was cleaning a statue of St. Bruno, at the height of an ordinary church-steeple, stood on the shoulder of the figure, and could just rest his arm on the top of its head. Some marble cherubs, that looked like children, were in high relief against a pier near me, and laying my hand on the hand of one of them, I found it like that of an infant in comparison. All this aided the sense of vastness. The *baldacchino*, or canopy of bronze, which is raised over the great altar, filled the eye no more than a pulpit in a common church; and yet I knew its summit was as lofty as half the height of the spire of Trinity, New York, or about a hundred and thirty feet, and essentially higher than the tower. I looked for a marble throne that was placed at the remotest extremity of the building, also as high as a common church-tower, a sort of poetical chair for the popes: it seemed distant as a cavern on a mountain.

To me there was no disappointment. Every thing appeared as vast as feet and inches could make it; and as I stood gazing at the glorious pile, the tears forced themselves from my eyes. Even little P—— was oppressed with the sense of the vastness of the place, for he clung close to my side, though he had passed half his life in looking at sights, and kept murmuring, *"Qu-est-ce que c'est?—qu'est que c'est? Est-ce une église?"*

It was getting dark, and perhaps the gloom magnified the effect. The atmosphere even—for this stupendous pile has an atmosphere of its own, one different from that of the outer world, —was soothing and delicious; and I turned away impressed with the truth that if ever the hand of man had indeed raised a struc-

ture to the Deity, in the least worthy of his majesty, it was this!
. . . The singing of St. Peter's has a reputation far and near,
and strangers are accustomed to go there to hear it. There is a
particular chapel in which a service is sung (vespers, I presume)
every Sunday afternoon, and where one can hear the finest vocal
church music in the world, music even finer than that of the
Royal Chapel at Dresden. At the latter place, however, the music
is chiefly instrumental; whereas here it is principally by voices.
One who has never seen such a temple, or heard a combination
of science, skill, and natural, I may say *artificial* power, can form
no just notion of the sensations that arise on walking among the
wonders of the church and listening to the heavenly chants.
Sometimes I withdraw to a distance, and the sounds reach me
like the swells of airs in another world: and at times I go near
the door of the chapel, and receive the full bursts of its harmony.
Operas, concerts, and conservatoires sink into insignificance before this sublime union of the temple and its worship; for both
may be considered as having reached the limits of human powers,
so far as the senses are concerned.

Around the door of this chapel, which is, I believe, called the
Chapel of the Choir, strangers assemble in crowds. Here, I regret
to say, they laugh, chat, lounge, and amuse themselves, much
as well-bred people amuse themselves in an evening party anywhere else. There is not much noise certainly, for well-bred
people are not often noisy; but there is little or no reverence.
After making all possible allowances for the difference between
Catholic and Protestant worship, this want of respect for the
altar and the temple is inexcusable. Happily, I have never seen
an American indulging in this levity. The fact speaks volumes in
reply to those who heap obloquy on the nation as wanting in
religion. The larger American sects manifest a great disrespect
for the mere house of God: they hold political meetings in their
churches, even concerts and exhibitions, all of which I deem
irreverent and unsuited to the place; but whenever anything like

worship is commenced, silence and decency prevail. This feeling they have brought abroad with them; but other Protestants, especially the English, who are such observers of the decencies at home, do not appear to entertain the same feelings.

Still, it must be admitted that the Catholics themselves do not always set a good example. I was strolling lately through the vast temple, equally impressed with reverence and delight, when a cardinal entered by a side door. He was a young man, with a marked air of gentility; and I presume his early rise in the church was owing to his high birth. He was in his official dress, and carried the red hat pressed against his bosom. As he entered from the Vatican, I presume he had just been in the presence of the Pope. Four attendants followed, two of whom were in black, and were a species of clerical esquires, though their official appellation is unknown to me; and two were common livery servants. The cardinal advanced to the great altar, beneath the celebrated *baldacchino,* and, kneeling, he prayed. Nothing could be better than his whole manner, which was subdued, gentle, and devout. So far all was well. The two *esquires* kneeled behind the cardinal on the pavement, put their hats to their faces, and appeared also to pray. The two lackqueys kneeled behind the esquires, the distance between the respective parties being about twenty feet: and they too raised their hats before their faces,—but it was to laugh and make grimaces at each other! This buffoonery was so obvious as to amount to mockery, and one near them might see it.

—Gleanings in Europe.

MR. MORSE GROWS WEARY

Wednesday in Holy Week, 1830

❀ WE WENT TO THE PIAZZA NAVONE, being market-day, in search of prints. The scene here is very amusing: the variety of wares exposed, and the confusion of noises and tongues, and now and then a jackass swelling the chorus with his most exquisite tones.

At three o'clock went to St. Peter's to see ceremonies at the Sistine Chapel. Cardinals asleep; monotonous bawling, long and tedious; candles put out one by one, fifteen in number; no ceremonies at the altar; cardinals present nineteen in number; seven yawns from the cardinals; tiresome and monotonous beyond description.

After three hours of this most tiresome chant, all the candles having been extinguished, the celebrated *Miserere* commenced. It is, indeed, sublime, but I think loses much of its effect from the fatigue of body, and mind, too, in which it is heard by the auditors. The *Miserere* is the composition of the celebrated Allegri, and for giving the effect of wailing and lamentation, without injury to harmony, it is one of the most perfect of compositions. The manner of sustaining a strain of concord by new voices, now swelling high, now gradually dying away, now sliding imperceptibly into discord and suddenly breaking into harmony, is admirable. The imagination is alive and fancies thousands of people in the deepest contrition. It closed by the cardinals clapping their hands for the earthquake.

Holy Thursday, 1830

Having examined the splendid chair in which he was to be borne, and while he was robing in another apartment, we found that, although we might have a complete view of the Pope and the ceremonies before and after the benediction, yet the principal effect was to be seen below. We therefore left our place at the balcony, where we could see nothing but the crowd, and hastened below. On passing into the hall we were so fortunate as to be just in season for the procession from the Sistine Chapel to the Pauline. The cardinals walked in procession, two by two, and one bore the host, while eight bearers held over him a rich canopy of silver tissue embroidered with gold.

Thence we hastened to the front of St. Peter's, where, in the center upon the highest step, we had an excellent view of the balcony, and, turning around, could see the immense crowd which had assembled in the piazza and the splendid square of troops which were drawn up before the steps of the church. Here I had scarcely time to make a hasty sketch, in the broiling sun, of the window and its decorations, before the precursors of the Pope, the two large feather fans, made their appearance on each side of the balcony, which was decorated with crimson and gold, and immediately after the Pope, with his miter of gold tissue and his splendid robes of gold and jewels, was borne forward, relieving finely from the deep crimson darkness behind him. He made the usual sign of blessing, with his two fingers raised. A book was then held before him in which he read, with much motion of his head, for a minute. He then rose, extending both his arms—this was the benediction—while at the same moment the soldiers and crowd all knelt; the cannon from the Castle of St. Angelo was discharged, and the bells in all the churches rang a simultaneous peal.

The effect was exceedingly grand, the most imposing of all the ceremonies I have witnessed. The Pope was then borne back again. Two papers were thrown from the balcony for which there was a great scramble among the crowd.

—*Letters and Journals.*

THE POET'S EYE

THE MORNING of this happy day I must endeavor to perpetuate by a few lines, and at least by description to impart to others what I have myself enjoyed. The weather has been beautiful and calm, quite a bright sky, and a warm sun. Accompanied by Tischbein, I set off for the Piazza of St. Peter's, where we went about first of all from one part to another; when it became too hot for that, walked up and down in the shade of the great obelisk, which is full wide enough for two abreast, and eating grapes which we purchased in the neighborhood. Then we entered the Sistine Chapel, which we found bright and cheerful, and with a good light for the pictures. "The Last Judgment" divided our admiration with the paintings on the roof by Michael Angelo. I could only see and wonder. The mental confidence and boldness of the master, and his grandeur of conception, are beyond all expression. After we had looked at all of them over and over again, we left this sacred building, and went to St. Peter's, which received from the bright heavens the loveliest light possible, and every part of it was clearly lit up. As men willing to be pleased, we were delighted with its vastness and splendor, and did not allow an over-nice or hypercritical taste to mar our pleasure. We suppressed every harsher judgment: we enjoyed the enjoyable.

Lastly we ascended the roof of the church, where one finds in little the plan of a well-built city. Houses and magazines, springs (in appearance at least), churches, and a great temple all in the air, and beautiful walks between. We mounted the dome, and saw glistening before us the regions of the Apennines, Soracte, and towards Tivoli the volcanic hills, Frascati, Castelgandolfo, and the plains, and beyond all the sea. Close at our feet lay the whole city of Rome in its length and breadth, with its mountain palaces, domes, etc. Not a breath of air was moving, and in the upper dome it was (as they say) like being in a hot-house. When we had looked enough at these things, we went down, and they opened for us the doors in the cornices of the dome, the tympanum, and the nave. There is a passage all round, and from above you can take a view of the whole church, and of its several parts. As we stood on the cornices of the tympanum, we saw beneath us the pope passing to his mid-day devotions. Nothing, therefore, was wanting to make our view of St. Peter's perfect. We at last descended to the area, and took in a neighboring hotel a cheerful but frugal meal, and then set off for St. Cecilia's.

It would take many words to describe the decorations of this church, which was crammed full of people; not a stone of the edifice was to be seen. The pillars were covered with red velvet wound round with gold lace; the capitals were overlaid with embroidered velvet, so as to retain somewhat of the appearance of capitals, and all the cornices and pillars were in manner covered with hangings. All the entablatures of the walls were also covered with life-like paintings, so that the whole church seemed to be laid out in mosaic. Around the church, and on the high altar, more than two hundred wax tapers were burning. It looked like a wall of lights, and the whole nave was perfectly lit up. The aisles and side altars were equally adorned and illuminated. Right opposite the high altar, and under the organ, two scaffolds were erected, which also were covered with velvet, on one of which were placed the singers, and on the other the instruments, which kept up one unbroken strain of music. The church was crammed full.

I have heard an excellent kind of musical accompaniment,

just as there are concerts of violins, or of other instruments, so here they had concerts of voices; so that one voice—the soprano, for instance—predominates, and sings solo, while from time to time the chorus of other voices falls in, and accompanies it, always of course with the whole orchestra. It has a good effect. I must end, as we in fact ended the day. In the evening we came upon the Opera, where no less a piece than "I Litiganti" was being performed, but we had all the day enjoyed so much of excellence, that we passed by the door. . . .

Of the beauty of a walk through Rome by moonlight it is impossible to form a conception, without having witnessed it. All single objects are swallowed up by the great masses of light and shade, and nothing but grand and general outlines present themselves to the eye. For three several days we have enjoyed to the full the brightest and most glorious of nights. Peculiarly beautiful at such a time is the Coliseum. At night it is always closed; a hermit dwells in a little shrine within its range, and beggars of all kinds nestle beneath its crumbling arches: the latter had lit a fire on the arena, and a gentle wind bore down the smoke to the ground, so that the lower portion of the ruins was quite hid by it, while above the vast walls stood out in deeper darkness before the eye. As we stopped at the gate to contemplate the scene through the iron gratings, the moon shone brightly in the heavens above. Presently the smoke found its way up the sides, and through every chink and opening, while the moon lit it up like a cloud. The sight was exceedingly glorious. In such a light one ought to see the Pantheon, the Capitol, the Portico of St. Peter's, and the other grand streets and squares:— and thus the sun and moon, like the human mind, have quite a different work to do here from elsewhere, where the vastness and yet the most elegant of masses present themselves to their rays.

—Goethe's Travels in Italy.

I LOVE ST. PETER'S

April 3, 1833
Wednesday

THE FAMOUS *Miserere* was sung this afternoon in the Sistine Chapel. The saying at Rome is, that it cannot be imitated, not only by any other choir, but in any other chapel in the world. The Emperor of Austria sent Mozart to Rome on purpose to have it sung at Vienna with like effect, but it failed.

Surely it is sweet music, and sounds more like the Eolian harp than anything else. The pathetic lessons of the day relate the treachery of Judas and apply select passages from the prophets and psalms to the circumstances of Jesus. Then whilst the choir chaunt the words *"Traditor autem dedit eis signum, dicens, Quem osculatus fuero, ipse est, tenete eum,"* all the candles in the chapel are extinguished but one. During the repetition of this verse, the last candle is taken down and hidden under the altar. Then out of the silence and the darkness rises this most plaintive and melodious strain (the whole congregation kneeling), *"Miserere mei, Deus,"* etc. The sight and the sound are very touching.

Everything here is in good taste. The choir are concealed by the high fence which rises above their heads. We were in Michel Angelo's chapel which is full of noblest scriptural forms and faces.

[Holy] Thursday

These forms strike me more than I expected, and yet how do they fall short of what they should be. Today I saw the Pope wash the feet of thirteen pilgrims, one from each nation of Christendom. One was from Kentucky. After the ceremony, he served them at dinner; this I did not see. But Gregory XVI is a learned and able man; he was a monk and is reputed of pure life. Why should he not leave one moment this formal service of fifty generations and speak out of his own heart—the Father of the Church to his children,—though it were but a single sentence or a single word? One earnest word or act to this sympathetic audience would overcome them. It would take all hearts by storm.

Tonight I heard the *Miserere* sung in St. Peter's and with less effect than yesterday. But what a temple! When night was settling down upon it and a long religious procession moved through a part of the church, I got an idea of its immensity such as I had not before. You walk about on its ample, marble pavement as you would on a common, so free are you of your neighbors; and throngs of people are lost upon it. And what beautiful lights and shades on its mighty gilded arches and vaults and far windows and brave columns, and its rich-clad priests that look as if they were the pictures come down from the walls and walking.

Thence we came out (I was walking with two painters, Cranch and Alexander) under the moon and saw the planet shine upon the finest fountain in the world, and upon all the stone saints on the piazza and the great church itself. This was a spectacle which only Rome can boast,—how faery beautiful! An Arabian Night's tale.

[Easter] Sunday

This morning the Pope said mass in St. Peter's. Rich dresses, great throngs, lines of troops, but not much to be said for the service. It is Easter, and the curtains are withdrawn from the pictures and statues to my great joy, and the Pope wears his triple crown instead of a miter.

At twelve o'clock the benediction was given. A canopy was hung over the great window that is above the principal door of

St. Peter's, and there sat the Pope. The troops were all under arms and in uniform in the piazza below, and all Rome and much of England and Germany and France and America was gathered there also. The great bell of the church tolled, drums beat, and trumpets sounded over the vast congregation.

Presently, at a signal, there was silence, and a book was brought to the Pope, out of which he read a moment and then rose and spread out his hands and blessed the people. All knelt as one man. He repeated his action (for no words could be heard), stretching his arms gracefully to the north and south and east and west, pronouncing a benediction on the whole world. It was a sublime spectacle. Then sounded drums and trumpets, then rose the people, and everyone went his way.

This evening I have seen the illumination of the church. When it was dark, I took the well-known way and on reaching the Bridge of St. Angelo found the church already hung with lights from turret to foundation. But this was only partial. At the moment when the bell in the tower tolled eight o'clock, out flashed innumerable torches in the air and the whole edifice blazed with fires which cast the first lamps into shade and lit up every face in the multitude of the piazza as with daylight. But it is very melancholy to see an illumination in this declining church and impoverished country.

I love St. Peter's church. It grieves me to think that after a few days I shall see it no more. It has a peculiar smell from the quantity of incense burned in it. The music that is heard in it is always good and the eye is always charmed. It is an ornament of the earth. It is not grand, it is so rich and pleasing; it should rather be called the sublime of the beautiful.

—*Journals of Ralph Waldo Emerson.*

A CRITICAL GUEST

❧ POOR LITTLE Numero Cinque Via del Gambero has seldom, I imagine, known so violent a sensation as that it experienced when, on the day of the Immaculate Conception, the Armenian Archbishop rolled up to the door in his red coach. The master of the house had always seemed to like us; now he appeared with profound respect suffusing, as it were, his whole being, and announced, "Signore, it is Monsignore come to take you to the Sistine Chapel in his carriage," and drew himself up in a line, as much like a series of serving-men as possible, to let us pass out. There was a private carriage for the ladies near that of Monsignore, for he had already advertised us that the sex were not permitted to ride in the red coach. As they appeared, however, he renewed his expressions of desolation at being deprived of their company, and assured them of his good-will with a multiplicity of smiles and nods, intermixed with shrugs of recurrence to his poignant regret. But! In fine, it was forbidden!

Monsignore was in full costume, with his best ecclesiastical clothes on, and with his great gold chain about his neck. The dress was richer than that of the western archbishops; and the long white beard of Monsignore made him look much more like a Scriptural monsignore than these. He lacked, perhaps, the fine spiritual grace of his brother, the Archbishop of Venice, to whose letter of introduction we owed his acquaintance and untiring civilities; but if a man cannot be plump and spiritual, he can be plump and pleasant, as Monsignore was to the last degree. He enlivened our ride with discourse about the Armenians at Venice, equally beloved of us; and, arrived at the Sistine Chapel, he marshaled the ladies before him, and won them early entrance through the crowd of English and Americans crushing one another at the door. Then he laid hold upon the captain of the Swiss Guard, who was swift to provide them with the best places; and in no wise did he seem one of the uninfluential and insignificant priests that About describes the archbishops at Rome to be. According to this lively author, a Swiss guard was striking back the crowd on some occasion with the butt of his halberd, and smote a cardinal on the breast. He instantly dropped upon his knees with, "Pardon, Eminenza! I thought it was a monsignore!" Even the chief of these handsome fellows had nothing but respect and obedience for our Archbishop.

The gentlemen present were separated from the ladies, and in a very narrow space outside of the chapel men of every nation were penned up together. All talked—several priests as loudly as the rest. But the rudest among them were certain Germans, who not only talked but stood upon a seat to see better, and were ordered down by one of the Swiss with a fierce *"Giù, signori, giù!"* Otherwise the guard kept good order in the chapel, and were no doubt as useful and genuine as anything about the poor old Pope. What gorgeous fellows they were, and, as soldiers, how absurd! The weapons they bore were as obsolete as the Inquisition. It was amusing to pass one of these play-soldiers on guard at the door of the Vatican—tall, straight, beautiful, superb, with his halberd on his shoulder—and then come to a real warrior outside, a little, ugly, red-legged French sentinel, with his Minié on his arm.

Except for the singing of the Pope's choir,—which was angelically sweet, and heavenly far above all praise,—the religious ceremonies affected me as tedious and empty. Each of the cardinals, as he entered the chapel, blew a sonorous nose; and was received standing by his brother prelates—a grotesque company of old-womanish old men in gaudy gowns. From where I stood I saw the Pope's face only in profile: it was gentle and benign enough, but not great in expression, and the smile on it almost degenerated into a simper. His Holiness had a cold; and his *recitative*, though full, was not smooth. He was all *prete* when, in the midst of the service, he hawked, held his handkerchief up before his face, a little way off, and ruthlessly spat in it!

—*Italian Journeys.*

RUS IN URBE

❧ OF COURSE we have been to the monster Church of St. Peter, frequently. I knew its dimensions. I knew it was a prodigious structure. I knew it was just about the length of the capitol at Washington—say seven hundred and thirty feet. I knew it was three hundred and sixty-four feet wide, and consequently wider than the capitol. I knew that the cross on the top of the dome of the church was four hundred and thirty-eight feet above the ground, and therefore about a hundred or may be a hundred and twenty-five feet higher than the dome of the capitol. Thus I had one gauge. I wished to come as near forming a correct idea of how it was going to look as possible; I had a curiosity to see how much I would err. I erred considerably. St. Peter's did not look nearly so large as the capitol, and certainly not a twentieth part as beautiful, from the outside.

When we reached the door, and stood fairly within the church, it was impossible to comprehend that it was a *very* large building. I had to *cipher* a comprehension of it. I had to ransack my memory for some more similes. St. Peter's is bulky. Its height and size would represent two of the Washington capitol set one on top of the other—if the capitol were wider; or two blocks or two blocks and a half of ordinary buildings set one on top of the other. St. Peter's *was* that large, but it could and would not look so. The trouble was that everything in it and about it was on such a scale of uniform vastness that there were no contrasts to

judge by—none but the people, and I had not noticed them.
They were insects. The statues of children holding vases of holy
water were immense, according to the tables of figures, but so
was everything else around them. The mosaic pictures in the
dome were huge, and were made of thousands and thousands of
cubes of glass as large as the end of my little finger, but those
pictures looked smooth, and gaudy of color, and in good proportion to the dome. Evidently they would not answer to measure
by. Away down toward the far end of the church (I thought it
was really clear at the far end, but discovered afterward that it
was in the center, under the dome) stood the thing they call the
baldacchino—a great bronze pyramidal frame-work like that
which upholds a mosquito-bar. It only looked like a considerably
magnified bedstead—nothing more. Yet I knew it was a good
deal more than half as high as Niagara Falls. It was overshadowed
by a dome so mighty that its own height was snubbed. The four
great square piers or pillars that stand equidistant from each
other in the church, and support the roof, I could not work up
to their real dimensions by any method of comparison. I knew
that the faces of each were about the width of a very large dwell-
ing-house front (fifty or sixty feet), and that they were twice as
high as an ordinary three-story dwelling, but still they looked
small. I tried all the different ways I could think of to compel myself to understand how large St. Peter's was, but with small
success. The mosaic portrait of an Apostle who was writing with
a pen six feet long seemed only an ordinary Apostle.

But the people attracted my attention after a while. To stand
in the door of St. Peter's and look at men down toward its further
extremity, two blocks away, has a diminishing effect on them;
surrounded by the prodigious pictures and statues, and lost in
the vast spaces, they look very much smaller than they would if
they stood two blocks away in the open air. I "averaged" a man
as he passed me and watched him as he drifted far down by the
baldacchino and beyond—watched him dwindle to an insignifi-

cant school-boy, and then, in the midst of the silent throng of
human pigmies gliding about him, I lost him. The church had
lately been decorated, on the occasion of a great ceremony in
honor of St. Peter, and men were engaged now in removing the
flowers and gilt paper from the walls and pillars. As no ladders
could reach the great heights, the men swung themselves down
from balustrades and the capitals of pilasters by ropes, to do this
work. The upper gallery which encircles the inner sweep of the
dome is two hundred and forty feet above the floor of the
church—very few steeples in America could reach up to it. Visitors always go up there to look down into the church because one
gets the best idea of some of the heights and distances from that
point. While we stood on the floor one of the workmen swung
loose from that gallery at the end of a long rope. I had not supposed, before, that a man *could* look so much like a spider. He
was insignificant in size, and his rope seemed only a thread.
Seeing that he took up so little space, I could believe the story,
then, that ten thousand troops went to St. Peter's once to hear
mass, and their commanding officer came afterward, and not finding them, supposed they had not yet arrived. But they were in
the church, nevertheless—they were in one of the transepts.
Nearly fifty thousand persons assembled in St. Peter's to hear
the publishing of the dogma of the Immaculate Conception. It is
estimated that the floor of the church affords standing room for—
for a large number of people; I have forgotten the exact figures.
But it is no matter—it is near enough.

In this connection I wish to say one word about Michael
Angelo Buonarotti. I used to worship the mighty genius of
Michael Angelo—that man who was great in poetry, painting,
sculpture, architecture—great in everything he undertook. But I
do not want Michael Angelo for breakfast—for luncheon—for
dinner—for tea—for supper—for between meals. I like a change,
occasionally. In Genoa, he designed everything; in Milan he or

his pupils designed everything; he designed the Lake of Como; in Padua, Verona, Venice, Bologna, who did we ever hear of, from guides, but Michael Angelo? In Florence, he painted everything, designed everything, nearly, and what he did not design he used to sit on a favorite stone and look at, and they showed us the stone. In Pisa he designed everything but the old shot-tower, and they would have attributed that to him if it had not been so awfully out of the perpendicular. He designed the piers of Leghorn and the custom-house regulations of Città Vecchia. But, here—here it is frightful. He designed St. Peter's; he designed the Pope; he designed the Pantheon, the uniform of the Pope's soldiers, the Tiber, the Vatican, the Coliseum, the Capitol, the Tarpeian Rock, the Barberini Palace, St. John Lateran, the Campagna, the Appian Way, the Seven Hills, the Baths of Caracalla, the Claudian Aqueduct, the Cloaca Maxima—the eternal bore designed the Eternal City, and unless all men and books do lie, he painted everything in it! Dan said the other day to the guide, "Enough, enough, enough! Say no more! Lump the whole thing! say that the Creator made Italy from designs by Michael Angelo!"

I never felt so fervently thankful, so soothed, so tranquil, so filled with a blessed peace, as I did yesterday when I learned that Michael Angelo was dead.

But we have taken it out of this guide. He has marched us through miles of pictures and sculpture in the vast corridors of the Vatican; and through miles of pictures and sculpture in twenty other palaces; he has shown us the great picture in the Sistine Chapel, and frescoes enough to fresco the heavens—pretty much all done by Michael Angelo. So with him we have played that game which has vanquished so many guides for us—imbecility and idiotic questions. These creatures never suspect—they have no idea of a sarcasm.

He shows us a figure and says: "Statoo brunzo." (Bronze statue.)

We look at it indifferently and the doctor asks: "By Michael Angelo?"

"No—not know who."

Then he shows us the ancient Roman Forum. The doctor asks: "Michael Angelo?"

A stare from the guide. "No—a thousan' year before he is born."

Then an Egyptian obelisk. Again: "Michael Angelo?"

"Oh, *mon dieu,* genteelmen! Zis is *two* thousan' year before he is born!"

He grows so tired of that unceasing question sometimes, that he dreads to show us anything at all. The wretch has tried all the ways he can think of to make us comprehend that Michael Angelo is only responsible for the creation of a *part* of the world, but somehow he has not succeeded yet. Relief for overtasked eyes and brain from study and sightseeing is necessary, or we shall become idiotic sure enough. Therefore this guide must continue to suffer. If he does not enjoy it, so much the worse for him. We do.

—*The Innocents Abroad.*

ROMAN MOSAICS

🌷 THE GARDENS of the Pincio are small, but a fairer spot it would be hard to find anywhere. The grounds are most beautifully laid out, and so skillfully arranged that they seem of far larger extent then they really are. Splendid palm-trees, aloes, and cactuses give a tropical charm to the walks; rare exotics and bloom-laden trees of genial climes, flashing fountains, and all manner of cultivated beauty, enliven the scene; while the air blows fresh and invigorating from the distant hills. From the lofty parapet of the city-wall, which bounds it on one side, you gaze into the green meadows and rich wooded solitudes of the Borghese grounds, that look like some rural retreat a score of miles from the city; and from the stone balustrade on the other side you see all Rome at your feet with its sea of brown houses, and beyond the picturesque roofs and the hidden river rising up the great mass of the Vatican buildings and the mighty dome of St. Peter's, which catches like a mountain peak the last level gold of the sunset, and flashes it back like an illumination, while all the intermediate view is in shadow.

No wonder that the Pincian Hill is the favorite promenade of Rome, and that on week-days and Sunday afternoons you see multitudes of people showing every phase of Roman life, and hundreds of carriages containing the flower of the Roman aristocracy, with beautiful horses, and footmen in rich liveries, crowding the piazza below, ascending the winding road, and

driving or walking round between the palms and the pines, over
the garden-paths, to the sound of band music. And thus they
continue to amuse themselves till the sun has set, and the first
sound of the bells of Ave Maria is heard from the churches; and
then they wind their way homewards.

—*Roman Mosaics.*

SKYLINE

❧ JUST AS THE THEATER, dancing, music, were a part or appendage of the State religion, so the Church has taken to itself all that is finest in spectacle, all that is rarest in singing. Those perfumed and golden gifts of the three old Magi to the young Christ, the gift of the world and its delicacies, were not given in vain. All the churches in Rome are full of incense and gold. To see St. Peter's is to realize all that is strongest, most Roman, nothing that is subtle or spiritual, in the power of the Church. This vast building, the largest church in the world, imposes itself upon you, wherever you are in Rome; you see the dome from the Alban or the Sabine hills, from which the whole city seems dwindled to a white shadow upon a green plain. Before it lies all Rome, behind it the vague desolation of fruitless fields, ruinous houses, a mouldering wall, a few ragged trees.

I climbed one evening, about sunset, on a day when the sky itself had the desolation of brooding storms, to the strip of narrow, untrodden ground behind it, which rises from the Via Scaccia, going down on the other side to the Via della Zecca. It stood there hiding the whole city and half the sky, a vast gray bulk; now and again the moon, looking through a rift in the clouds, touched the leaden roof with a finger of light; the cypresses, seeming to lean against the white walls at the base, turned blacker; a few gas lamps shone about it like gold candles about the high altar; and gradually, as I watched, light after light sprang up

[117]

out of the deep streets and precipitous houses, the hills grew
darker, and more vague, and the solid mass itself, now a loom-
ing grayness, seemed to float like a great shadow into the depths
of the night.

And always, by day, looked at from within or without, it is
by its immensity, its spectacular qualities, that it is impressive.
To walk across the floor is like taking a journey; voices chanting
in a side chapel can only just be heard from the opposite aisle;
and, looking at the four piers which support the dome, one remembers that the church of San Carlino alle Quattro Fontane,
by no means a small church, is exactly the size of one of those
four piers. Everything, the whole decoration, in order that it
may be in proportion to the scale of the building, is exaggerated,
and almost no detail bears an intimate examination, or can give
one a separate sensation of pleasure; for the few lovely things,
like Michelangelo's Pietà, are lost in the little chapels, where
they exist quietly, in their corners, like a fine, silent criticism of
all this display, these florid Popes and angels, this noisy architectural rhetoric. And St. Peter's, impressing you, as it certainly
does, with its tremendous size, strength, wealth, and the tireless,
enduring power which has called it into being, holds you at a
distance, with the true ecclesiastical frigidity.

You learn here how to distinguish between what is emotional
and what is properly ecclesiastical in the Catholic Church. St.
Peter's is entirely positive, dogmatic, the assertion of the su-
premacy of the Church over the world; never mystic, as in
one of those dim Spanish cathedrals, that of Barcelona, for instance; nor yet fantastic, full of strange, precious wonders of the
world, brought from far off, as in St. Mark's. It is florid, spectacular, but never profane; suggesting, as it does, what is the
strength, and what are also the metaphysical limitations of the
Church, it never suggests, as St. Mark's does, the human curios-
ities which may become a strange vice, as easily as a singular
virtue. Nor is it, like St. Mark's, in the midst of the city, where

the heart of the city beats, where one sees a homely crowd wandering in and out all day long, looking in on the way home from market, as one might look in for a moment at a friend's house.

High Mass at St. Peter's, as I saw it on Christmas Day, said by Cardinal Rampolla, was an impressive ceremony, indeed, but it was said mainly to a crowd of curious strangers. The large, rigid figure in the red robes and the gold miter, who sat there under his golden vestments, lifting a white-gloved hand on whose third finger shone the emerald ring set with diamonds, performed the sacred functions with a dignity which was a little weary, and in the priest's expressionless way, with that air of fixed meditation (as of a continual commerce with heaven) which is the Church's manner of expressing disapproval of the world. Where I seemed to see a real devotion was in the peasants from the Campagna, who passed with their rough cloaks rolled round them, and kissed St. Peter's foot devoutly, leaning their foreheads against it; the women carefully rubbing the toe with their handkerchiefs before kissing it.

I saw the same deep feeling in a fifteenth-century church into which I went that afternoon, S. Agostino, a church famed for its devotion. A whole wall was covered with little gilt-framed votive offerings, silver hearts, and pious vows, and in front of them many poor old women sat and knelt, praying with closed eyes; others lifted their children to kiss the foot of Sansovino's patrician Virgin, the compassionate Madonna del Parto. I found a different, but perhaps not less sincere, company of worshippers in San Luigi dei Francesi, before the screen of candles, like burning gold, gold light rising flamelike out of gilt candlesticks, which enshrined for their devotion the unseen presence of the Sacrament.

But at the midnight Mass in the same church, which was attended by a special permission, I was once more in that atmosphere of positive, unspiritual things which I had breathed in St.

Peter's, and which seemed to me so typical of Rome. The church was filled to its farthest corner by a brilliant crowd; the music, played by organ, harp, and strings, and sung by somewhat uncertain voices, was florid and brilliant; and far off, at the golden end of the church, white against the gold light, seven rows of candles, rising like an arch of pure gold, the priests moved through the sacred ritual. Near me were some Italians, two of them women of the finest aristocratic type, with faces carved like cameos, a touch of cruelty in their dark, vivid, reticent dignity; and these faces, looking on as at a show, and prepared to look away the moment it was no longer amusing, seemed to bring all the strength of the world's hold on one into the perfumed atmosphere of the place. Looking, as I could not but look, at these beautiful Pagan faces, perfect as Roman medals, I felt that they were Rome, and that Rome was at least sure of this world, whatever her admiration, her curiosity, her possible dreams, of another.

To realize the greatness of Rome, it is not enough to have seen the Colosseum, St. Peter's, the churches, palaces, ruins, squares, fountains, and gardens; you may have seen all these, and yet not have seen the most beautiful possession of Rome: the Campagna. Seen from the Alban hills, Rome is a mere cluster of white houses in a desert, a desert as variable in color as the sky. Lost in that wilderness, a speck between that wilderness and the sky, it seems a mere accident in a visible infinity. And now remember that this vast Campagna is simply the pleasure park of Rome: that it is left there, feverous and unproductive, the loveliest of ruins, in order that Rome may have the pride of possessing it; and think if any city in the world possesses so costly and magnificent a luxury.

It is one of the many delicate surprises of Rome to come suddenly, at the end of a street which had seemed lost in the entanglements of the city, upon a glimpse of the Campagna or the hills. And those hills, rising up from the plain to the sky, their soft lines, under certain weather, indistinguishable from either, opalescent, changing color as the wind scatters or heaps the clouds as sunlight or *scirocco* passes over them, have something of the untiring charm, the infinite variety, of the sea. Drive a little way into the Campagna, and you might be on the Pampas, or in the desert which is about the ruins of Thebes. An almost audible silence descends upon you, in which the world seems asleep. A shepherd leans motionless upon his staff; the sheep move drowsily about him; and you hear the tinkle of the bell.

To see Tivoli, loud and white with waterfalls, a little gray town set upon gray and cloven rocks, fringed with the silvery green of olive trees; to see any one of the *castelli*, one would willingly cross a whole country; and they lie, Frascati, Albano, Genzano, Marino, Ariccia, Rocca di Papa, at the very gates of Rome, within the compass of one day's drive. These *castelli* are all fantastic and improbable; white, huddled, perched like flights of white birds that have settled there; hanging over volcanic chasms that have burst into lakes, fertilized into vines and olives; wild trees, their gray trunks leaning this way and that, seeming to face up and down the hillside, like armies meeting in battle; each *castello* with its own rococo villas, like incrustations upon the rock; each *castello* set on its own hill, as if it had drawn up the ladder after having climbed there: a little city of refuge from the perils of the plain.

They hold the Alban Lake between them, and Lake Nemi, which sleeps with the deepest sleep of any lake I have ever seen, in the most restful arms of land. And each has its own aspect. Frascati, as one turns in and out of its street, opening sullenly on vague glimpses, as if cut by the sides of a frame, is like a seaside village; and one cannot help imagining the wash of waves, instead of the grassy plain of the Campagna, at the end of those coiling streets. Rocca di Papa is like an eagle's nest, perched high on the mountain, with its shady square in front of the little church where you hear old women praying aloud. Marino has an

air of the country, with its fierce men, its somewhat bold, handsome women, its thronging children. Ariccia hangs picturesquely
against the very side of the hill, jutting out into space. Each
has its variety of primitive life, of rococo architecture, of running
water, of trees, of volcanic rock, of lake scenery. And for those
who care greatly for the delicate shading of colors as they change
over a sensitive landscape, to look from these heights is to look
down, from dawn till sunset, upon a paradise of the daintiest
colors in the world, in that jewelled desert which lies about Rome.

But the Campagna is most wonderful, most itself, at sunset;
and sunset in Rome should be seen from the Via Appia, as I
saw it during a memorable drive in mid-winter. Looking back
from the mound beyond the Casal Rotondo, Rome seemed far
off, dwindled by distance, all its towers and domes and roofs
white, set in the hollow of the hills. Nearer to me, Frascati, a
white sparkle upon the dark Alban hills; between, along the
sky, the Apennines, their snow lying caressingly against the
clouds; and below, all around me, the desert of the Campagna,
the long gray line of the aqueducts seeming to impress itself, with
a certain insistency, upon the otherwise timeless waste of the
great plain. A church bell sounded faintly, like the sound of a
cow-bell, from a little white church on the Via Appia Nuova; the
air was still, clear, cold, with a marvelous serenity in its soft
brightness; and as I looked across the Campagna, going out
desolately towards the sea, I could just distinguish a light shining
along the line of dark trees at the edge of the horizon.

Hearing a slow creaking of wheels, I looked down, and saw
in a road two lounging oxen drawing a load of silvery ilex boughs.
Two peasants went by, lounging like the oxen, in their long-
haired garments of undressed skins; shepherds who had come
down from the Apennines for the winter, with their flocks and
herds, and had encamped upon the plain, in the little conical
huts which rise out of it so strangely. Sunset was beginning, and,
as we drove back along the Via Appia, the clouds which had

obscured the sun cleared away, and the sky seemed to be washed with colors which were at once fiery and watery; greens of an inexpressibly luminous delicacy, paler and softer than any grass or leaf that ever grew, but with the ardor in them of growing things; pinks that were like the inner petals of rose-leaves, flushing on the horizon to a fierce golden red, which burned in the tops of the trees like a conflagration, and at the edges floating away into paler and paler gold, and from that into a blue which was the color of shallow water under very faint sunlight, a blue which deepened overhead into the vast outstretched dome of the sky.

The air grew chill, with that intense cold which seems to come down out of the sky upon Rome for an hour after sunset. We drove back, along the straight road, between the ruined tombs which had once stood at the gates of the villas of Romans, and which stand now, in their ruins, seeming to look as the Romans loved to look, on the road which was the world's highway; that long road leading into the Eternal City (upon which, indeed, the ends of the earth are still visibly come) out of the vague world. In so beautiful a desolation, at which the soul shivers away into that loneliness which is the soul's ecstasy before eternal things, I said to myself that here, if anywhere upon earth, God and man had worked together to show at one glimpse all the glory of the world.

—*Cities of Italy.*

THE ODOR OF SACRIFICE

❦ IN FEBRUARY 1902 Pope Leo the Thirteenth celebrated his jubilee. I heard him officiate at Mass at the Sixtine Chapel, and also went—although I forget if this was later or not—to High Mass at St. Peter's, when the Pope was carried in on his chair and blessed the crowd. I had a place under the dome. At the elevation of the Host the Papal Guard went down on one knee, and their halberds struck the marble floor with one sharp, thunderous rap, and presently the silver trumpets rang out in the dome. At that moment I looked up and my eye caught the inscription, written in large letters all round it: *"Tu es Petrus,"* and I reflected the prophecy had certainly received a most substantial and concrete fulfillment. Not that at that time I felt any sympathy with the Catholic Church; indeed, it might not have existed for me at Rome at that time. I thought too, that the English Catholic inhabitants of Rome were on the look-out for converts, and were busy casting their nets. Of this, however, I saw no trace, although I met several of them at various times.

But that ceremony in St. Peter's would have impressed anyone. And when the Pope was carried through St. Peter's, with his cortege of fan-bearers, and rose from his chair and blessed the crowd with a sweeping, regal, all-embracing gesture, the solemnity and the majesty of the spectacle were indescribable, especially as the pallor of the Pope's face seemed transparent, as if the veil of flesh between himself and the other world had been refined and attenuated to the utmost and to an almost unearthly limit.

During Holy Week I attended some of the ceremonies at St. Peter's, and I think what impressed me most was the blessing of the oils on Maundy Thursday, and the washing of the altar, when that great church is full of fragrant sacrificial smells of wine and myrrh, and when the vastness of the crowd suddenly brings home to you the immense size of the building which the scale of the ornamentation dwarfs to the eye.

—*The Puppet Show of Memory.*

A VATICAN SERMON

❧ UNDER THE GAY SKY of a winter Sunday, nearly all the cabs in Rome were scurrying towards St. Peter's. There was one long parade of them returning along the Tiber embankment, having discharged their loads, and there was an endless double file of the reckless little flea-bitten *vetturas* trotting into the Borgo, these overcrowded with laughing Italian families—grandmothers, parents, daughters-in-law, and children, heaped up pleasantly like fruit and flowers in peddlers' carts. They crossed the St. Angelo bridge, passing that statue of St. Peter which, Pasquino said, once grew so alarmed at the number of people Pope Sixtus V was hanging, for petty offences, from the battlements of the castle near by, that it called over to the statue of St. Paul: "I fear I must be leaving. Sixtus will surely hang me for cutting off Malchus's ear!" When the double file reached the piazza in front of the church, it broke into brisk disorder: the pathetic little horses galloped for the arch to the left, which leads into the Via delle Fondamenta, the iron tires making an intolerable clatter on the uneven flagstones. They passed through the arch, and so on, round St. Peter's to the Swiss Gate of the Vatican, where the people dismounted hurriedly and joined the pedestrians. Every one held in his hand a slip of white paper—a printed invitation. These were presented for the inspection of the Papal Gendarmes and the Swiss Guards—the former fine enough with their cocked hats and white belts, the latter more mediaeval-looking than the

Yeomen of the Guard, gaudier than bumblebees, and showing no
signs of overwork.

The stream of people went through the gate, through a small
court and a couple of passages, to emerge upon a great court,
the Cortile di San Damaso, which is enclosed partly by the
palace, partly by a large open gallery. The roof of the latter was
now crowded, the figures of the people silhouetted to the view
of those below, against the bright blue sky that curves down
over Italy on a clear day, almost as rich, almost as blue, as the
summer sky over the United States. The court itself was not
crowded by the eight or nine thousand persons who were standing about in groups, the murmur of their chatter and laughter
rising through the warm air to those who were leaning from open
windows of the palace.

Against the arcade, opposite the gallery, stood a very large
platform, higher than the heads of the spectators. It was hung
with red velvet and gold, and between two columns which rose
over a dais on the platform long red velvet curtains depended,
underneath the papal arms carven upon the stone front of a
small balcony. The dais supported a great red and gold chair, the
papal throne. Upon each side of the throne stood rigidly a tall,
steel-helmeted Swiss Guard in his brilliant stripes, long pike in
hand. In spite of the stateliness of this pair, the whole picture
was (to an American) so strangely theatrical that it seemed only
plausible that the two guards would presently draw the curtains to
disclose an old-fashioned tableau: "Marmion and Constance"
possibly, or "Joan of Arc before her Judges," to be followed by
a declamation, "I speak not to implore your grace," for the bene-
fit of the Ladies Missionary Adjunct.

The Society of the Daughters of Mary had entered in procession, girls in white dresses with long veils; and with the banners
of the society borne proudly in the van, they took places nearest
the platform, for it was to them, particularly, that the Pope
would speak.

Seated upon the steps of the arcade, to the left, were twenty or thirty young girls in gray, with lace scarfs upon their heads, a choir of novices; beyond them was a band of many pieces. The girls whispered, gossiped, chuckled, now and then breaking into open laughter, which did not shock, as it might from a choir in church; yet the court was a church at the time, since the day was Sunday and the Pope was coming there to preach. Their laughter was but part of the murmur of gayety that was everywhere.

But the people were waiting for the Pope happily. Even the papal lay nobles, in their evening dress and silk hats, with gold chains and orders clinking together across their white shirt-fronts, looked cheerful. There were many country people, and many poor, but they were the "respectable" poor; there were no beggars, no cripples, none of the deformity, rags, and dirt that make so much of Rome only less hideous than parts of Naples. Better still, there were no postal-sellers, no venders of cheap cameos nor peddlers of folding photogravures encircling the spectator. Florentines, Neapolitans, soft-spoken Venetians, and a few dark Sicilians were there with the Roman crowd. There were Germans wearing the Emperor's mustache, and Frenchmen with heavily rimmed monocles. There were about a hundred or so tall Americans and English, the former eagerly interested and looking so, the latter the same but not looking so.

Where the crowd was thinnest and the open spaces were largest, below the gallery, stood two young people whose nationality was marked—partly by their keen, humorous, expectant eyes; somewhat, too, by the fashion of their clothes. The young man was broad-shouldered, but he wore a short coat two inches broader and flared, slightly, above the hips; the girl's plain long coat "gave her a waist," and her shoes were, perhaps, too dainty. More than their nationality was marked, however, in her way of keeping her slim gray glove tucked through his arm all the while, and in their both showing openly that while they dwelt in a more exalted sphere, still the world was a beautiful, if remote, spectacle, fondly arranged for the two to look at, now and then, as a momentary diversion from their permanent vocation of looking at each other. They were a Chicago bride and groom on their wedding-journey; and they had been given tickets by Father Murphy of the American College "to see the Pope."

They looked about them with the unreasonable surprise that Americans might be expected to feel in such a place: the sense of unreality that much velvet and gold and a throne flanked by guards in helmets and long hose must produce on people who naturally expect raw planking, bunting, and a glass of water on a deal table to furnish the color of public dignity. But they did not look very long, and fearing that they were recklessly consuming too much of eternity in loose observation of the evanescent, were turning to each other again, when the young man was made aware of a hand fluttering at him over the heads of a group near by, and of a frenzied voice that cried:

"Hi! 'Ere! Zees way!"

Quite at a loss, the youth could but stare, until the owner of the hand and the voice, a small, dapper Italian, was at his side, plucking earnestly at his sleeve and repeating: "Zees way! 'Ere!"

"What is the trouble? Are we in the way?"

"In *what* way? No! Come weetha *me!*" exclaimed the sacrilegious intruder. "You too far back! I show good place! Come!"

He was all staccato; and he made use of more gestures in twenty seconds than many a legislative orator might employ in a whole session. He turned sharply and began to work a path toward the red platform—an easy task of which he made as much as possible, vociferating in Italian to his countrymen, calling greetings to acquaintances here and there, and saying everything thrice over with shoulders, arms, and hands; looking back, continually, to shout cordial encouragements to the bewildered Americans, who followed him without knowing why.

"'Ere! Squeege! Push! I show you! Keep your both elbow out alway, in crowd, like me! Shove! You see? Push! Elbow out

both side; nobody can press you, lady, w'en you keep both elbow
out. Shove! Good for zees pipple to get some shove!"

Thus heartening his passive followers, he led them to within
a few feet of the red platform, stopping at a vantage-point whence
they faced the throne.

"Aha, gentiman! Is it better? You satisfy? Behole wair you
are! Now you can see Pawp nice w'en 'e come. I 'ave arrive you
'ere, becaus' w'y? Eh? You trav' all ze way from Cincinnat' to
see Pawp, I sink you mus' see 'im *nice*. So I arrive you 'ere."

In the space of three minutes he had taken as complete possession of the pair as if he had bought them. They offered no
resistance, and finding themselves in a better position, were grateful. Their bustling little proprietor was neatly dressed and, except
for his trifling mustache, clean-shaven. He was calm and self-
contained for his kind—which means that had he been an American he must have been thought to labor unsuccessfully with
overmastering emotion. When, from a far corner of the court,
came the wail of a baby (of course there were babies there), he
leaped as high as he could to shake his forefinger at it and
ejaculate, " 'Sh!" as if a baby could not cry at a Pope! He was
not alone in this action, however. Half the Italians present exhibited their sense of responsibility for the baby's conduct, and
the multitudinous " 'Sh!" and the sight of so many people jump-
ing up and down and waving their hands either amused or horrified the child into instant silence.

A gentleman coming quietly out of the palace into the arcade
created a stir among the various officials and unofficials lounging
there. A dozen of these hurried forward to greet him. He was a
stout, elderly man; his frock coat was trim, almost dandified, and
not new; his silk hat had known many ironings; his gray mustache
had a slight, cavalier upward twist; and he looked very happy.
Deferential groups followed him and surrounded him; and when
he paused to address any person, that person took on, at once, an
air of profound attention, bending forward a head cocked to

pelican solemnity, as if called into a consultation of state—the manner of the county chairman to whom the United States Senator says something just before the speech.

" 'Tis ze Pawp brozzer!" exclaimed the new guardian of the young Americans. "Look how all gentimans bow! He not reech: Pawp family poor pipple; not fine, reech family—ver' poor,—but like many here. No diff' now! See all gentimans make bow and bow. An' look,—see yo'ng gentiman black mustache, bal' head in front, lean agains' marber colun? He Pecci. Gentimans don' run and bow so much to 'eem, now. Treat ver' nice, but not like new Pawp brozzer. An' look—other way—see gentiman w'ite 'airs, w'ite mustache, front of ze ban'; he great composer, great musician, gr-r-reat frien' of me; goin' lead ze ban'. Yo'ng girl, all in same clothes—novice—they goin' sing. That w'y I am 'ere. My frien', that great composer, he make special compozitzion for to-day. He write to me, las' night, to me, his gr-r-reat frien', that I shall be 'ere for his great special compozitzion. An' w'y? Beckoss I am jawnlis!"

"Jawnlis?" The young couple could make nothing of the word.

"Jawnlis! Yes. Me, I am jawnlis. Make report to newspape'! You un'stan'?" He jerked a pencil from one pocket, a crumpled sheet of blank paper from another, and made, in half a minute, half a hundred imitations of a man writing, including all the gyrations incidental to the act as he conceived it—writing furiously for a second, pursing his lips with energy; pausing then, plunged into abysmal thought in the effort of composition; pirouetting out of it, happily relieved by a shining idea; writing again more violently, turning the sheet to go down the other side, not forgetting to stab it with periods and slash it with dashes, his hand fluttering to high poises, then swooping down like that of an old-fashioned piano-pupil "showing technique," and completing the masterpiece almost as quickly as a melodrama heroine does her letter of farewell to the cruel guardian.

"Write!" he cried. "Write, write, write! You un'stan? Write!

So! Write in newspape'! Jawnlis! So! Critichise compozitzion make for to-day. 'E write me special. W'y? You can imaginate! I am jawnlis, man of newspape'! An' I am his gr-r-reat frien'. You un'stan'. Yes, I am jawnlis." With that the journalist laid his forefinger along his nose—a gesture which, in Italy, usually denotes not a sly or facetious intention, but the contrary.

"It take brain," he said, impressively, but with an undercurrent of melancholy expressive of the loneliness of his isolation, "great brain. Sank God, I haf brain! Zees pipple all roun' you, zey haf not brain. No! Bigot! Stupid! Myself, I am a Liberal. But zees man, zees Pawp who is goin' come 'ere, I like 'eem! Ees a good man. 'E liberal inside. 'E frien' of ze King; I hear they eat dinner sometime long ago, an' make good frien' togeth'. Good man; not meddle politic, only preach; talk only spirchal power, no temporal. 'E belief all real Christian Kingdom ees spirchal; preach *ole* Christian doctun. Ev'rabod' like 'eem, excep' only some cardinals. If 'e goin' be temporal, come out Vatican, try to get temporal power, I be firs' to 'ate 'eem; I be ze firs' to 'it 'eem—I knock 'eem down! I am a Liberal! No bigot! You expec' *me* go to confessional? Tell my troub' to *priest*? Pouf! Aha! Whoo! You no fool *zees* chick! Ha, ha! You 'eer? 'No fool zees chick!' I been America; I know ze slank. Bell-boy teach me. Yes! Been at Cincinnat'! See!" He laid violent hands upon the collar of his coat and threw it forward to expose the trademark of a Cincinnati clothing-house sewn into the lining of the collar. His attitude may be easily translated to the familiar. It was: "Behold the birthmark! I am your father, the Duke."

"Only three time I wear 'eem," he continued. "That 'ow I know you. My clothe' made in Cincinnat'. I see you far back in crowd. 'Ha! Fine lady,' I say, 'good family. American! Cannot see.' I bring you good place. I would lay down my life for American! I am gentiman—gentiman troo and troo!" His voice shook; he hovered on the verge of pathos, but suddenly adopted the gallant as more becoming. He placed his left hand upon his right chest, bowed, and repeated:

"Gentiman troo an' troo! You see, I say it from my hearts, weetha my 'and on my hearts!"

A bell within the palace tinkled. There had been an agreeable sound of chatter, sounding from everywhere in the court, but the bell was a signal for the mere murmur to heighten in pitch and rise to a sudden resonant noisiness, which was like the coming of heavy April rain through sunshine to fall on a tin roof. It increased again, like a quick rattle of hail, as with a wide flash of brass and silver, the instruments rose simultaneously to the mouths of the musicians. The Papal Anthem leaped out jubilantly from the horns; a kind of reverent quickstep it is; and the great melody of it took its way through the clamor of the ten thousand, like a soul-stirring procession passing down a shouting street. Another bell was struck. At that, into the anthem there broke a deep and splendid roll of drums. These were the heralds of the coming of the presence. They rolled out their long salute, while a dozen stately and glittering officers filed slowly out upon the platform and ranged themselves in a semicircle, flanking each side of the dais. They were followed by as many ecclesiastics in purple and red; and now the clamor of the crowd grew into an uproar, then suddenly rose to thunder as there appeared a single figure, all in magnificent white, amidst the mass of red and gold and purple. There was a storm of hats and handkerchiefs on the air, and the cheering filled the court like a solid as the Pope passed to his throne. The officers and ecclesiastics knelt as he went by them; and to the young Americans, who had, all at once, found inexplicable tears in their eyes, it seemed quite natural that these dignitaries should kneel.

For Pius X has the effect of pathos; perhaps it is the transparent and touching quality of the simple goodness that is in his face. Many a town in the United States has been blessed with a citizen (but usually not more) whose look was of this type; a strong and kindly "Uncle Billy Jackson," an old fellow carrying the radiance of a life spent in good works, the service of those in need; one whose hale greeting on the street made that rare thing, a genial philanthropist, whose heart and hand and scanty store were not for the orphan alone, not for the unhighly-educated alone, but for all who lacked, or sinned, or mourned; for the grieving child, the lame dog, the drunkard, for the stranger fallen sick.

Looking upon the Pope, one feels the great pity of it that the man should be a prisoner; for a prisoner he is, not merely out of sentiment, as so many lightly think, or voluntarily, or because of his own sense of right, not even because it is his policy; but because the policy of the powers of his organization confine him. The satisfaction of being his own jailer, which was his predecessor's, is denied to Pius X. One remembers well his sorrow in the great trust which he had not sought, and thinks of that beloved Venice which he will never see again.

There was something about him, too, which made the little bride lean closer to her young husband, as she said, huskily: "He seems so like the good bishop in *Les Miserables*. I know he'd have given Jean Valjean the stolen silver!"

The Pope stood in front of the throne, smiling a little, and looking down upon his people; for his they were, from the moment they saw him. Nor was it difficult to be sure he liked them. You hear, in Rome, that it will not be long before Pius X will be as difficult of access as was his predecessor; but, in whatever manner his present small liberties may come to be curtailed, one thing is certain: that he will always want the people to come to him. He would go to them, if he could. Perhaps one might add, he will if he can. . . .

Pius X is of a good height, strongly made, even stout, and has a fine grace of carriage; his dignity is as great as his position, but utterly without haughtiness or pomposity or pride of office. He has none of the "magnetism" of the "popular preacher," actor, or orator; nevertheless, he is remarkably magnetic; it is the magnetism of unmistakable goodness and good-will to all the world.

"Viva il Papa!" thundered the crowd. Everyone was laughing with excitement and the sheer pleasure of seeing him, and because he smiled a little.

"See!" cried the journalist, seizing the arm of the young man from Chicago. "Look, my frien' the composer; 'e will speak to me! Aha! I am 'ere, my frien'!" He waved his crumpled bit of paper over the heads of the people, shouting reassuringly to the leader of the band, who, looking very anxious, was now mounted upon a stool in front of the novices, baton in hand. The leader nodded affably. " 'E speak to me, you see? Great composer! Excuse. I must make attensh' for my critichism."

The full joyful voices of the novices rose in the open air over the pulsing instruments. It was as if the young girls had, all at once, bloomed gloriously into music. The people listened intently; yet no one looked at the singers; rarely an eye wandered even for a moment from the Pope.

"It is like music set not to words," whispered the little bride, "but to a face."

The journalist made some hieroglyphics upon his sheet of paper, spread upon his elevated knee—a storklike attitude perfectly at variance with the ponderous responsibility of his expression, which would have made that of Atlas, in comparison, seem a vacation schoolboy's. He listened in silence for three minutes, but the strain was too great. He thrust the paper in his pocket and turned to the Americans.

The composer, his air of anxiety replaced by one of relief and pleasure, was acknowledging the hearty plaudits of the people. The Pope bowed and smilingly waved his hand to him; at which the cheering broke out again, lasting until the Pope came forward and stood, near the edge of the platform, to speak to the Daughters of Mary—and to all the people. Silence fell instantly; there was only the faint, multitudinous rustle as everyone leaned forward a little, intent to listen.

His voice, mellow, clear and resonant, yet gentle, has in it the quality of lofty and practical goodness that is in his face. It is a strong voice, too, with the strength of the man who could give an incorrigible lout a fine beating for the good of his soul; and it is what might be called a "brave" voice. A man with that kind of voice will not be afraid of anything that might happen to himself only. But, more than these things, it carries to one who hears it the benediction that exhales from the spirit of Pius X, to all the world, all the time.

While he was speaking, the great clock, high over his head, belled out the hour, four. So intent were the people not to lose a syllable that a thousand unconscious whispers reproved each solemn stroke, saying " 'Sh!" to the bell.

Quite silently, and without so much as the sound of a foot scruffing the pavement, the crowd had drawn forward and closer, leaving no groups and open spaces, until, at last, they formed a dense press; so that when the Pope raised his arms for the benediction and the people knelt to receive his blessing, the whole mass surged back like one large receding wave.

The Chicagoans were expecting the congregation to file out in decorous silence after the benediction, and they were infinitely surprised, and delighted as well, when the people, rising, began to cheer again with all their hearts. The enthusiasm which had greeted the coming of the Pope burst out, many times intensified by the silence which had pent it up; and it was the greater because the feeling for the man had grown deeper every second. His coming had thrilled the people; at first sight they had liked him; now they loved him. Women were crying and laughing and shouting, "Viva il Papa!" at the same time; the handkerchiefs were out again, overhead, like whitecaps on a running sea. The music flared up, only to be drowned, and above everything sounded the regular, volleyed cheering of the students of the American College.

Pius X smiled down upon it all from the red throne. One of his attendants had brought him a beautiful red hat and long red coat, for now the western hills were casting their cold shadows over the city.

The journalist had lost his charges in the confusion, and they were making their way, slowly, toward the arch through which they were to descend to the Bernini steps. The little bride, awed and full of many thoughts, walked lingeringly, her head over her shoulder, looking back wistfully. She pressed her husband's arm.

"Jim, *you* don't believe they'd hurt him, that Curia, or anybody, do you?"

"No, no; all that's just talk," answered the Chicagoan, reassuringly. "Some people like to talk that way; they think it makes them more interesting. Besides, I don't think a man that looks like the Pope would be apt to try to do anything he couldn't do. He looks pretty strong, to me."

"There's something so sad about him," she said, "something so sad and so kind!"

They reached the arch, and she stopped for a last look at the picture they would never see again. The racing sea of whitecaps was still beating up to the red wall of the platform; above it the banners tossed and rocked like stricken sails. The silver-shot blue of the late afternoon sky bent in like a canopy over the brown palace walls; the brilliant semicircle of officers, helmeted guards, and prelates glittered about the red throne, whereon sat the central figure of all the world—so it seemed at that moment—the good and simple-hearted old man in his gorgeous white and red, his kindly eyes beaming good-will from under the splendid hat.

"Ah, isn't he wonderful!" said the little bride; and then, in her girlish tenderness and admiration, she found the inadequate and incongruous word that is luminous with the human meaning the Pope of Rome had for her: "Oh, isn't he a *dear!*"

—"A Vatican Sermon," *Harper's Monthly Magazine,*
    June, 1904.

EMPORIA INVICTA

❦ IN ROME we saw the Pope at one of the great spectacles of the Church, the Beatification of Joan of Arc. My mother had been born a Catholic, but had never taken her first communion. A Congregational family took her when she was a little girl, perhaps twelve or thirteen, I don't know, and gave her a home. She went with them to Galesburg, Illinois, where Knox College took her in, a Congregational school. As a child I often heard her talk bitterly of the Catholics around her birthplace in Oswego because they had not helped her when she was helpless. Nevertheless, when she came to Rome, she had one ambition. It was to see the Pope. I could see the old faith stirred in her heart as she stood beside me in the tremendous crowd; and the power of the great spectacle, as we were jammed together in it, was moving her Irish heart profoundly. I watched her. In a way she was a spectacle herself, seventy-nine years old, as vigorous as a woman of fifty, able to do a full day's work at any task she knew. I saw her face light up and then suddenly, just as the Pope was passing in the climax of the day, in mounting passion I saw wrath, deep Irish rage, illuminate her face. I saw her grab a hatpin, though how she got her arms up, Heaven knows. Then a strange thing happened. She ducked slightly, and I saw a man standing near her, in back of her, a weasel-eyed, middle-aged little Italian, suddenly rise up from the throng, a miniature earthquake, and shatter the crowd around her. She had bumped him with her behind, and she hissed as he came down: "He'll not pinch my leg again!"

I looked again, and Heaven knows how the man disappeared, possibly dissolved in the fury of her wrath, but she certainly gave him a catapult shove from her bottom with a voltage that must have disarmed him and she waved her hatpin like the sword of a conqueror as the Pope passed on. She did not take her eyes from the Pope through it all. The dual drama of the glorious pageant and the insulted Irish peasant's daughter passed in almost the twinkling of an eye.

She watched calmly while the Pope, in a cloud of glory, was wafted down the aisle. The crowd about her thinned a little. She turned to me after the climax and said:

"These dirty Italians! These dirty Italians!" And that was all.

The heavenly choir resounded in the vaulted doors. The celestial color of a great spectacle still held its form. Ten minutes more the Pope sat on his mounted throne, giving his languid blessing with the two-finger sign that in my boyhood days had been an invitation to go swimming. Except for its utter lack of enthusiasm, the drama of it went on. Joan's spirit would have been called from the farthest star by the joy and beauty of this pageant. It was sustained happily, climaxing in the final act of beatification. In all the world, in all history, no other organization of man's device under God's blessing has been able to put together so much formal richness with such authentic fame and joy, mixed in one high moment of massed ecstasy.

When it was over, my mother and I walked together out of the great building in silence. Never again did she mention "the dirty Italians," and in her life she rarely spoke of the high and holy hour in St. Peter's. I don't know why. She went to the Congregational Church, the church of her girlhood and youth, though she never was a pious person and never seemed in her conscious moments to regret that she had sat under the altar of Henry Ward Beecher and his brother Edward, at Knox College, and had heard

the preachments of the great Congregationalists in the first half of
the nineteenth century. But nevertheless I am sure that to her
dying day that picture in St. Peter's remained in her heart, a
sacred memory symbolizing her childhood days.

—*The Autobiography of William Allen White.*

A ROMAN HOLIDAY

❧ WE ARRIVED in Rome late at night, and after taking a walk and a couple of drinks rolled into the hay. The next morning we were up bright and early, and on our way to St. Peter's. There we put in two or three hours admiring its wonders, especially the immense *pissoir* on the roof—the largest in Europe—, and by noon we found ourselves in the alley between the cathedral and the Vatican, thumbing through postcards at a stand there set up. While we were so engaged an American we had met on the ship strolled up, and the four of us decided to lunch together. But before we could set off for an eating-house we noticed a group of people gathered about a priest a little farther up the alley, with the priest haranguing them violently. It seemed worth looking into, so we approached the group and I noted that the priest was talking German. From his remarks it quickly appeared that his customers were pious pilgrims from Vienna, that they had been forty-eight hours in day-coaches on the way—I could well believe it by their smell—, that they had an appointment to be received by the Pope, that the time set was only a few minutes hence, and that their pastor was giving them a last-minute refresher course in Vatican etiquette. Over and over again he explained to them the stage management of a papal audience, and cautioned them to behave in a seemly and Christian manner. They would be lined up on their knees he said, and His Holiness would walk down the line, blessing them as he went and offering

them his ring to kiss. Under no circumstances were they to at-
tempt to kiss his hand, but only the ring. "Nicht die Hand!" he
kept on repeating. "Küsst den Ring!" Nor did he stop with this
brief, almost military order: he also went into the consideration
lying behind it. What a scandal it would be, he said, if the illustrious Pope of Rome, the spiritual father of the whole universe,
were exposed in his own almost sacred person to the lewd oscula-
tion of the vulgar! What an insult to His Holiness, and what a
source of obscene joy to the vast hordes of infidels! His ring was
provided as a means of warding off any such calamity. It, and
not his hand, was to be kissed. "Nicht die Hand, Kinder! Küsst
den Ring!"

So saying, he signaled the pilgrims to follow him. As they
moved over toward a door making into the Vatican I looked at
Mac, Mac looked at Ed, Ed looked at the stranger from the *Laconia*, and the stranger looked at me. Why not, indeed? The group
was large enough for us to be lost in it, and the pilgrims seemed to
be of very low mental visibility. As for the priest, he was marching
ahead of them, with his back to them and us. We therefore
ducked among them, and in a minute we were marching down
one of the long corridors of the Vatican, headed for the audience
chamber. I expected to see a large hall elegantly turned out, with
maybe a couple of pictures by Raphael or Leonardo on its walls,
but the priest actually led us into a series of modest rooms that
looked like parlors in a bourgeois home. They were arranged *en
suite* and the Pope, I gathered, would traverse them one after
another. The priest was in the room nearest His Holiness's entrance, but when he issued a command that we fall on our knees
it was relayed down the line, and we all obeyed. Mac kneeled
to my left and Ed to my right and beyond Ed was the stranger.
We waited patiently, but in some uneasiness. What if we were
detected? Would the Swiss guards who stood at every door simply
throw us out, or would it be a matter for the police? We had
not long to suffer, for in a minute there was a murmur in the

room beyond us and in another minute the Pope was passing before us, holding out his ring to be kissed.

He was Pius X, born Sarto, already an ancient man and beginning to break up. From the floor where we kneeled he looked tall, but I doubt that he was so in fact. His skin was a startling whiteness, and he stooped from the effects of a large swelling at the back of his neck—not, of course, a goitre, but of the same general dimensions and aspect. As he came into our room, preceded by a chamberlain and followed by two guards, an ormolu clock on the marble mantelpiece struck twelve. He moved slowly and with effort, and appeared to be almost unaware of his visitors, though he held out his hand for the kissing of his ring, and smiled wanly. Save for the whispered words of his blessing he said nothing, and neither did any of the pilgrims. He had been Pope, by now, for eleven years, and was close to eighty years old. A man of deep piety and simple tastes, he had resisted, back in 1880, an effort to make him Bishop of Treviso, but a few years later he had been caught by the cogs of the Roman escalator and by 1893 he was the Cardinal Patriarch of Venice and ten years later he was Pope. His reign, alas, had not been any too peaceful: there had been struggles with France, turmoils among the Italian bishops, and all sorts of vexatious disputes—about the powers and jurisdictions of the Papal courts, the text of canon law, the nomination of bishops, the reform of the breviary and of church music, and so on without ceasing. He looked immensely old as he passed so slowly before us, and pretty well worn out. But he walked without help, and in less than two minutes he was gone. This was in May, 1914. Two months later a shot was fired at Sarajevo in faraway Bosnia, and on August 2 World War I began. His Holiness survived that blasting of all his hopes of peace on earth by less than three weeks. On August 20 he was dead.

Once he vanished, Mac, Ed, the stranger and I made tracks out of the room, for we feared that the priest might come back

and discover us. Without anyone to guide us, we got lost at
once, and were presently astonished to find ourselves in the
Sistine Chapel. It was quite empty, and we hid there for ten
minutes—long enough to throw off the scent. Then we tried
the first long corridor that offered, and at its end found a door
which took us out into the glare of noontime Rome. A horse-
hack was waiting nearby, and in it we rode grandly to our
hotel. There was a large assemblage of *Laconia* passengers
in the dining-room, and some of them asked us where we had
been. When we replied that we had been undergoing the honor
of an audience with the Pope there were sniffs of incredulity,
and mingled with that incredulity there was not a little hostility.
Some of those other passengers were pious Catholics come to
Rome for the express purpose of paying their respects to His Holiness, but when they had gone to the American College that
morning to apply for an audience they had been told that it would
involve a great many onerous formalities and probably a long
wait. So many applications were piled up, in fact, that the best
the clergy at the college could promise, even to a ninth-degree
Knight of Columbus and his lady, was a possible look-in some
time in July. Actual bishops, it appeared, were hanging about for
weeks before their numbers turned up. Moreover, all the lay
applicants were warned that their appointments, if, when and as
obtained at all, would be for designated weeks, not for specific
days, and that they might have to stand by from end to end of
those weeks, the men in boiled shirts and tail coats and the ladies
in black gowns with long sleeves. If, at the moment of their sum-
mons, they were not so arrayed, they would miss their turns, and
maybe have to wait three months before they were called again.

All of this, naturally enough, had filled the pilgrims with un-
pleasant sentiments, and they were in no mood to listen with
any appreciation to the tale of our own exploit. It was already
very hot in Rome, and they could well imagine what it would be
like in July or August to sit in unventilated hotel rooms for a

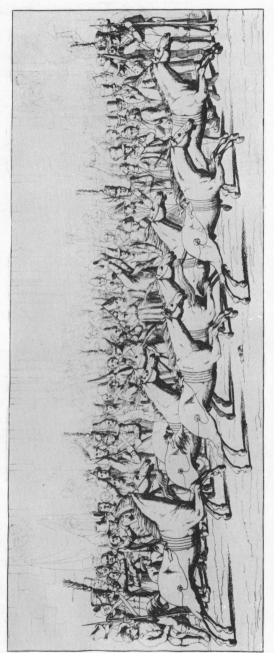

1. Hjalmar von Moerner, "Il Carnevale di Roma" (Carnival in Rome), Rome 1820
See "The Roman Weather" p. 23

2. Giuseppe Agustino Vasi, "Basilica de S. Pietro in Vaticano" (Basilica of St. Peter in the Vatican)

3. Giuseppe Agustino Vasi, "Basilica di S. Maria Maggiore" (Basilica of St. Mary Major)

4. Giuseppe Agustino Vasi, "Basilica di S. Giovanni in Laterano" (Basilica of St. John in the Lateran)

5. Piranesi, "Piazza Navona"

6. Piranesi, "Piazza di Spagna"

7. Piranesi, "Fontana di Trevi" (Fountain of Trevi)

8. Piranesi, "Castel Sant'Angelo"

week on end, clad in boiled shirts and long sleeves. At the start, they eased their minds by denouncing us as liars of unparalleled effrontery, but as we added various details in support of our narrative, they had to admit that we were probably telling something more or less resembling the truth, and thereupon they took refuge in the theory that our uninvited visit was not only an insult to the Pope, but also a carnal and blasphemous attack upon Holy Church itself, and upon the True Faith that it inculcated. The Knights of Columbus present were all too old and bulky to hope to beat us up, but they talked darkly of employing Black Handers for the purpose, and even hinted that they knew a Jesuit who could supply the Black Handers. We replied primly that there was a lawyer in our outfit, and that if any such threats were carried out he would know how to launch the secular law upon all persons responsible. This seemed to daunt the knights, who had a high reverence for the police of all nations, and they gradually subsided into mutterings about the impertinence of Protestants, and, even worse, of infidels, and the need of laws barring them from the capital of Christendom. All we could reply to that was that Teddy Roosevelt and William Jennings Bryan were both Protestants, and that Thomas Jefferson had been an infidel. It was a somewhat feeble argument, and we did not press it. In consequence, the debate gradually petered out, and when we left at last the knights and their ladies had gone back to discussing the discomforts of boiled shirts and long sleeves in hot weather.

—Heathen Days.

CASTELLI ROMANI

🌸 BUT WHEN THE DAY comes for farewell, climb before sunset to the farther Janiculum, for those seductive hours when evening prepares to wrap the city in darkness. Climb by the easier gradient of the northern end, and on the hillside luxuriate in a neighborhood sacred to the poet Tasso. The way is by the steep Salita Sant' Onofrio. Near the top stands the church and monastery of that same saint. Here Tasso spent his last days. In a restful courtyard a fountain drips a cool poem under arched oaks. An open colonnade shelters frescoes by Domenichino. Inside the little monastery is shown the cell where Tasso died, other cells near by treasure tangible souvenirs of the poet, and in the church one finds his tomb. Just beyond, on the hillside, is "Tasso's Oak," a venerable tree which lightning has done its best to shatter and science has done its best to save. Tasso came here and sat in its shade and looked down on Rome, and like as not, in passing, you will find lounging here a young Italian poet seeking inspiration at the same source.

Once on the crest of the Janiculum, you are on the highest of all the Seven Hills. From any point here Rome is more revealing than from any other outlook. This is Rome without reservation. Not only Rome but her vast setting. Everything seen in the morning, though reversed, is seen again. The *cuppolone* (the great dome), the modern Roman's dialectic name for his St. Peter's, hides itself a little behind the flanking trees, but the Castle Saint

Angelo raises its trumpeting angel nearer than ever to the sky. The Tiber, too, is more evident between its stone-paved banks, and nearly all its thirteen bridges may be distinguished, including, beyond the solitary island to the south, near the exquisite Temple of Fortune, the lone arch which is the surviving veteran of the Æmelian Bridge put there in 181 B.C. Just opposite by the riverside, most conspicuous of all the medieval houses built by the great Italian families, is the Farnese Palace, distinguishable by its high loggia and its vast roof.

Here the southern end of the city is not screened by the vast white monument. It presents its slender flank and is more graceful in this modesty. The Capitoline group rises in a buff mass from which stands out the broad façade of that church which, on its eyry, at the top of one hundred and twenty-four steps, deserves its name, the quaintest in Rome, Santa Maria in Aracoeli (Saint Mary in the Rainbow); next it is the campanile of the yellow Campidoglio; and between them in the distance are the two cupolas and the tower of Santa Maria Maggiore. Beyond this group three hollow arches rise nakedly above an unseen valley. The arches are the survival of the Basilica of Constantine and they look down into the vale of the Roman Forum. Next, upper tiers of the Colosseum come in view, and farther off a monumental mass trumpets its presence. One even makes out a line of giant statues on its high façade. It is the basilica of Saint John Lateran, and here, until 1870, the popes were crowned. Somewhere in the plain this side, among the thick clutter of habitations, is the site of the Circus Maximus where in the time of Augustus two hundred thousand spectators might find seats at one time to watch the races, the games and the gladiators.

Behind Rome and giving this view a character all its own, one sees from here the noble reredos of mountains, the Romans' refuge from the summer heat. The southerly group are the Alban Hills, dotted with white towns of which, one is assured, the largest and whitest is Frascati. Far away, across the Capitoline, a wraith

on the horizon is the twin peak of Monte Velino. It is dwarfed
by nearer hills, but, halfway to the Adriatic, or fifty miles away,
it may be seen because it rises 8,165 feet above the sea. On the
right of it are the Tiburtini Hills, up whose flank is Tivoli and
the Villa d'Este and Hadrian's Villa, and on the left bank the
dark heights of the delectable Sabine Mountains, whose praise
was so often on Horace's pen.

In the morning light of the high sun Rome was a motley of
orange and tan, buff and brown, ecru, gray and white. The same
sun in its last moments, before descending behind the Janiculum,
bathes the city in a glow of rose, and the roofs and domes and
monuments are picked out in a delicate pink which softens slowly
till the city seems a bed of broken coral. One by one familiar
objects fade. By some magician's touch long lines of light show
where the greater arteries of life reach out and the glow of pools
of incandescence from invisible sources show where the broad
piazzas are.

This is the time to leave here, descend into the city as the sun
disappears, and cut through the smaller streets, among shadows
with the gray of lead and the brown of bronze. The way for the
most part is marked by corner brackets whose flickering tapers
pierce the darkness only to accent it. A lesser glow reflects from
the tinsel of old wall shrines. Archways open into moonlit courts.
Broad doorways open to dim crowded rooms alive with chatter to
the obbligato of a soft guitar.

Leave Rome, so, as you came, in the night, and let the morning
light wake you far away, among other scenes, your memory of
her an undisturbed dream.

—An Italian Holiday.

BENEDICTION[1]

✿ ALTHOUGH MRS. ENGEL was not a Catholic, she felt that to be in Rome and not see the Pope was to miss something essential. It was like eating an artichoke and ignoring the heart, she thought, but she had no practical idea how to rectify it. She was aware that the Pope gave a daily benediction from his window overlooking St. Peter's Square, but she and her husband had never been there at the right hour, which was approximately noon. The thing to do was to plan for it and go, she knew, but she was shy about suggesting it, for while she was an Episcopalian, Mr. Engel was a Congregationalist, when he remembered it, and she was not sure how he would take to being publicly blessed. She would go alone some morning when he was having his hair cut, or something, she promised herself, and then, one afternoon, she ran into Miss Murphy.

Half an hour later, she burst in on Mr. Engel, who was sitting on his bed with a number of lira notes spread around him. "What do you think?" she demanded, her eyes shining.

"I know one thing I think," Mr. Engel replied. "Something ought to be done about these ten-thousand-lira notes. No one will change them, and I've got to have something to tip with."

"I know, it's a shame, but who do you think I met buying postcards from the porter?" said his wife, in one breath. "Do you remember Miss Murphy?"

---

[1] Permission the author copr. © 1957 The New Yorker Magazine, Inc.

"No," said Mr. Engel.

"Yes, you do. She was on the boat with us coming over. She wore the suit with the funny pockets, and she has a sister who's a nun. Don't you remember her? You danced with her once."

"I never danced with a nun," said Mr. Engel definitely.

"I meant with Miss *Murphy*, the time they had that change-partners waltz. *She* remembers it. She spoke of it twice. Well, anyway, that's who she is, and she's staying right here in the hotel—and where do you think she's taking me?"

"I don't know," said Mr. Engel. "Waltzing?"

"*No*," said Mrs. Engel. "I *wish* you wouldn't spoil things."

Mr. Engel relented. "Where, then?" he asked, gathering his money together.

"Well," said Mrs. Engel, "she's taking me to an audience." Mr. Engel looked vague. "The *Pope*. She's taking me to see the Pope."

"Oh," said Mr. Engel.

"I can't *believe* it," his wife went on. "It won't be like seeing him from the Square, the way anyone can. This is *indoors*." She paused. "Not indoors in his *apartments*. That's only for very small groups. This one is for several groups combined, so it's sort of biggish. It's to be in St. Peter's."

"The church?"

"The Basilica," Mrs. Engel amended.

"That's more than sort of biggish, that's big. How will you be able to see him there?"

Mrs. Engel glowed. "Miss Murphy has tickets for places in a special stand, like a royal box, or something—I suppose because her sister's a nun. The tickets are a special color. Wasn't it wonderful that she had two? She was going to return one when she met *me*."

"When is it to be?"

"Tomorrow, at noon, but we're going to get there at eleven, because they don't *reserve* the seats in the box, and we want to be right in front." She beamed at Mr. Engel. "Aren't you excited?"

"Excited?"

"Well, *interested*, then."

"I suppose so," said Mr. Engel, putting his money in his wallet.

Mrs. Engel hesitated. "Do you—do you *mind* my going?" she asked tentatively.

"*I* don't mind," her husband answered. "I just thought you didn't like crowds."

"We have *seats*," Mrs. Engel said. "We even go in by a private entrance. This isn't a *crowd*—this is an *audience*." She let the word linger, and then went to her wardrobe and surveyed her dresses. "*Now* the thing is, what am I going to wear? Of course, *she's* going to wear black with a mantilla, the way they do, but I don't think *I* should. . . . Anyway, I haven't *got* a mantilla," she added a little wistfully.

"I don't see why you have to dress up for it," said Mr. Engel.

Before Mrs. Engel answered this, she somehow managed to give the impression that she had counted up to ten. "It wouldn't be dressing up if I wore a mantilla. It would be *manners*—like wearing three feathers when you're presented at court." She pushed her dresses along the hanger rail. "My black is too cocktaily. Do you think my dark-blue would do, with my black hat, if I took the flowers off?"

Mr. Engel had collected a dacron shirt, and a box of soap flakes, which he shook experimentally. "Remind me to get some more of these," he said, and retired to the bathroom.

Mrs. Engel examined her black hat. Without its trimming, it would be no more than a head covering, but, after all, that was the idea, she supposed. She had one brief vision of herself correct and remote in the mystery of drifting black lace, and dismissed it. Mantillas and Mr. Engel would not mix, she decided. But before she reached for her scissors, she telephoned an order to the porter.

If a mantilla was beyond her, the hotel car service was not, and the deference of a limousine she could, and would, contribute.

The next morning, at ten-thirty, Mr. Engel helped Miss Murphy into the symbolic limousine and asked his invariable questions of Mrs. Engel. "Have you got everything? Bag, money, glasses?"

Mrs. Engel, whose mouth was oddly dry, nodded.

"Medals," said Miss Murphy. "Have you your medals?"

Mrs. Engel looked bewildered. "Medals?" She thought of Mr. Engel's Purple Heart. "I'm afraid not. Not *with* me."

"Ah, that's too bad," said Miss Murphy. "Any religious article you carry or wear will get the blessing." She indicated a small parcel tucked under her arm. "Rosaries and medals to take home."

"Oh," said Mrs. Engel. "You mean *saints*! I have a St. Christopher medal"—Miss Murphy smiled tolerantly—"but it's on the car at home. Oh dear, I would so love to have a *blessed* St. Christopher." She looked wildly down the street toward the shops. "I suppose there isn't time to—"

"There isn't," said Mr. Engel, "and you're blocking the taxis."

Mrs. Engel looked at him imploringly. "If only I had thought of it in time," she said.

"You'll be late," said Mr. Engel. He urged her in, nodded to the chauffeur, and stood, half waving, as the car started away.

"He's a fine-looking man," said Miss Murphy, "and a grand waltzer. He didn't remember me, though; he didn't know me from Adam."

Mrs. Engel wrenched herself from St. Christopher. "It was your mantilla," she invented hastily. "He's more used to you in a hat." She gave a side glance at Miss Murphy. Remembering some of her less fortunate shipboard costumes, Mrs. Engel thought that the Pope's ruling on dress had much to be said for it. It was not only modest, it was helpful. Miss Murphy looked actually distinguished, Mrs. Engel acknowledged—and wished she could think the same of herself. The denuded hat, softened with a veil

ripped from another hat, looked better than she had hoped, and
her dark dress was simple, but the total effect, she was afraid,
was no more than unobtrusive.

"I would have worn a mantilla, too," she told Miss Murphy,
"but I wasn't sure that I *should*."

"It isn't obligatory, it isn't obligatory at all," Miss Murphy
assured her, just touching her own black lace. "The Holy Father
has relaxed the rule considerably. Of course, this is a public audience. A private one would be another matter altogether."

"Have you been to one like that?" asked Mrs. Engel.

"I've not been to one of any kind," said Miss Murphy, "but
there's established procedure for all."

"Is it difficult?" asked Mrs. Engel, seeing herself backing out
of St. Peter's. "Will I be able to do it properly?"

"You'll not have to do anything," said Miss Murphy. "Just sit
in your place and don't stir till we kneel for the blessing."

"But when the Pope—when the Holy *Father*—comes in," said
Mrs. Engel, "don't we do anything then?"

"Well, he won't *come* in, he'll be carried in on his chair," Miss
Murphy said. "It may be that we'll stand then, but we'll be told
about that, I've no doubt. So relax, now, Mrs. Engel. We've no
cause to worry ourselves." She laughed, a shade too brightly, and
touched a cross at her throat with trembling fingers. "I'll say a
prayer to St. Peter; he'll not let us disgrace him."

Maybe she ought to include St. Christopher, Mrs. Engel
thought. He got you places safely; maybe he got you *through*
things safely. She didn't know, but she wished again that she had
one of his medals. Then she forgot the medal and everything
else, for the car was approaching St. Peter's Square, and she saw
how it teemed with people. "We'll never get there!" she exclaimed. "There isn't even room to walk!"

But the car ignored the congested Square and swept to a
gateway at its left, where Swiss Guards made splotches of red
and yellow against gray stone. A note from Mrs. Engel's guide-

book leaped to her memory, and she recognized the entrance they were approaching. It's the Arch of the Bells, she thought, and we're going through it to see the Pope. She caught sight of herself in the car mirror, and made a final, token gesture. Taking her handkerchief, she quickly, almost with one movement, rubbed off her lipstick.

As Miss Murphy presented her special tickets, the guards at the Arch saluted, and as the car rolled through it to a courtyard inside, Mrs. Engel bowed to them in return. It *is* like royalty, she thought. Now they drove up to a wide door, where they waited while a car ahead of them discharged three ladies in long mantillas and a man with a ribbon round his neck, from which hung a gold cross. Other crosses and medals were pinned to the breast of his dark suit. A Papal Count, Mrs. Engel decided, or a Knight of the Realm—no, of Malta, she corrected herself. Well, anyway, he was *someone*, she was sure, and she wondered if he would be in their stand. His car moved on, and it was her own and Miss Murphy's turn to alight. A man with gloves and a badge approved their tickets with a low bow, and Mrs. Engel, her heart thumping perceptibly, followed Miss Murphy up a short flight of steps toward the unknown.

Almost at once, there were people. Not guards—not chamberlains, as Mrs. Engel had half expected—but ordinary, everyday people, all in what was unmistakably a tearing hurry. "Where did *they* come from?" Miss Murphy asked as she and Mrs. Engel headed with the rest down a long stone corridor. Feet sounded behind them, and four nuns with winged coifs like flying birds passed on the double. Six young men in bright-red cassocks went by like a flash fire. "Seminarians. They're always rushing," said Miss Murphy. Two Norwegians and an American soldier skirted Mrs. Engel with the effect of being on skis. "I wonder if we're in the right place," said Miss Murphy, and waved her special tickets for the attention of an official stationed on the way. "*Si, si,*" he responded. "*Avanti, avanti.*" Mrs. Engel thought he sounded impatient, but she reminded herself that most Italians did.

"*Avanti!*" cried a man with a sword, and this time there was no doubt.

Unconsciously, Miss Murphy increased her speed, infecting Mrs. Engel, and soon they were almost running. Dignity was receding, and more and more people were overtaking them, all with the look of men and women who had just been told that the dam had burst. "Where do they think they're *going?*" asked Miss Murphy, rebounding from the impact of several small but solid little girls in white First Communion dresses.

If Mrs. Engel had an answer, it was smothered by an Italian family that converged on her and bore her through an opening into the arms of a man in a cocked hat. "*Avanti!*" he commanded, and Mrs. Engel found that she was out of the corridor and in the immensity of the church.

"We're all right," said Miss Murphy breathlessly. "We've come around a back way. We're in the transept, and the stand can't be far off."

Although the crowds kept them moving, Mrs. Engel could recognize, now, where she was. She was near the canopied High Altar, and the dome was just above. She looked up, and gasped. From top to bottom, for as far as she could see, the church was hung with blazing red and studded with lighted candelabra, as if scarlet ribbons had been pinned to the arches with diamond brooches, and there, in front of the lamp-lined tomb of St. Peter, she could just see a dais on which stood a tall chair, its pointed back glinting with gold. She stopped dead.

"*Avanti!*" protested a little man, who was behaving as if he were directing a line of fire buckets.

"We go to the *stand,*" said Miss Murphy, waving her tickets again.

"*Si, si, va bene,*" said someone soothingly, and Mrs. Engel and Miss Murphy were propelled up a step or two onto a railed platform covered by what seemed to be a low ceiling, and so choked with occupants that Mrs. Engel could only think of what she had heard of the New York subway at the rush hour. But before she could do more than notice that at least the front rows were decorous with long lines of motionless nuns, a hoarse injunction compelled her on. *"Di sopra!"* it said. *"Di sopra.* Up, please, up."

She nudged Miss Murphy, who was standing stock-still. "We have to go up," Mrs. Engel said. Miss Murphy turned, looking as if she were about to cry. "Up," Mrs. Engel repeated. "We go up."

The press of people impelled them to a stairway, narrow and quivering, that ran eerily up behind the platform and led to a tier above it—a balcony, which Mrs. Engel had mistaken for a ceiling. "It's as bad here," said Miss Murphy, like a Celtic Cassandra. "There's no hope for us at all."

Mrs. Engel looked around her. The first rows up here, like those she had noticed below, were neat with the black-and-white of nuns. Over in one corner, the man with all the medals cowered crestfallen, his ladies crushed against him. Anywhere one could sit, people sat, and where they couldn't sit, they stood. "We should have come earlier," said Miss Murphy inadequately.

"Mi scusi," said a Roman matron, squeezing herself into a space where none had existed.

"Prego," said Mrs. Engel, and wished she hadn't.

"Pardon," said an American voice, and a man with three cameras flattened her as he pushed by.

"We should have come earlier," said Miss Murphy again, standing as stiff and weighted as the statue of St. Andrew against which the stand was erected.

"Look!" said Mrs. Engel.

At the very back, on a line with St. Andrew's knees, she had spotted a bench that offered a suggestion of space. She steered Miss Murphy, who seemed incapable of independent action,

toward it. It was mainly in possession of the Italian family that
had engulfed Mrs. Engel in the corridor. "No, no!" they cried
in concerted defense. "We save!"

Mrs. Engel took courage. "*Non capisco.* No understand," she
said, and hoped it was all right to fib in church. "Well," she said
when she had inserted herself and Miss Murphy in the space,
"this isn't so bad."

The balcony was crammed, but it sloped steeply, and it was
possible to see the dais. "And there's no one behind us, so we
can stand up to see better," she said. She thought a moment. "I
mean, if that would be correct. Will people *do* that?"

Miss Murphy looked at the excited crowd about her. "I don't
know *what* they'll do," she said through tight lips. "I'd put nothing past them."

Mrs. Engel attempted comfort. "They'll settle down," she
said, raising her voice against the chatter of several languages.
"They'll be wonderful. Look at all those nice nuns."

Miss Murphy stared stonily at the veils and coifs that had
preempted the front rows of seats. "Why wouldn't they be nice?"
she said. "All in the best places, like that."

"Maybe they got here *very* early," Mrs. Engel offered placat-
ingly.

"I'd not be surprised if they'd slept here," said Miss Murphy
witheringly.

Mrs. Engel gave up. Miss Murphy was disappointed, and so
was she, but, after all, it was worse for Miss Murphy, because
the Pope was *her* Pope. Surely, when the time came, it would be
all right. Finally putting aside her ideas of royal boxes and velvet
chairs, Mrs. Engel admitted to herself that at least the position
of the stand was enviable. It faced the dais below, and when
the Pope was there, and everyone was quiet, they would see
him well. She craned for confirmation, and drew a breath at
what she saw. The transept was checkered with groups of nuns,
priests, children, and—"laymen" she supposed was the word—

in orderly, squared-off sections. But away from these, stretching back beyond her vision, were masses and masses of people, so dwarfed by the vast space and distances that they had only the dark, packed quality of a homogeneous sticky substance. "Caviar," Mrs. Engel said to herself. "The church is full of caviar." Above the crowd's blackness, the Basilica soared in the brilliance of its decorations like a flaming, protective bird. Under the dome, the chair dominated, still waiting for the hush she was sure would herald the coming of the Pope. Dotted near it were Swiss Guards, their uniforms—so improbable by daylight—now as right as votive candles.

"Michelangelo knew what he was doing when he designed those uniforms," Mrs. Engel murmured, to distract Miss Murphy, who sniffed.

"I've read that he did it one day when he was annoyed," she said coldly. "And whoever designed this stand must have been in the same state. It's not safe. Listen to that, will you?"

The stairs were creaking under the strain of heavily ascending feet. "Someone ought to *stop* them," said Mrs. Engel. "It was full long ago."

A young Irish priest standing near heard her and grinned. "In Italy, there's no such word as full," he said.

"If you ask *me*," said Miss Murphy darkly, "the nuns are the worst. There's twice as many now as there were."

The priest chuckled. "They have a system," he said. "They spread themselves out, with their veils and all, and then move close together when other nuns come. They're a caution!"

They talk about them as if they were *people*, Mrs. Engel noted, amazed, but she supposed it was like being in a family. However, she argued to herself, they surely had more right to good places than—well, someone like herself. Or *sightseers*, she added scathingly as two stolid British tourists, complete with binoculars, increased the standees. If the nuns had their rights, then so had Miss Murphy hers, and she ought to assert them.

Mrs. Engel was getting confused, but she was also getting angry. She glared at the binoculars and turned to Miss Murphy, who had subsided into misery.

Mrs. Engel couldn't bear it. "Get down there, Miss Murphy," she ordered peremptorily. "Get right down there in front."

"Me?" said Miss Murphy, startled. "There's no room there."

"*Make* it!" said Mrs. Engel. "Everyone else does, and you have more right. Go *on*. Tell them your sister's a nun." Miss Murphy looked uncertain. "*Per favore, attenzione,*" said Mrs. Engel to the air. "*La sorella della signorina—*" She stopped. "I don't know the Italian for 'nun,' " she said, "but you go *on down.*"

Miss Murphy, suddenly spurred, thrust herself forward. Mrs. Engel watched as she edged and pressed and insinuated herself, inch by inch, down through people, between people, until she was miraculously in a corner of the lower tier, by the railing, where at first she clung, and then knelt, to lean over it for an unobstructed view. Mrs. Engel sighed with relief.

"Why don't you have a go at it yourself?" asked the young priest, who had been watching with amusement.

Mrs. Engel shook her head. "I couldn't," she said and hoped he would understand. "You see, I'm not a *Catholic.*"

The priest smiled. "Better stay where you are now, anyway," he said. "It's almost time Holy Father was here."

Mrs. Engel froze. In her concern for Miss Murphy, she had almost forgotten the Pope, and he was *coming.* She straightened her hat and tried to wedge herself more firmly onto the bench. Soon everything would be quiet, she knew, and she wouldn't want to move then, or disturb anyone.

"*Mama!*" cried the Italian family beside her, and reached ecstatic hands toward a panting old woman, hung with rosaries, who made her way to them. They pulled her down to the bench, almost obliterating Mrs. Engel, and burst into the volubility of people reunited after many years. "They'll stop any moment now," Mrs. Engel told herself as she was pushed to the very end of the bench. She thought of the hush, and the Pope borne high to the dais, and she gripped her hands together to stop them from shaking. Then, all at once, as if some wordless signal had been given, the shuffling and the chatter were arrested, and a strange intensity took their place, as if something unseen were gathering itself in. From far back in the church came a murmur.

"He's coming," said the young priest, almost to himself, and Mrs. Engel saw his face whiten. The murmur rose and became a clamor. "*Viva!*" Mrs. Engel heard. "*Viva il Papa!*" The cry rose and was repeated. "*Viva il Papa!*" screamed a woman near her in the stand, and Mrs. Engel felt the crowd go mad around her. Everyone was standing, leaning forward; the shouting grew until it was a wall of sound. The Pope was there, below her, she thought, and she couldn't *see* him. Some people clambered onto the benches, to stand. She tried to climb onto hers, but there was no room there. She was in a well, she thought, a tight, dark well, while the people around her, who made the well, roared an acclamation to the Pope she couldn't see. Then the noise lessened, and a voice floated out and up. The Pope was speaking, she realized, and she strained frantically to hear him. A half-understood phrase here and there told her he was welcoming the groups below in their several languages, going from one to another quite easily. Then, almost before she could take them in, the words came in English, pure and almost unaccented: ". . . our blessing to you and all your family and friends. . . ."

"Oh, *please*," she heard herself say aloud. "I want to *see*." She actually whimpered, and, from behind her, hands clasped her waist, and she was lifted into the air. She had one dazed glimpse of the figure in white rising from the chair on the dais before she was put down again. She turned and saw who had lifted her. It was the father of the Italian family, who was standing above her on the bench. "*Mille grazie,*" she said, but he didn't hear her. He was looking out and down, his middle-aged eyes childlike with tears. The people were now getting down from the benches. Mrs. Engel felt panic. It's over, she thought. It's all over, and I've missed the blessing. But no one left, and the complete hush that Mrs. Engel had imagined would come when the Pope first entered came at last. All around her, and down in the church, the thousands dropped to their knees as one person, with a curious sound, like snow slipping from a roof. For a moment, Mrs. Engel stood alone, looking over the bowed heads before her, and now she saw the figure in white clearly. She saw the sweeping sign of the cross, and, light though the hand was that made it, it seemed to fill the length and breadth of the church. Then she, too, knelt.

The next half hour was a blur. Mrs. Engel knew vaguely when the Pope left the dais and was carried down the nave; she followed his progress by the diminishment of the cheering. It stopped, and he was gone. Finally, Miss Murphy appeared, pale and tear-stained, her mantilla awry, her parcel of medals clutched in a death grip. Together they made their way out to the courtyard, where the car was waiting, and rode back to the hotel in shaken silence.

Mr. Engel was in the lobby, ready to take them to lunch. Miss Murphy refused. "I'm destroyed," she said. "I'll just have a cup of tea in my room above." She looked at them both. "It wasn't the way I thought it would be, it wasn't the way at all," she said. "All that pushing and shoving and screaming at him, and himself a saint!"

Mrs. Engel thought back on the shouting and the intensity and the tears. She touched Miss Murphy's hand. "Maybe that's the reason for it," she said.

Miss Murphy's eyes filled. "Well, anyway, we *saw* him," she said, and an unexpected humor creased her face into a smile, "in spite of our special seats."

The Engels went alone to the garden for lunch. "What did *you* do this morning?" Mrs. Engel asked after she had given an account of hers.

"I saw the Pope," said Mr. Engel.

Mrs. Engel flushed. "I don't think it's very funny to joke about it, after all I've told you."

"I'm not joking," said Mr. Engel, prodding a piece of pastry. "I went to St. Peter's and saw the Pope. Here." He took a medal from his pocket and slid it across the table to her.

She took it up. "It's a St. Christopher," she said.

"Isn't that what you wanted?"

"Of course."

"It's blessed," said Mr. Engel severely, "so don't lose it."

"But how? How did you *get* it blessed?"

"I told you. You wanted a medal, so I got one and took it to St. Peter's."

"But how did you get in? It was jammed."

"There was a crowd," said Mr. Engel judiciously, "but I went in, in back of it."

"*How* in back of it?"

"The crowd was all in the big center aisle," said Mr. Engel patiently, "but the side ones were sort of empty. I just walked up one till I got to where the Pope was speaking. When he was all through, he walked around by the railing where I was, and that's when I saw him near to."

"You mean you were *close* to him?"

"Not very—about like that." He indicated a tub of geraniums some six feet away.

"You mean without a ticket, without waiting, without *anything,* you just walked in and saw him?"

"Certainly."

Mrs. Engel drank a glass of water. "What was he like, close to? Were you impressed?"

Mr. Engel retreated from the query. "I don't know what you mean by 'impressed.' "

Mrs. Engel changed her approach. "I just meant *imagine* seeing him so *close.* What a shame you didn't have a camera."

Mr. Engel took on what his wife called his Rock of New England look. "I wouldn't have used it," he said stiffly.

"But why not?"

"It wouldn't have been respectful," said Mr. Engel.

His wife looked down at her plate, satisfied with his answer. It was how she had felt about wearing lipstick, only she couldn't explain why. She turned the St. Christopher medal in her hand; if it had been blessed, she suddenly thought, then so had Mr. Engel. She looked at him and smiled, and then put the medal into her handbag.

Mr. Engel caught the movement. "Be careful of it, now," he said. "Don't lose it."

"I won't," said Mrs. Engel. "I promise I won't."

—*The New Yorker*, July 13, 1957.

ARRIVEDERCI, ROMA

❧ EACH TIME I have left this city, the City, eternally urban, eternally beckoning, it has been with the solemn resolve to return. But it would be foolish to take unnecessary chances. So one afternoon I took the family to the Trevi fountain and we ceremoniously threw pennies over our shoulders. And now as we leave we are all convinced that we will return—but probably never again en famille.

Nevertheless, I have achieved a fatherly ambition. I have introduced the children to the ancient home of their culture and of their faith. Long after I am gone, I hope that they will remember their stay here, and when they do come back will recall the day they stood by the fountain with their parents and tossed pennies into the waters. But they will have other things to remember too.

I do not think they will quickly forget their audience with Pope John XXIII. There was great excitement in our household when the Vatican messenger arrived one afternoon with the announcement that the Holy Father would receive us next morning at Castel Gandolfo. We got up early, the children were all scrubbed and shining, and we went off to the railroad station to get the interurban train to the Pope's summer residence. Through a mixup, Terence, the oldest, missed the train. We waited anxiously until the last minute, but the train left without him. Everyone was sad about it, though it was solemnly agreed that at least he would learn a lesson from the disappointment.

After we got to the tiny railroad station at Castel Gandolfo, there was an interminable climb up the hill to the Pontifical Palace. When finally we reached the palace, our stalwart Terence was awaiting us. The younger children cheered. Admiration for their big brother shone in their eyes. A mishap that was going to teach him a lesson only established his adolescent independence more solidly. They knew he did not have any money of his own. How did he do it? Simple. He explained his plight to a Roman cab driver who agreed that the only thing to do was to drive him out there. I would like to report that the cab driver, his work of mercy completed, quietly disappeared. But he was waiting with a bill.

The Pope, as warmly human and fatherly as we expected him to be, asked if they were all ours. When we said yes he clapped his hands, "Bravo, Bravissimo." He gave individual attention to each one. He told Joan that he had the same name; he told Ann that her name meant Grace; he found the Italian form for Terence, etc. He said that maybe one of the boys would be a priest, adding "who knows?" when not one of the four announced a vocation on the spot.

In the confusion Christopher never got a chance to kiss the Fisherman's ring, but Monsignor Ryan, the Pope's secretary, noted his disappointment, and after the Pope finished with the others in the room he led the Holy Father back to Chris. All received the papal blessing and Pope John smilingly left us. The children were elated with their good fortune when we climbed down the steep hill to get the train back to Rome.

Though this was the high point of the trip, there were other things for them to remember. There was the day Chris found some old coins buried under a rock in the Coliseum and was sure he had uncovered priceless relics. On closer inspection, the coins turned out to be French francs from the Occupation and generally worthless. But this aroused a numismatic enthusiasm that ultimately led him to the Roman flea market where he purchased a whole handful of misshapen coins, supposedly antique, for a few lire.

Both girls were horrified by the Capuchin cemetery on the Via Veneto where the skeletal remains of dead friars are piled up in what the guide books straight-facedly describe as artistic patterns. But the boys were intrigued by it all. They all even began to get interested in churches, or at least in counting up the number they visited, which was considerable, and they trudged dutifully if somewhat hastily through the Vatican Museum and stood goggle-eyed before the wonders of the Vatican Treasury.

I can not really say what they got out of the trip. I suppose that its value was rather cumulative and that it will be some time before we know what was learned. Perhaps considerably less than I hoped for. For one thing is sure. Rome puts demands on its visitors. One must be steeped in history, art, architecture, even theology, to get what Rome has to give.

But I hope that this first trip to Rome will serve as an introduction to many things for our children. Most of all, I hope that we have all come home a little more tolerant of other people's customs and ways than we were when we left. I hope we have all gained a deeper sense of history, which is something else again from mere knowledge of historical events. I hope that we have a larger view of Catholicism and a keener appreciation of the variety of humanity who for religious reasons alone feel at home in the Eternal City.

Though we will all be glad to get back to the familiarity of our own land, the wonder of Rome is also a little familiar now, too. There is a sense in which we are all Romans, for it is here in this city that the West has its most venerable home.

—The Commonweal, March 25, 1960.

III

Easter in Rome

"AT THESE grand ceremonies which the Roman Church exhibits at Christmas, I looked on as a Protestant," Thackeray has Clive Newcome write from Rome. "Holy Father on his throne or in his palanquin, cardinals with their tails and their train-bearers, mitered bishops and abbots, regiments of friars and clergy, relics exposed for adoration, columns draped, altars illuminated, incense smoking, organs pealing, and boxes of piping soprani, Swiss guards with slashed breeches and fringed halberds;—between us and all this splendor of old-world ceremony there's an ocean flowing."

Though one would have to go back almost beyond history to find the year when there were no Englishmen living in Rome, it is safe to say that most of them found Clive Newcome's "stormy gulf" rolling between the two cultures. The selections gathered in this chapter are a good cross-section of the impressions of the Northerners who came to sun-blest Rome to find health or political asylum, to paint or to check off the basilicas and museums in Baedeker, or, like Keats, to die.

For all of them, the sight of St. Peter's etched in fire against the night sky was an experience which took the emotions by storm. Ruskin, who would have coined the jibe "Quod non fecerunt barbari fecerunt Barberini" if it had not been said before, was as susceptible as any: "The whole of the twenty minutes' burst of changing fire, *taking place, as it does, among architectural outlines of the noblest scale and character, and assisted by the roar of the artillery of the fortress, is still unequalled, and I never expect to see any piece of mere spectacle produced by human art fit to be named in the same day with the illumination of St. Peter's."*

THAT IS FAITH, THAT IS POWER

I WAS LUCKY ENOUGH to see the Pope here on Easter Sunday. He seems a harmless, infirm, fretful old man. I confess I should feel little ambition to be at the head of a procession, at which the ignorant stare, the better informed smile. I was also lucky enough to see St. Peter's illuminated to the very top (a project of Michael Angelo's) in the evening. It was finest at first, as the kindled lights blended with the fading twilight. It seemed doubtful whether it were an artificial illumination, the work of carpenters and torch-bearers, or the reflection of an invisible sun. One half of the cross shone with the richest gold, and rows of lamps gave light as from a sky. At length a shower of fairy lights burst out at a signal in all directions, and covered the whole building. It looked better at a distance than when we went nearer it. It continued blazing all night.

What an effect it must have upon the country round! Now and then a life or so is lost in lighting up the huge fabric, but what is this to the glory of the church and the salvation of souls, to which it no doubt tends? I can easily conceive some of the wild groups that I saw in the streets the following day to have been led by delight and wonder from their mountain-haunts, or even from the bandits' cave, to worship at this new starry glory, rising from the earth. The whole of the immense space before St. Peter's was in the afternoon crowded with people to see the Pope give his benediction. The rich dresses of the country people, the strong features and orderly behavior of all, gave this assemblage a decided superiority over any thing of the kind I had seen in England.

I did not hear the *Miserere* which is chaunted by the Priests, and sung by a single voice (I understand like an angel's) in a dim religious light in the Sistine Chapel; nor did I see the exhibition of the relics, at which I was told all the beauty of Rome was present. It is something even to miss such things. After all, St. Peter's does not seem to me the chief boast or most imposing display of the Catholic religion. Old Melrose Abbey, battered to pieces and in ruins, as it is, impresses me much more than the collective pride and pomp of Michael Angelo's great work. Popery is here at home, and may strut and swell and deck itself out as it pleases, on the spot and for the occasion. It is the pageant of an hour. But to stretch out its arm fifteen hundred miles, to create a voice in the wilderness, to have left its monuments standing by the Teviot-side, or to send the midnight hymn through the shades of Vallombrosa, or to make it echo among Alpine solitudes, that is faith, that is power. The rest is a puppet-show!

I am no admirer of Pontificals, but I am a slave to the picturesque. The priests talking together in St. Peter's, or the common people kneeling at the altars, make groups that shame all art. The inhabitants of the city have something French about them— something of the cook's and the milliner's shop—something pert, gross, and cunning; but the Roman peasants redeem the credit of their golden sky. The young women that come here from Gensano and Albano, and that are known by their scarlet boddices and white head-dresses and handsome, good-humored faces, are the finest specimens I have ever seen of human nature. They are like creatures that have breathed the air of Heaven, till the sun has ripened them into perfect beauty, health, and goodness. They are universally admired in Rome. The English women that you see, though pretty, are pieces of dough to them. Little troops and whole families, men, women, and children, from the Campagna and neighboring districts of Rome, throng the streets during Easter and Lent, who come to visit the shrine of some favorite Saint, repeating their *Aves* aloud, and telling their beads with all the earnestness imaginable. Popery is no farce to them. They surely think St. Peter's is the way to Heaven. You even see priests counting their beads, and looking grave. . . .

I forgot to mention, in the proper place, that I was quite delighted with the external deportment of the ecclesiastics in Rome. It was marked by a perfect propriety, decorum, and humanity, from the highest to the lowest. Not the slightest look or gesture to remind you that you were foreigners or heretics—an example of civility that is far from being superfluous, even in the capital of the Christian world. It may be said that this is art, and a desire to gain upon the good opinion of strangers. Be it so, but it must be allowed that it is calculated to this end. Good manners have this advantage over good morals, that they lie more upon the surface; and there is nothing, I own, that inclines me to think so well of the understandings or dispositions of others, as a thorough absence of all impertinence. I do not think *they* can be the worst people in the world who habitually pay most attention to the feelings of others; nor those the best who are endeavoring every moment to hurt them.

—*Notes on a Journey through France and Italy.*

ST. PETER'S ON FIRE

❧ BROWNING HAS GIVEN the best picture of St. Peter's on a festival-day, sketching it with a few verses in his large style. And doubtless it is the scene of the grandest spectacles which the world can see in these latter days. Those Easter pomps, where the antique world marches visibly before you in gilded mail and crimson doublet, refresh the eyes, and are good so long as they continue to be merely spectacle. But if one thinks for a moment of the servant of the servants of the Lord in cloth of gold, borne on men's shoulders, or of the children receiving the blessing of their Holy Father, with a regiment of French soldiers to protect the father from the children, it becomes a little sad. If one would feel the full meaning of those ceremonials, however, let him consider the coincidences between the Romish and the Buddhist forms of worship, and remembering that the Pope is the direct heir, through the Pontifex Maximus, of rites that were ancient when the Etruscans were modern, he will look with a feeling deeper than curiosity upon forms which record the earliest conquests of the Invisible, the first triumphs of mind over muscle.

To me the noon silence and solitude of St. Peter's were most impressive, when the sunlight, made visible by the mist of the ever-burning lamps in which it was entangled, hovered under the dome like the holy dove goldenly descending. Very grand also is the twilight, when all outlines melt into mysterious vastness, and the arches expand and lose themselves in the deepening shadow. Then, standing in the desert transept, you hear the far-off vespers swell and die like low breathings of the sea on some conjectured shore.

As the sky is supposed to scatter its golden star-pollen once every year in meteoric showers, so the dome of St. Peter's has its annual efflorescence of fire. This illumination is the great show of Papal Rome. Just after sunset, I stood upon the Trinità dei Monti and saw the little drops of pale light creeping downward from the cross and trickling over the dome. Then, as the sky darkened behind, it seemed as if the setting sun had lodged upon the horizon and there burned out, the fire still clinging to his massy ribs. And when the change from the silver to the golden illumination came, it was as if the breeze had fanned the embers into flame again.

Bitten with the Anglo-Saxon gadfly that drives us all to disenchant artifice, and see the springs that fix it on, I walked down to get a nearer look. My next glimpse was from the bridge of Sant' Angelo; but there was no time nor space for pause. Foot-passengers crowding hither and thither, as they heard the shout of *Avanti!* from the mile of coachmen behind, dragoon-horses curtsying backward just where there were most women and children to be flattened, and the dome drawing all eyes and thoughts the wrong way, made a hubbub to be got out of at any desperate hazard. Besides, one could not help feeling nervously hurried; for it seemed quite plain to everybody that this starry apparition must be as momentary as it was wonderful, and that we should find it vanished when we reached the piazza. But suddenly you stand in front of it, and see the soft travertine of the front suffused with a tremulous, glooming glow, a mildened glory, as if the building breathed, and so transmuted its shadow into soft pulses of light.

After wondering long enough, I went back to the Pincio, and watched it for an hour longer. But I did not wish to see it go out. It seemed better to go home and leave it still trembling, so that I could fancy a kind of permanence in it, and half believe I should find it there again some lucky evening. Before leaving it altogether, I went away to cool my eyes with darkness, and came back several times; and every time it was a new miracle, the more so that it was a human piece of faëry-work. Beautiful as fire is in itself, I suspect that part of the pleasure is metaphysical, and that the sense of playing with an element which can be so terrible adds to the zest of the spectacle. And then fire is not the least degraded by it, because it is not utilized. If beauty were in use, the factory would add a grace to the river, and we should turn from the fire-writing on the wall of heaven to look at a message printed by the magnetic telegraph. There may be a beauty in the use itself; but utilization is always downward, and it is this feeling that makes Schiller's Pegasus in yoke so universally pleasing. So long as the curse of work clings to man, he will see beauty only in play. The capital of the most frugal commonwealth in the world burns up five thousand dollars a year in gunpowder, and nobody murmurs. Provident Judas wished to utilize the ointment, but the Teacher would rather that it should be wasted in poem.

—*Fireside Travels.*

JOHN BULL DISAPPROVES

❦ THE HOLY WEEK in Rome is supposed to offer great attractions to all visitors; but, saving for the sights of Easter Sunday, I would counsel those who go to Rome for its own interest, to avoid it at that time. The ceremonies, in general, are of the most tedious and wearisome kind; the heat and crowd at every one of them, painfully oppressive; the noise, hubbub, and confusion, quite distracting. We abandoned the pursuit of these shows, very early in the proceedings, and betook ourselves to the Ruins again. But, we plunged into the crowd for a share of the best of the sights; and what we saw, I will describe to you.

At the Sistine chapel, on the Wednesday, we saw very little, for by the time we reached it (though we were early) the besieging crowd had filled it to the door, and overflowed into the adjoining hall, where they were struggling, and squeezing, and mutually expostulating, and making great rushes every time a lady was brought out faint, as if at least fifty people could be accommodated in her vacant standing-room. Hanging in the doorway of the chapel was a heavy curtain, and this curtain, some twenty people nearest to it, in their anxiety to hear the chanting of the *Miserere,* were continually plucking at, in opposition to each other, that it might not fall down and stifle the sound of the voices. The consequence was, that it occasioned the most extraordinary confusion, and seemed to wind itself about the unwary, like a Serpent. Now, a lady was wrapped up in it, and couldn't be unwound. Now, the voice of a stifling gentleman was heard inside it, beseeching to be let out. Now, two muffled arms, no man could say of which sex, struggled in it as in a sack. Now, it was carried by a rush, bodily overhead into the chapel, like an awning. Now, it came out the other way, and blinded one of the Pope's Swiss Guards, who had arrived, that moment, to set things to right.

Being seated at a little distance, among two or three of the Pope's gentlemen, who were very weary and counting the minutes—as perhaps his Holiness was too—we had better opportunities of observing this eccentric entertainment, than of hearing the *Miserere*. Sometimes, there was a swell of mournful voices that sounded very pathetic and sad, and died away, into a low strain again; but that was all we heard.

At another time, there was the Exhibition of the Relics in Saint Peter's, which took place at between six and seven o'clock in the evening, and was striking from the cathedral being dark and gloomy, and having a great many people in it. The place into which the relics were brought, one by one, by a party of three priests, was a high balcony near the chief altar. This was the only lighted part of the church. There are always a hundred and twelve lamps burning near the altar, and there were two tall tapers, besides, near the black statue of St. Peter; but these were nothing in such an immense edifice. The gloom, and the general upturning of faces to the balcony, and the prostration of true believers on the pavement, as shining objects, like pictures or looking-glasses, were brought out and shown, had something effective in it, despite the very preposterous manner in which they were held up for the general edification, and the great elevation at which they were displayed; which one would think rather calculated to diminish the comfort derivable from a full conviction of their being genuine.

On the Thursday, we went to see the Pope convey the Sacrament from the Sistine chapel, to deposit it in the Capella Paolina,

another chapel in the Vatican;—a ceremony emblematical of
the entombment of the Saviour before His Resurrection. We
waited in a great gallery with a great crowd of people (three-
fourths of them English) for an hour or so, while they were
chaunting the *Miserere,* in the Sistine chapel again. Both
chapels opened out of the gallery; and the general attention was
concentrated on the occasional opening and shutting of the door
of the one for which the Pope was ultimately bound. None of
these openings disclosed anything more tremendous than a man
on a ladder, lighting a great quantity of candles; but at each and
every opening, there was a terrific rush made at this ladder and
this man, something like (I should think) a charge of the heavy
British cavalry at Waterloo. The man was never brought down,
however, nor the ladder; for it performed the strangest antics in
the world among the crowd—where it was carried by the man,
when the candles were all lighted; and finally it was stuck up
against the gallery wall, in a very disorderly manner, just before
the opening of the other chapel, and the commencement of a
new chaunt, announced the approach of his Holiness. At this
crisis, the soldiers of the guard, who had been poking the crowd
into all sorts of shapes, formed down the gallery: and the procession came up, between the two lines they made.

There were a few choristers, and then a great many priests,
walking two and two, and carrying—the good-looking priests at
least—their lighted tapers, so as to throw the light with a good
effect upon their faces; for the room was darkened. Those who
were not handsome, or who had not long beards, carried *their*
tapers anyhow, and abandoned themselves to spiritual contempla-
tion. Meanwhile, the chaunting was very monotonous and dreary.
The procession passed on, slowly, into the chapel, and the drone
of voices went on, and came on, with it, until the Pope himself
appeared, walking under a white satin canopy, and bearing the
covered Sacrament in both hands; cardinals and canons clustered
round him, making a brilliant show. The soldiers of the guard

knelt down as he passed; all the bystanders bowed; and so he
passed on into the chapel; the white satin canopy being removed
from over him at the door, and a white satin parasol hoisted over
his poor old head, in place of it. A few more couples brought up
the rear, and passed into the chapel also. Then, the chapel door
was shut; and it was all over; and everybody hurried off headlong, as for life or death, to see something else, and say it wasn't
worth the trouble.

I think the most popular and most crowded sight (excepting
those of Easter Sunday and Monday, which are open to all classes
of people) was the Pope washing the feet of Thirteen men,
representing the twelve apostles, and Judas Iscariot. The place
in which this pious office is performed, is one of the chapels of
St. Peter's, which is gaily decorated for the occasion; the thirteen
sitting, "all of a row," on a very high bench, and looking particularly uncomfortable, with the eyes of Heaven knows how
many English, French, Americans, Swiss, Germans, Russians,
Swedes, Norwegians, and other foreigners, nailed to their faces
all the time. They are robed in white; and on their heads they
wear a stiff white cap, like a large English porter-pot, without a
handle. Each carries in his hand, a nosegay, of the size of a fine
cauliflower; and two of them, on this occasion, wore spectacles:
which, remembering the characters they sustained, I thought a
droll appendage to the costume. There was a great eye to character. St. John was represented by a good-looking young man.
St. Peter, by a grave-looking old gentleman, with a flowing brown
beard; and Judas Iscariot by such an enormous hypocrite (I could
not make out, though, whether the expression of his face was
real or assumed) that if he had acted the part to the death and
had gone away and hanged himself, he would have left nothing
to be desired.

As the two large boxes, appropriated to ladies at this sight, were
full to the throat, and getting near was hopeless, we posted off,
along with a great crowd, to be in time at the Table, where the

Pope, in person, waits on these Thirteen; and after a prodigious struggle at the Vatican staircase, and several personal conflicts with the Swiss guard, the whole crowd swept into the room. It was a long gallery hung with drapery of white and red, with another great box for ladies (who are obliged to dress in black at these ceremonies, and to wear black veils), a royal box for the King of Naples and his party; and the table itself, which, set out like a ball supper, and ornamented with golden figures of the real apostles, was arranged on an elevated platform on one side of the gallery. The counterfeit apostles' knives and forks were laid out on that side of the table which was nearest to the wall, so that they might be stared at again, without let or hindrance.

The body of the room was full of male strangers; the crowd immense; the heat very great; and the pressure sometimes frightful. It was at its height, when the stream came pouring in, from the feet-washing; and then there were such shrieks and outcries, that a party of Piedmontese dragoons went to the rescue of the Swiss guard, and helped them to calm the tumult.

The ladies were particularly ferocious, in their struggles for places. One lady of my acquaintance was seized round the waist, in the ladies' box, by a strong matron, and hoisted out of her place; and there was another lady (in a back row in the same box) who improved her position by sticking a large pin into the ladies before her.

The gentlemen about me were remarkably anxious to see what was on the table; and one Englishman seemed to have embarked the whole energy of his nature in the determination to discover whether there was any mustard. "By Jupiter there's vinegar!" I heard him say to his friend, after he had stood on tiptoe an immense time, and had been crushed and beaten on all sides. "And there's oil! I saw them distinctly, in cruets! Can any gentleman, in front there, see mustard on the table? Sir, will you oblige me! *Do* you see a Mustard-Pot?"

The apostles and Judas appearing on the platform, after much expectation, were marshaled, in line, in front of the table, with Peter at the top; and a good long stare was taken at them by the company, while twelve of them took a long smell at their nosegays, and Judas—moving his lips very obtrusively—engaged in inward prayer. Then, the Pope, clad in a scarlet robe, and wearing on his head a skull-cap of white satin, appeared in the midst of a crowd of Cardinals and other dignitaries, and took in his hand a little golden ewer, from which he poured a little water over one of Peter's hands, while one attendant held a golden basin; a second, a fine cloth; a third, Peter's nosegay, which was taken from him during the operation. This his Holiness performed, with considerable expedition, on every man in the line (Judas, I observed to be particularly overcome by his condescension); and then the whole Thirteen sat down to dinner. Grace said by the Pope. Peter in the chair.

There was white wine, and red wine: and the dinner looked very good. The courses appeared in portions, one for each apostle: and these being presented to the Pope, by Cardinals upon their knees, were by him handed to the Thirteen. The manner in which Judas grew more white-livered over his victuals, and languished, with his head on one side, as if he had no appetite, defies all description. Peter was a good, sound old man, and went in, as the saying is, "to win"; eating everything that was given to him (he got the best: being first in the row) and saying nothing to anybody. The dishes appeared to be chiefly composed of fish and vegetables. The Pope helped the Thirteen to wine also: and, during the whole dinner, somebody read something aloud, out of a large book—the Bible, I presume—which nobody could hear, and to which nobody paid the least attention. . . .

On Easter Sunday, as well as on the preceding Thursday, the Pope bestows his benediction on the people, from the balcony in front of St. Peter's. This Easter Sunday was a day so bright and blue: so cloudless, balmy, wonderfully bright: that all the pre-

vious bad weather vanished from the recollection in a moment.
I had seen the Thursday's Benediction dropping damply on some
hundreds of umbrellas, but there was not a sparkle then, in all the
hundred fountains of Rome—such fountains as they are!—
and on this Sunday morning they were running diamonds. The
miles of miserable streets through which we drove (compelled to
a certain course by the Pope's dragoons: the Roman police on
such occasions) were so full of color, that nothing in them was
capable of wearing a faded aspect. The common people came
out in their gayest dresses; the richer people in their smartest
vehicles; Cardinals rattled to the church of the Poor Fisherman
in their state carriages; shabby magnificence flaunted its thread-
bare liveries and tarnished cocked hats, in the sun; and every
coach in Rome was put in requisition for the Great Piazza of St.
Peter's.

One hundred and fifty thousand people were there at least!
Yet there was ample room. How many carriages were there, I
don't know, yet there was room for them too, and to spare. The
great steps of the church were densely crowded. There were
many of the Contadini, from Albano (who delight in red), in
that part of the square, and the mingling of bright colors in the
crowd was beautiful. Below the steps the troops were ranged.
In the magnificent proportions of the place they looked like a
bed of flowers. Sulky Romans, lively peasants from the neighboring country, groups of pilgrims from distant parts of Italy, sightseeing foreigners of all nations, made a murmur in the clear
air, like so many insects; and high above them all, plashing and
bubbling, and making rainbow colors in the light, the two
delicious fountains welled and tumbled bountifully.

A kind of bright carpet was hung over the front of the
balcony; and the sides of the great window were bedecked with
crimson drapery. An awning was stretched, too, over the top,
to screen the old man from the hot rays of the sun. As noon
approached, all eyes were turned up to this window. In due time,

the chair was seen approaching to the front, with the gigantic
fans of peacock's feathers, close behind. The doll within it (for
the balcony is very high) then rose up, and stretched out its tiny
arms, while all the male spectators in the square uncovered, and
some, but not by any means the greater part, kneeled down. The
guns upon the ramparts of the Castle of St. Angelo proclaimed,
next moment, that the benediction was given; drums beat,
trumpets sounded, arms clashed; and the great mass below, suddenly breaking into smaller heaps, and scattering here and there
in rills, was stirred like parti-colored sand.

What a bright noon it was, as we rode away! The Tiber was
no longer yellow, but blue. There was a blush on the old bridges,
that made them fresh and hale again. The Pantheon, with its
majestic front, all seamed and furrowed like an old face, had
summer light upon its battered walls. Every squalid and desolate
hut in the Eternal City (bear witness every grim old palace, to
the filth and misery of the plebeian neighbor that elbows it, as
certain as Time has laid its grip on its patrician head!) was fresh
and new with some ray of the sun. The very prison in the
crowded street, a whirl of carriages and people, had some stray
sense of the day, dropping through its chinks and crevices: and
dismal prisoners who could not wind their faces round the
barricading of the blocked-up windows, stretched out their hands,
and clinging to the rusty bars, turned *them* towards the overflowing street: as if it were a cheerful fire, and could be shared in,
that way.

But, when the night came on, without a cloud to dim the full
moon, what a sight it was to see the Great Square full once
more, and the whole church, from the cross to the ground, lighted
with innumerable lanterns, tracing out the architecture, and
winking and shining all round the colonnade of the piazza! And
what a sense of exultation, joy, delight, it was, when the great
bell struck half-past seven—on the instant—to behold one bright
red mass of fire, soar gallantly from the top of the cupola to the

extremest summit of the cross, and the moment it leaped into its place, become the signal of a bursting out of countless lights, as great, and red, and blazing as itself, from every part of the gigantic church; so that every cornice, capital, and smallest ornament of stone, expressed itself in fire; and the black solid groundwork of the enormous dome seemed to grow transparent as an eggshell!

A train of gunpowder, an electric chain—nothing could be fired more suddenly and swiftly, than this second illumination; and when we had got away, and gone upon a distant height, and looked towards it two hours afterwards, there it still stood, shining and glittering in the calm night like a jewel! Not a line of its proportions wanting; not an angle blunted; not an atom of its radiance lost.

The next night—Easter Monday—there was a great display of fireworks from the Castle of St. Angelo. We hired a room in an opposite house, and made our way, to our places, in good time, through a dense mob of people choking up the square in front, and all the avenues leading to it; and so loading the bridge by which the castle is approached, that it seemed ready to sink into the rapid Tiber below. There are statues on this bridge (execrable works), and, among them, great vessels full of burning tow were placed: glaring strangely on the faces of the crowd, and not less strangely on the stone counterfeits above them.

The show began with a tremendous discharge of cannon; and then, for twenty minutes or half an hour, the whole castle was one incessant sheet of fire, and labyrinth of blazing wheels of every color, size, and speed; while rockets streamed into the sky, not by ones or twos, or scores, but hundreds at a time. The concluding burst—the Girandola—was like the blowing up into the air of the whole massive castle, without smoke or dust.

In half an hour afterwards, the immense concourse had dispersed; the moon was looking calmly down upon her wrinkled image in the river; and half a dozen men and boys, with bits of lighted candle in their hands: moving here and there, in search of anything worth having, that might have been dropped in the press: had the whole scene to themselves.

—American Notes; Pictures from Italy.

SANCTUARIES

❦ Displeasing as is the presence of most of the English-speaking tourists one meets in Rome, there are two places where they delight to congregate, which yet have charms for me that not even Cockney vulgarity or Yankee irreverence can destroy. The church of the convent of Trinità de' Monti wins me, in spite of the throng that fills its nave at the hour of evening every Sunday and festival day. Some years since, when I first visited Rome, the music which was heard there was of the highest order of merit. At present the nuns of the Sacred Heart have no such great *artistes* in their community as they had then, but the music of their choir is still one of those things which he who has once heard can never forget. It is the only church in Rome in which I have heard female voices; and, though I much prefer the great male choirs of the basilicas, there is a soothing simplicity in the music at Trinità de' Monti which goes home to almost every heart. I have seen giddy and unthinking girls, who laughed at the ceremonial they did not understand, subdued to reverence by those strains, and supercilious Englishmen reduced to the humiliating necessity of wiping their eyes. Indeed, the whole scene is so harmoniously impressive that its enchantment cannot be resisted. The solemn church, lighted only by the twilight rays, and the tapers upon the high altar,—the veiled forms of the pious sisterhood and their young pupils in the grated sanctuary,—the clouding of the fragrant incense,—the tinkling of that silvery bell and

of the chains of the swinging censer,—those ancient and dignified
rites,—and over all, those clear angelic voices praying and prais-
ing, in litany and hymn—all combine to make up a worship, one
moment of which would seem enough to wipe away the memory
of a lifetime of folly, and disappointment, and sorrow.

The Sistine Chapel is another place to which I am bound by
an almost supernatural fascination. My imperfect eyesight will
not permit me to enjoy fully the frescoes that adorn its lofty
walls; but I feel that I am in the presence of the great master
and some of his mightiest conceptions. I do not know whether
the chapel is most impressive in its empty state, or when thronged
for some great religious function. In the former condition, its
fine proportions and its simplicity satisfy me so completely, that
I hardly wish for the pomp and splendor which belong to it on
great occasions. I know of nothing more grand than the sight
of that simple throne of the Sovereign Pontiff, when it is occupied by that benignant old man, to whom more than two hundred
millions of people look with veneration as to a father and a
teacher,—and surrounded by those illustrious prelates and princes
who compose a senate of moral and intellectual worth, such as all
the world beside cannot parallel. Those venerable figures—
those gray hairs—those massive foreheads, and those resplendent
robes of office, seem to be a part of some great historical picture,
rather than a reality before my eyes.

There is nothing more severe in actual experience, or more
satisfactory in the recollection, than Holy Week in the Sistine
Chapel. The crowd, the fatigue, and the presence of so many
sight-seers, who have come with the same feeling that they would
attend an opera or a play, are not calculated to increase one's
bodily comfort, or to awaken the sentiments proper to so sacred
a season as that which is then commemorated. But after these
have passed away, there remains the recollection, which time
does not diminish, but makes more precious, of that darkening
chapel and the bowed-down heads of the Pope and cardinals,

of the music, "yearning like a god in pain," of the melodious woe of the *Miserere*, the plaintive majesty of the Lamentations and the Reproaches, and the shrill dissonance of the shouts of the populace in the gospel narrative of the crucifixion. These are things which would outweigh a year of fatigue and pain. I know of no greater or more sincere tribute to the perfections of the Sistine choir, and the genius of Allegri and Palestrina, than the patience with which so many people submit to be packed, like herring in a box, into that small chapel. But old and gouty as I am, I would gladly undergo all the discomforts of that time to hear those sounds once more.

. . . It is a sad thing to leave Rome. I have seen people who have made but a brief stay there shed more tears on going away than they ever did on a departure from home; but for one who has lived there long enough to feel like a Roman citizen— to feel that the broken columns of the Forum have become a part of his being—to feel as familiar with St. Peter's and the Vatican as with the King's Chapel and the Tremont House—it is doubly hard to go away.

—*My Unknown Chum.*

THE SISTINE CHAPEL

🌸 THE LAST WEEK of Lent was come, and strangers streamed back towards Rome. Carriage after carriage rolled in through the Porta del Popolo and the Porta del Giovanni. On Wednesday afternoon began the *Miserere* in the Sistine Chapel. My soul longed for music; in the world of melody I could find sympathy and consolation. The throng was great, even within the chapel— the foremost division was already filled with ladies. Magnificent boxes, hung with velvet and golden draperies, for royal person- ages and foreigners from various courts, were here erected so high, that they looked out beyond the richly carved railing which separated the ladies from the interior of the chapel. The papal Swiss guards stood in their bright festal array. The officers wore light armor, and in their helmets a waving plume: this was particularly becoming to Bernardo, who was greeted by the hand- some young ladies with whom he was acquainted.

I obtained a seat immediately within the barrier, not far from the place where the papal singers were stationed. Several English people sat behind me. I had seen them during the carnival, in their gaudy masquerade dresses: here they wore the same. They wished to pass themselves off for officers, even boys of ten years old. They all wore the most expensive uniforms, of the most showy and ill matched colors. As for example, one wore a light blue coat, embroidered with silver, gold upon the slippers, and a sort of turban with feathers and pearls. But this was not anything new at the festivals in Rome, where a uniform obtained for its wearer a better seat. The people who were near smiled at it, but it did not occupy me long.

The old cardinals entered in their magnificent violet-colored velvet cloaks, with their white ermine capes; and seated themselves side by side, in a great half circle, within the barrier, whilst the priests who had carried their trains seated themselves at their feet. By the little side door of the altar the holy father now entered in his purple mantle and silver tiara. He ascended his throne. Bishops swung the vessels of incense around him, whilst young priests, in scarlet vestments, knelt, with lighted torches in their hands, before him and the high altar.

The reading of the lessons began. But it was impossible to keep the eyes fixed on the lifeless letters of the Missal—they raised themselves, with the thoughts, to the vast universe which Michael Angelo has breathed forth in colors upon the ceiling and the walls. I contemplated his mighty sibyls and wondrously glorious prophets, every one of them a subject for a painting. My eyes drank in the magnificent processions, the beautiful groups of angels: they were not to me painted pictures; all stood living before me. The rich tree of knowledge from which Eve gave the fruit to Adam; the Almighty God, who floated over the waters, not borne up by angels, as the old masters had represented him—no, the company of angels rested upon him and his fluttering garments. It is true I had seen these pictures before, but never as now had they seized upon me. The crowd of people, perhaps even the lyric of my thoughts, made me wonderfully alive to poetical impressions; and many a poet's heart has felt as mine did!

The bold foreshortenings, the determinate force with which every figure steps forward, is amazing, and carries one quite away! It is a spiritual Sermon on the Mount, in color and form. Like Raphael, we stand in astonishment before the power of Michael Angelo. Every prophet is a Moses like that which he formed in marble. What giant forms are those which seize upon our eye and our thoughts as we enter! But, when intoxicated with this view, let us turn our eyes to the background of the chapel, whose whole wall is a high altar of art and thought. The great chaotic picture, from the floor to the roof, shows itself there like a jewel, of which all the rest is only the setting. We see there the *Last Judgment.*

Christ stands in judgment upon the clouds, and the apostles and his mother stretch forth their hands beseechingly for the poor human race. The dead raise the grave-stones under which they have lain; blessed spirits float upwards, adoring to God, whilst the abyss seizes its victims. Here one of the ascending spirits seeks to save his condemned brother, whom the abyss already embraces in its snaky folds. The children of despair strike their clinched fists upon their brows, and sink into the depths! In bold foreshortening, float and tumble whole legions between heaven and earth. The sympathy of the angels; the expression of lovers who meet; the child, that, at the sound of the trumpet, clings to the mother's breast, is so natural and beautiful, that one believes one's self to be one among those who are waiting for judgment. Michael Angelo has expressed in colors what Dante saw and has sung to the generations of the earth.

The descending sun, at that moment, threw his last beams in through the uppermost window. Christ, and the blessed around him, were strongly lighted up; whilst the lower part, where the dead arose, and the demons thrust their boat, laden with damned, from shore, were almost in darkness.

Just as the sun went down the last lesson was ended, and the last light which now remained was removed, and the whole picture-world vanished from before me; but, in that same moment, burst forth music and singing. That which color had bodily revealed arose now in sound: the day of judgment, with its despair and its exultation, resounded above us.

The father of the Church, stripped of his papal pomp, stood

before the altar and prayed at the holy cross: and upon the wings
of the trumpet resounded the trembling quire, *"Populus meus,
quid feci tibi?"* Soft angel tones rose above the deep song, tones
which ascended not from a human breast: it was not a man's
nor a woman's: it belonged to the world of spirits: it was like
the weeping of angels dissolved in melody.

In this world of harmony my soul imbibed strength and the
fullness of life. I felt myself joyful and strong, as I had not been
for a long time. Annunciata, Bernardo, all my love, passed before
my thought. I loved, in this moment, as blessed spirits may love.
The peace which I had sought in prayer, but had not found,
flowed now, with these tones, into my heart.

The Improvisatore.

IV

Sede Vacante

"PRETTY much everything published about the Vatican is untrue," gloomily observes Francis MacNutt, the papal chamberlain, and he cites the imaginary striking of the brow of the dead Pontiff with a silver hammer. Though much of the fiction about the Papacy has appeared in the guise of newspaper reportage (the silver hammer legend is indestructible), yet the protocol for the election and enthronement of a Pope is usually reported accurately.

From the millions of words which have been written about the papal election, two impressions have been selected. Hugh Walpole's lively account, written from a vantage point in St. Peter's Square, catches the pressure of suspense and the climactic eagerness which pervade the great piazza as the eyes and camera lenses of the world focus on the ridiculous stovepipe protruding from the Sistine. Cortesi's has all the high comedy of a Moss Hart play, and illuminates the character of an extraordinary reporter who once, when applying for a job with a news service, confidently gave as his references the Pope and the King of Italy.

WHEN THE POPE DIES

❦ THE PREPARATIONS to cover with success the final illness and death of Leo XIII lasted over ten years. I had realized that at the first signal that the Pope was nearing his end the greatest interest and anxiety would be felt in the whole world and that the ablest newspapermen would rush to Rome, where there would be the keenest competition to secure the best information. Accordingly, I laid my plans years ahead, forming many intimate friendships in both Vatican and ecclesiastical circles, and among the Pope's private acquaintances and relations.

The election of Cardinal Pecci to the Pontificate under the name of Leo XIII was among the most interesting that ever occurred. Upon the death of Pius IX, the last Pope who was also a temporal ruler, the Sacred College was divided into several parties, all unable to reconcile their views with those of the others. Finally they decided to elect Cardinal Pecci, who looked so pale, frail, and thin, that nobody expected him to live for more than six months, at the end of which time the College of Cardinals would have been better prepared to elect the pontiff whom they really desired. Pecci himself was convinced that his would not be a long life, for at the end of the second scrutiny, when it became evident that he would be elected, he turned to Cardinal Pellegrini, who was sitting next to him, and said: "So you want to have a second Adrian V," alluding to the fact that this Pope reigned for only thirty-eight days. It would be interesting to know why Leo, who was a profound scholar of Church history, chose as his example just Adrian V and not some other pope whose pontificate was even shorter, such as Leo XI, who reigned twenty-seven days; Pius III, twenty-six; Boniface XI, fifteen; or St. Stephen, who died three days after he was elected.

When, immediately after his election, Leo was being robed for the benediction of the crowd from the interior balcony of St. Peter's, turning to those who were dressing him, he said: "Hurry, or I shall die before you have finished." However, in spite of all prevision, Leo buried all the cardinals but one who had participated in his conclave, and reigned for twenty-five years and five months, which, excepting that of Pius IX, is the longest pontificate known.

These facts, coupled with the influence and prestige which the Catholic Church had gained under the direction of Leo's powerful and brilliant mind, gave a special importance to the disappearance of this extraordinary man.

My first step in the elaborate preparations for being quickly and correctly informed in case of any complications at the Vatican was taken in 1893, ten years before the death of Leo, when I started to pay a weekly visit to Professor Giuseppe Lapponi, the Pope's physician. Lapponi and I soon became good friends, and the weekly visit became a pleasure and an excuse for many friendly chats, instead of remaining the stiff interview it was at first. I remember that I found out from these talks I had with Lapponi that the post of Vatican physician is not the sinecure and the remunerative job one might expect. First of all, the Pope's doctor cannot call his time his own, for not only does the Vatican work take up many hours of the day, but the rest of his time is given up to answering calls from all the journalists and important personages in Rome who are perpetually inquiring as to the Pope's health. "This would still be bearable," Lapponi told me, "if only all these people would limit themselves to asking for their information during the day. Most of them, to be surer of finding me at home, have the bad habit of ringing me up on the telephone in the middle of the night." Added to these inconveniences, the Vatican doctor has to sustain a considerable expense in answering all the telegrams of inquiry which, owing to the high station of the senders, he cannot afford to ignore.

The salary of the Vatican physician used to be in those days simply absurd. The Vatican still paid the same fees that had been established about a couple of centuries before, and which were exactly six hundred dollars a year. The only privilege allowed to the official doctor was a carriage to drive him backward and forward between his house and the Vatican. Lapponi used to be very loud in his complaints to me, and in answer to my exclamations of wonder that he did not resign from the post, he used to say:

"You know, I have become rather fond of the old Pope. He is really a very nice man and, except in the matter of the salary, treats me exceptionally well. I am so much in his confidence that to threaten him with my resignation unless he raises my salary would seem to me very much like blackmail. This morning, for instance," Lapponi would go on telling me, to illustrate the degree of confidence he enjoyed, "the Pope and I were in the library and he wanted me to see a particular book which was on a high shelf. I tried to get it by standing on a chair, but I could not reach it. The Pope himself then insisted on getting on to the chair and stretching for the book, which he easily reached, as he is considerably taller than I am. He did this, mind you, in spite of his nearly ninety years and of my protests as his physician."

Besides the Pope's physician, I also made a point of becoming very well acquainted with his family, of whom I already knew Cardinal Giuseppe Pecci, his brother. Giuseppe Pecci was a Jesuit, and, though very earnest and kind, was not of the same mental caliber as the Pope. The two brothers loved each other dearly and Giuseppe told me that one of the greatest privations in his life was that of not being able to be in as close relations with his brother as he had been before the latter's elevation to the pontificate. Leo was a very strict observer of etiquette, and Giuseppe, for instance, never again had a meal with his brother after the latter became Pope.

The rest of the Pecci family lived at Carpineto, a small town fifty miles from Rome, perched on the top of a hill about three thousand feet above sea level. The journey to Carpineto from Rome was one of the severest imaginable, as the roads were beyond words, and the only means of conveyance was a miserable coach pulled by two even more miserable horses in the last stages of emaciation. Perhaps for this reason nobody ever went to Carpineto and nobody ever used to move from Carpineto, with the result that the town was more or less in the same condition as the Pope's regime had left it in the Middle Ages. The most elementary rules and hygienic necessities were unknown. Even in the chief house of the town, called the Palace, where the Pecci family lived, a bathroom was a thing nobody had ever dreamed of having. Good drinking water had never been brought to the town, where everybody drank either rain water or wine. Still, under these conditions I found that the citizens of Carpineto were an exceptionally robust crowd of people who invariably managed to live to a great age. From these visits dates my great skepticism regarding the microbe theory and the propagation of disease.

At Carpineto lived one of the Pope's nephews, Count Ludovico Pecci, who spent his life as a country gentleman, looking after his property. He always used to receive me with the greatest cordiality, glad, I think, to hear what was going on in the outside world.

There was another nephew of the Pope, Count Camillo Pecci, who was the member of the family I knew best. He had married a Cuban lady and was at the same time the *enfante gâte* and the *enfante terrible* of his uncle. He got into all sorts of trouble and

always had recourse to the Pope to put things right. Leo used
to work himself up into terrible fits of anger, but always ended up
by contenting his spoiled nephew. Camillo was up to all sorts
of tricks to soften the Pope's heart. Once when he required
assistance very soon after a previous call upon his generosity he
had the idea of sending his wife to speak to his uncle. Countess
Pecci, who was a very accomplished singer, was to say that as
they lacked money she would be obliged to go on the stage to
earn her living. They hoped that Leo would be horrified at the
idea of his niece singing in music halls, a very shocking thing
for ladies to do in Italy in those days, and that he would therefore
again help them. Leo, however, took the news very calmly,
perfectly realizing the trick, and, to the lady's great indignation,
in his nasal voice replied: "I am only sorry for one thing, my
dear, I shall not be able to come and listen to you." On a full
confession of the real state of affairs he again thundered in a
paroxysm of fury, but eventually as usual, settled everything.

Leo appointed Count Camillo general of the papal army.
Camillo told me that once, when he visited Havana, the Cuban
government held a military review in his honor, at which he
naturally was present in full-dress uniform. All went well until
they wanted to present him with an address beginning with the
words: "To General Count Camillo Pecci, who won his rank on
the battle field." "For heaven's sake," Camillo interrupted,
"don't say that, or I shall never have the cheek to go back to
Rome. I have never even seen a gun fired." "Then," it was suggested, "we will say, 'who won his rank on the field of honor.'"
"Worse still, worse still," exclaimed Camillo, horrified. He
begged so insistently to be let off the address that this part of the
ceremony was omitted.

I also made it my duty to know intimately as many members
of the Vatican household as possible. At the slightest hint of
an indisposition of the Pope my whole army of reporters was
mobilized, and I had not only the Pontiff's private chaplain and

chamberlain keeping me informed of the Pope's condition, but also the cardinals and bishops who held important positions in the Vatican.

The first time I had need of using my complicated system of news-gathering was in 1899, when Leo was operated upon by Professor Mazzoni for the removal of a cyst, an operation which would have been of no importance had the patient not been the Pope, and had he not been eighty-nine years of age. I got my news with great promptness and exactness, though I had to work hard to obtain this result. Among other things I used to oblige my reporters to ring me up three times every night, whether there was any news or not. I became so accustomed to the ringing of the telephone next to my bed that I used to get hold of the receiver automatically, and when I realized there was nothing of importance going on I could go to sleep with the receiver on my pillow and the reporter still talking.

Eventually, however, the day came that Leo laid himself down never to rise again. As soon as I heard that the Pope had been obliged to take to his bed I set my whole organization moving, arranging a double service of communication by telephone and by messenger, to make quite sure that no news should escape me.

Leo was ill for eighteen days, and for eighteen days I never went to bed. I think that if the Pope had lived even a little longer I would have died before him. His illness began in July, just when all those who can leave Rome are far away enjoying a little coolness at the seaside or in the hills. I suddenly found myself with an immense amount of stuff and stories to be cast into shape and cabled to America. I was obliged to engage outsiders capable of writing English and of translating from the Italian the enormous quantity of news continually pouring into my office from the reporters whom I had stationed with a generous hand in the Vatican. The only typist I could obtain I had to get down from Florence, as there were none to be had in Rome in that season. Luckily, soon I was helped out by the cleverest European correspondents of the American news organization, who were rushed immediately out to Rome. Among these were Charles T. Thompson, one of the best balanced heads I have ever met, and an admirable organizer, and William A. M. Goode who, although he has now become Sir William Goode, still remains for his friends "Billy" Goode, and who still often sends to me, with a letter of introduction, some Minister of Foreign Affairs or some Premier from eastern Europe.

Thanks to the great number of acquaintances I had made in the Vatican, all of whom kept me informed of what was happening in various quarters, I was able to cable a day-to-day, in fact hour-to-hour, graphic description of what was going on at the deathbed of Leo XIII, enabling the American readers to follow, only a few hours after the events had actually occurred, the scenes at the Vatican, and to learn the words uttered by the Pope. The tension and suspense throughout the world, among Protestants as well as Catholics, were extraordinary. In one of the last days of the illness Mr. Melville E. Stone cabled to me that not only all the Catholic, but even some Protestant churches had rung their bells, had held special services, and had offered prayers for the recovery of the aged Pontiff. I forwarded the dispatch at once to Cardinal Rampolla, and the next day I received a reply from the then Monsignor Della Chiesa, who, nearly ten years later, became Benedict XV, saying that he had shown Mr. Stone's dispatch to the dying Pope, who, after reading it, exclaimed: "I die satisfied, as this shows that my idea of the reunion of all Christian Churches is not a dream."

My labor in connection with the illness and death of Leo was complicated by the fact that the Italian government had decided that no dispatch announcing the death of the Pope would be allowed to pass until the Vatican itself had had time to notify the papal representatives abroad. I had, however, arranged a system whereby not only could I have the news long before anyone else, but by which I could also transmit the news to America. On the fatal day everything went like clockwork.

According to Vatican rules a Pope is not officially dead until his private physician, by passing a lighted candle before his lips, has ascertained that he breathes no more. When the Pope died, Doctor Lapponi, going into the room adjoining the Pope's bed-chamber to get the candle for this rite, telephoned to me the news of the death. I was prepared, and had the following apparently harmless cable ready with the exception of the figures which I filled in from Lapponi's particulars.

"Melstone Newyork
Number missing bond 404
Montefiore."

The figures 404 indicated that the Pope had died at four minutes past four. Not daring to trust any messenger boy with the precious news I rushed personally to the Central Telegraph Office just as I was, collarless and with my shirt sleeves turned up (I remember it was July and broiling hot). It was one of the most memorable "beats" in the history of journalism. My code message, which I sent by all routes possible, reached New York in nine minutes, when, that is, nobody in Rome, except a few persons in the Vatican, yet knew that Leo XIII was no more. From New York the news was "flashed" not only through the States as far as San Francisco, but was also cabled back to Europe, enabling London, Paris, and Berlin newspapers to publish Leo's death before getting the report from their Rome Correspondents.

That night, for the first time after nearly three weeks, I slept in a bed, and the next day, for the first time since Leo had fallen ill, I went to the Vatican.

With the Pope's death the work, though naturally reduced, was by no means over. Then came the funeral and the election of the new Pontiff, both events proving of very great interest, the first for sentimental reasons, the second mainly for the contending interests in the Conclave.

On the evening in which the funeral of Leo was to take place, I found myself without an invitation ticket. Moreover, the Vatican had no more to give. I wished very strongly to be present, and said so to Commendator Puccinelli, the Master of the Apostolic Palace. Puccinelli, the Master, thought for a minute and then said: "Never mind about the ticket. Meet me at eight o'clock this evening in the Court of St. Damasus. I will arrange it for you." I did as I had been told, and to my surprise Puccinelli led me to where the funeral procession was being formed and placed me among the cardinals. When all was ready the procession moved into St. Peter's toward one of the side chapels where the actual service was to be held. This chapel is separated from the aisle of the church by bronze gates, and I noticed that these were shut as soon as the head of the procession formed by the cardinals, with me among them, had entered. The rest of the procession was left outside in the aisle and nave of the church. Thus I was the only one, besides the members of the Sacred College, to assist actually on the spot at that memorable and impressive ceremony. I wrote an account of the unforgettable scene in the chapel itself, so that at the end of the service I had already several thousand words ready to file, beating everybody else in exactness and speed.

The Conclave and the election of Pius X afforded even greater successes. As is known, the most severe measures are taken to insure the strictest secrecy concerning the Conclave. Even the doors leading to the Sistine Chapel and to the apartments occupied by the cardinals are walled up, leaving only a small aperture over which a very strict watch is kept. I remember Cardinal Logue, Archbishop of Armagh in Ireland, telling me that he and his conclavist were relegated to the very top of the Apostolic Palace in two little rooms, the windows of which had been walled up nearly to the top to avoid their looking over and signaling to outsiders. "I couldn't endure it," said His Eminence; "the heat and the closeness were too oppressive. I took to standing on a chair, by which device I managed to look out into St. Peter's

Square and see the beautiful fountains below that made me wish to have a splash in them."

I had taken many precautions and made many plans to circumvent the secrecy and the measures the Vatican authorities had adopted to keep all the events in the Conclave hidden. Many of my tricks were found out, but a sufficient number of them worked to enable me to cable twice daily a complete report of what had happened behind the walled doors, including the number of votes cast for each candidate at each ballot.

A set of carrier pigeons which were to carry reports to my office were not only found out, but were killed and eaten. This discovery roused the suspicions of the cardinals, who managed to catch several of my informants who were immediately cast out of the mysterious precincts. Other devices, fortunately, proved quite successful. The ones upon which I had to rely most were laundry lists and doctor's prescriptions, which were allowed to pass freely, none of those on watch realizing that these were really code messages by which I was enabled to follow the ballots in the Conclave. With these and other methods which I cannot reveal, since some of the people involved are still alive, I was able, at eleven o'clock on the 4th August, to wire to America that Giuseppe Sarto had been elected Pope a few minutes before, and that he had assumed the name of Pius X. On account of the difference in time between Europe and America, the news appeared in the Californian papers of that same morning. This time also the news was cabled back to Europe, beating the dispatches from Rome.

—*My Thirty Years of Friendships.*

THE WATCH ON ST. PETER'S SQUARE

ON THE FOLLOWING DAY we all attended to witness the last procession of the Cardinals before they were locked into the Conclave. After many altercations with policemen, showing of tickets, grinning at Swiss Guards, we found ourselves with a select number in a splendid hall that led from the Sistine to another chapel, packed together behind ropes, but very close to the pathway of the procession.

We were a motley crowd of journalists, ladies in black, gentlemen in evening dress, officers in uniform, priests and monks. We were all pressed very tightly together against the rope. Everyone chattered and pushed and laughed. The Noble Guards lined the aisle, and an officer, resplendent in gilt and embroidery, strutted up and down. The hall was magnificently painted with pictures of tremendous battles on sea and land. Behind me was a vast glowing canvas of high ships in flames, men struggling in the water and lurid waves lit at their edges with lightning. Everything glittered and shone. The heat was intense and there was a scent of musk and sweat. I was wedged between two fat priests and pressed upon by another. Although the chatter was of monkeys there was also an air of breathless expectation.

The heat, the thick scent, the pressure upon me of stout bodies created in me a kind of visionary unreality. I have never fainted

in my life, but I was perhaps not far from fainting now. And
yet I felt no weakness; although my hand was pushed against
the fat thigh of the priest next to me I felt no desire for his
support or, indeed, anyone's.

It was rather as though I had been translated into another
world and that an evil one. I was somewhere in a place of glittering richness and the thick enervating scent of hot-house flowers.
I saw the cartoon on the wall behind me quite clearly, but it
seemed to move as though the figures in the sea were alive, I
could almost hear their cries. The men and women pressing in
upon me were real and not real. Certain journalists I had learnt
by this time to know by sight, and I can remember a tall thin
man with pince-nez and hair *en brosse,* the elegant Englishman
representing *The Times* and my own Frank Gervasi with his
restless vitality and kindliness. I remember, too, the thick plump
body of the priest against whom I was, willy-nilly, pressing, the
thick red rolls of flesh at the back of his neck, the double chin,
the sleepy half-closed eyes. All these were real in their actuality,
but they were also figures in some play or pageant or masque.
In this masque I too was performing and it was a part evil and
sensuous. I not only acquiesced in this part but was glad of it.
And, as in *John Inglesant* at the court of the Duke of Umbria,
so I seemed to look on to a whirling tangle of lascivious figures
and know that in a moment or two I also would join the dance
and, dancing, lose my integrity.

This fantasy must seem exaggerated at this later time, but the
consciousness of splendid and rewarding evil was not exaggerated.
I remember that something within myself, as though I were in a
dream, said: "You have, through all these months, been fighting
your way to the center. Now you are there; and it is not God
that you have found but the Devil." For the Devil is very real,
at certain times, to anyone with imagination.

It was as in a dream that I heard the singing of the choir in
the distance, saw the Noble Guard stand at salute and, at the

same time, felt the whole loggia crammed with figures that were other than my own immediate companions. We were pressed in with witnesses and they were not the Saints of God.

Leaning against the rope as the procession passed I could, by stretching out my hand, have touched any of the members. First came the choir-boys and the priests, then the Cardinals. There were over sixty of them and the majority wore their splendid crimson. They advanced slowly, and around me, on every side, was the buzz of names. But I was more than ever in my dream and these were figures in it. Their faces were to me then like a page of grotesques drawn by Leonardo; and their bodies only bodies—fat ones, tall ones, thin ones, short ones. And of the faces I saw so very few that were holy—three or four at the most. Holy? I didn't wish them to be holy, and that was why I saw them as I did, for it is in ourselves that truth or falsehood lies.

It was a procession of grotesques, of phantasmagoria. Protruding chins, two, three, four chins, no chins at all, dented chins, bony chins, short noses, long noses, nostrils distended, nostrils tight and pinched, eyes staring and vapid, little eyes like dead pebbles, big staring eyes like those of glazed fish, bright burning lustful eyes, eyes of cold intelligence, and mouths tight and thrifty, mouths thick and sensual, mouths slack and aimless. All these within myself, created by me, hemmed in on every side by the masque of the decorated ghosts, by the dead who were living, and the living so nearly dead. One of these moving past me would soon be Pope, would have the destiny of nearly half the civilized world in his hands.

They moved into the further chapel and we heard the singing of the Mass. Through the hot sick disgust, miasmic and revolting, of myself I was conscious for a moment of the room at Castel Gandolfo and the Astronomer saying, "He would often have his meal here—fruit and cheese—and he would look at the charts of the stars while he was eating."

They were returning. I felt a vast, devastating depression. I had come all this way and this was all that I had found —I did not care who would be Pope. My body was sweating, in my nostrils a thick sweet stench, and in my heart a sad longing for any libertinage. I had come all this way to find only evil.

The procession had stopped, and so close to me that my hand could most easily close on his long thin arm was Pacelli, the late Pope's secretary. I had seen so many photographs of him that he did not seem a stranger. I knew that many thousands of men and women longed for him to be elected. It was the common rule that anyone who had been secretary to the last Pope could not be the new Pope, for it was always expected that, with the new Pope, there would be a fresh, original policy. I had heard many things for him, some things against him. He was very much more of a world-diplomat than Pius XI could ever have been. Not so simple a man. He was this and he was that.

Now, as I looked at him, standing so close to me, his thin beautiful fingers pressed together, his large brilliant eyes lost in his vision, his powerful lips moving in prayer, I forgot anything I had ever heard. It was as though he turned to me and with one quick gesture threw off from me all my burden of evil.

He did not, of course, turn or move. I have no wish to exaggerate. The confused evil unhappiness, the eagerness to surrender to temptation, the sense of many abnormal spirits driving in upon me during the last half-hour had been very real, not at all sentimentally imagined. Wishing to speak the truth and the truth only, I can but say that I was in contact, at this moment, quite suddenly, with a goodness and a spiritual integrity that I could not doubt any more than I could doubt the reality of the tortoiseshell spectacles upon the thick nose of the priest next to me.

Dramatically, and perhaps falsely, I might say that Pacelli's eyes shone with a fire of purpose, with a humility and with a

spiritual power that I had seen in no man's eyes before. But the
ecstatic vision in that face was no histrionic falsity. It was his
relation to myself, although he did not know that I was there, and
would never know, that lifted my burden so gloriously for me.
"Go down into Sodom and find one righteous man. It is enough."
I had gone down and I had found him.

He moved forward at last and it was as though I moved with
him.

This was on March 1st.

On March 2nd I got up very early and hustled along to our
Hearst Hiding-hole. About this something must be said.

Ever since Frank Gervasi had arrived in Rome from America
he and Bill Hillman had had but one thought between them—
namely, how could they get the name of the newly-elected Pope
to the outside world before anyone else? This was not so easy.
As everyone knows, the stove, into which Hillman and I had been
photographed pushing sticks, led to a chimney and the chimney
stretched up through the Sistine Chapel into the open sky. So
soon as any Cardinal received two-thirds of the votes at any
meeting of the Conclave a thin white smoke issued into the
sky from the chimney, and the whole world was certain that a
new Pope had been elected. There were two meetings every
day, and therefore twice every day—at twelve and at five—smoke
would issue from the chimney. When there was no election
the smoke would be black.

So much for the smoke. But there was more in it for us than
this. For about an hour after the smoke was perceived the identity
of the new Pope would still be a secret, would be a secret indeed
until an official appeared on the window-balcony of St. Peter's
and proclaimed the name. After that there would again be a
pause while the new Pope arrayed himself in a white robe—
white dresses of three sizes were held in readiness—before appearing in front of his people.

For Gervasi, therefore, two things were necessary. He must,

in one way or another, know that it was *white* smoke before
anyone else, and secondly he must have some secret information,
before anyone else, as to the identity of the new Pope. As to
the second of these I did not know then, I do not know now,
anything at all, but our preparations for the seeing of the smoke
were as romantic and decorative as *The Castle of Otranto* or *The
Mysteries of Udolpho.*

Gervasi rented a priests' chapel and lodging-house exactly
opposite St. Peter's, or rather one room in the lodging-house.
This was a little house, as it might be a hiding-place in any spy
story or romantic novel. Outside it was innocent enough, a shabby
house with a shabby door and in front of it a ruin of stones and
rubble where some houses had been destroyed to further Mussolini's plans for a great wide road to St. Angelo.

Passing through the shabby little door you found yourself
climbing some rough stairs towards a room full of ugly Madonnas
and crucifixes and paper flowers, a room that was for some
reason being repainted. Down a passage on the left was a kitchen,
and this place fascinated me because it was human and lively,
and hugged, with enjoyment, an enchanting smell of good
cooking. I would look through the doorway and see a stout
priest, his sleeves turned up, rocking pans over a slow fire,
absorbed and contented.

Up some more stairs you came to the narrow bedrooms of the
priests, and it was one of these bedrooms that we had hired.
The room was incongruously filled. In the middle of it was a
large telescope turned exactly on the slender chimney rising above
the Vatican roofs. There was a bed; there was a tin washing-stand;
there was a picture of Madonna and Child above the bed. There
was a table with telephones, a wireless and a typewriter, a sofa
and a chair.

Into this we all crowded, Michael grinning, Noyes kindly
and amiable as always, Gervasi as excited as though we were about
to discover, once and for ever, that there was life on Mars, and

myself with a Dante and a Penguin detective story to fill in time if nothing occurred.

Opposite us, in full and perfect view, were St. Peter's, the Square and the Vatican, and, at first, on that fine morning, the only life was composed of the pigeons, of a few loiterers, a taxi or two, a procession of priests and some tourists with a gesticulating guide. But, looking through the telescope, the fatal chimney was as brilliant and dramatic as the pointing finger of fate. I had it driven deep into my soul that if I were not the very first human being in the world to see the white smoke wheedling its way through that chimney I had failed in the whole purpose of my journey to Rome.

There had been much discussion as to how long this Conclave would last. There had been historic Conclaves that had lasted for months. There had been one such, I remembered, in *John Inglesant*. So long as the Conclave lasted I was a prisoner there. The authorities, however—those who really knew—said that this one would be short. The seriousness of the international situation demanded a new Pope as soon as possible. A week perhaps? Yes, possibly, a week. Gervasi, however, thought that, at the very most, it would be three days.

The morning began slowly and rightfully to swallow itself. Now only Gervasi and I were in the priest's bedroom. Michael was posted in the Square, beneath one of the pillars. From this position he could see the man on the wall opposite the chimney who would get a vision of the smoke before anyone in the Square. He would wave a hand to Michael, who would wave a hat to Gervasi, who would instantly telephone to New York.

I stared through the telescope at the chimney. The radio was turned on and, in a cultured Oxford accent, was spilling out German propaganda: "The Führer's love for all Germans wherever they may be, in the lost plains of China or in the darkest depths of Africa, cannot surely be abused by any lover of truth. That his heart should go out to those exiled sons. . . ."

At this moment Gervasi's own personal telephone sounded. He listened. I heard him say: "Christ, but it can't be true! Where did he see the notices? Send Garibaldi down . . . Maybe he didn't read them right . . . What! you say everyone's excited? Crowds gathering? Send Garibaldi down. . . . Yes. Pronto."

He turned round to me, his brown face puckered like a monkey's, his eyes glittering.

"War!"

"What!"

"Yes . . . Oh, hell . . . it can't be. But it must be. They've called up all the reservists. Notices up all down the Corso."

I stared through the telescope. It was half-past eleven.

"Big crowds now."

"They'll be bigger when they hear this news."

He was dictating messages through to London and New York. Then I heard his sharp cry:

"What! Only those years? . . . Why, that means nothing. They call them up in the natural. . . . Wait till I get to him to wring his bloody neck. . . ."

He turned round nonchalantly to me.

"It's only those two classes. . . . What the hell! . . . Getting me all het up . . . !"

My eye was still in the telescope—but, deep in my soul, I realized a curious thing. I had moved on, past hysteria. On that Tuesday evening of the Munich September, the Botts staying with me in Brackenburn, I had, at that last late 11.40 broadcast, turned to them and said:

"Yes. This really *is* War. This really *is* War!"

And Alan, looking at me in that half-alive, wholly-intelligent, indifferent spirit of his, said, with all the genius of divine prophecy, "Mussolini is the only man who can do anything now."

But I did then (and it was the only time) sink deep, deep into the waters of despair. I raged up and down the room crying out on the folly, the madness, the insane crime. . . . But beneath and behind these cries was the certain sure knowledge that France and ourselves were utterly unprepared. I happened to know, from some chance information, that our defense of London simply didn't exist. I foresaw as inevitable the most ghastly massacre of human beings in modern history, a possible panic submission, and so, after all, that world rule of force and tyranny, that nightmare to the freedom of mankind.

I admired and even loved the Czechs, but with that vision in front of me I would have readily sacrificed the Czechs to save the world—for they would, in any case, have been sacrificed with the rest of us. On the following day Neville Chamberlain did save the world.

This, however, is most certainly not a book of politics. I record this only because, during that lively moment when Gervasi moved into world war and out of it again, I knew that the panic of September 1938 was over, as far as Englishmen were concerned, for ever. Hitler should have struck then. During the months that followed we recovered our force, our balance, our confidence, our firm resolve.

"As there isn't going to be a war just now I think I'll go down into the Square."

I went down, stood beside Michael and watched. Twelve o'clock struck and shortly afterwards the smoke came out. The first curl or two seemed as white as Bernard Shaw's beard, but it darkened, it darkened. . . . Everyone sighed and turned away home.

I had a curious unnatural feeling that it was my fault that the smoke was black. Nay, worse than that, the wrong Pope would be chosen and I should be to blame. The whole world would be ruined (was it not hanging on the edge of ruin?) and it would be my fault. I had not discovered my Fountain. The Fountain was illusion. I was an ass and a sentimental, romantic, imagining-where-there-is-nothing kind of ass to boot. It is when I am tempted towards the realists that I am most miserable.

Jack Priestley, for whom I would do almost anything, thinks he
sees exactly what is what and that I never can. I write an article
about Freedom. He says it's a good article but not at all about
Freedom.

"My kind of Freedom."

"There's only one sort of Freedom."

"You want men to be free but have poor hopes of them. But I
have good hopes of them whether they are free or no. I'm more
of an ass than you about the ground I'm standing on, but wiser
in taking a long view."

He won't admit that, of course, and I remember that, at this
moment, as I went with my Dante and my Penguin under my
arm to the restaurant in the corner of the Square, I thought of
him, longed for his company as I so often do, and felt he was
right about everything. This is a bad world. Men are such fools.
They will elect a wicked Pope. That is the way the world is
going now. And over my macaroni I saw the burning eyes of
Pacelli darkening in sorrow. Out of the sunny gloom from the
pillars the four friends I had made in Rome came towards me—
Michael Angelo Buonarroti the sculptor, Keats the poet, Pius XI
the mountain-climber, Pacelli the friend of God and of man.
I was cheered. They seemed so close to me and so happy. Had
Jack Priestley been with me I would have introduced him. They
are exactly the kind of men he likes. The trouble with him is
that his standards are so dreadfully high.

But while I ate my luncheon I reflected, as I suppose hundreds
of thousands in Rome on that day were reflecting, that the
Cardinals, shut in there, seated each one under his canopy and
under the brilliant imaginings of Michael Angelo, were intriguing
and scheming and moving, as in a game of chess, from one
position to another. How near had anyone been, at that first
meeting this morning, to a required majority? Had parties by
now been formed behind this candidate and that? The disgust
remained with me.

I was unhappy during all that afternoon. Perhaps the false alarm that morning about the war had distressed me more deeply than I knew. The crowds began to gather again and they looked so innocent, so friendly, so humble, so eager to be good and to love their fellow-men.

The Italian, when he is not disturbed by any violent passion, is the most amiable of all mankind. He wants no trouble with anyone. He does not see why everything should not be perfectly all right to the end of time. An English crowd is as good-tempered as any, but there is a lack of imagination at the heart of it. It also is kindly, ready to be friendly, wanting only the best for everyone, but it is tepid about all humankind who are not English, tepid in understanding and a little pitying. But these Italians, now, many of them monks and priests, were waiting on a world-event and were praying for the whole Universe. All civilization was within their embrace, now, on this blue-gilt afternoon, looking steadfastly at the dove-colored façade of St. Peter's.

And I thought how awful it would be if aeroplanes, possibly from my own country, silently came up and smashed them as they stood there. They would not, in actual fact, be standing there and waiting, but thousands of Chinese, only in the last month, had been smashed in just that fashion, and in Barcelona children had run across the squares, screaming. . . .

I wanted, in fact, passionately that those enclosed Cardinals should do something that would help to save the world—that they choose a man who would, in his own time and fashion, be God's man. What happened in this Election would weigh the balance towards Salvation or Destruction. It appeared to me, as I crossed the sun-splashed Square, that the consequence of this event was heavy with importance. I was impotent. We were all impotent. Those Cardinals in the Sistine. . . .

And then, shortly after four o'clock, I left the Square and went back to the city office. It was a lazy, slack thing to do and

showed that I was not really a good journalist. But Gervasi,
telephoning at his table, said that he thought it unlikely there
would be a decision tonight.

I went, at a leisurely pace, up the dark staircase and wandered
into the office. As I passed the door I saw Hillman swerve towards
me. He screamed (yes, he screamed!):
"A Pope is elected! A Pope is elected! Go back! Go back!"
I turned, I flashed down the stairs, stumbling, gasping, risking
my neck in that half-gloom, pushed out into the twisting pattern
of Italians, grasped a taxi by its mane, shouted "St. Peter's" to the
driver and hung on to the window, praying that I might be in
time.
In time for what? I didn't quite know. After the smoke there
was, of course, an interval before the name of the new Pope was
announced. That name had, in all probability, been already
telephoned by Gervasi to New York and if I hurried to the
little priests' house I should learn it.
But, oddly enough, I didn't want to see Gervasi or the priests'
house or anything to do with any newspaper. I was dimly aware
that at some time that evening I should have to send an account
of this Election to America, but I wasn't thinking of that now.
All I wanted was to be with the crowd at St. Peter's. I repeated
aloud to myself over and over again, "In time. . . . In time. . . ."
The kind of chump I'd been to miss the white smoke after all!
But it didn't seem now to be the important thing—the important
thing was that I should be there when they announced the name
of the new Pope.
We were level with the priests' house when the taxi stopped.
The crowd had stopped it. From here, some quarter of a mile
from St. Peter's, a vast, packed, unstirring crowd stretched to
the foot of the church. Heads, heads, unmoving, staying as though
in a trance—a stagnant lake of heads up to the very walls of the
church.

I plunged into it and, very strangely, it opened wherever I pressed. There was no resistance—I had not to murmur a "*Prego.*" I was to see one other vast crowd in Rome before the end and that was to be in spirit and temper very different from this. This was, in fact, a quite new crowd in my experience. In all probability I shall never see another like it. As it parted so easily before me I moved, like a man swimming, almost to the bottom of the steps leading up to the great doors. There was a line of soldiers here.

I stopped and stayed, and looked forward to the balcony in front of the window where the announcer of the name of the new Pope would stand. I was aware, then, in the silence that was on every side of me, of a tense, an almost agonizing anxiety.

It was not only that priests on every side of me were praying, not only that, in all those eyes staring at the window high and far away, there was a beseeching, an imploring expression—there was also a tenseness, the sense in the air above us and around us of thousands upon thousands of souls beseeching God for something; the Israelites must have been thus when they waited for the rain to fall from heaven. Beside me was a young priest from the American College.

"There was no mistake, was there?" I asked. "It was the white smoke that came out."

"Oh, yes. It was the white smoke all right," he answered, grinning.

"Was it white from the start?"

"It was like a puff of cigarette smoke. That's what it was—cigarette smoke. It went wriggling up—gray at first, quite white at the end."

"Were you surprised?"

"Oh yes. Of course we were. They said it would be three or four days. I'm afraid it won't be Pacelli."

"Why not?"

"Yes. It must be Pacelli," another American boy broke in

quite furiously. "Don't you know they said that if he was going
to be elected it would be in the first two days? After that he
would have no chance. Well, here it is . . . the very first day . . ."

"All right. I know. But Pacelli hasn't all that following, you
know. The politicians. . . ."

Pacelli. Pacelli. Pacelli. Everywhere I heard the name breathed.
It hung in the air as though the wishes of all those hearts were
vocal.

Above that sea of heads the sky was turning a white-green
like the pale curve of a centuries-washen bowl. I gazed round
me as though I were seeing Bernini's wonderful Square for the
first time, and it was an absolute truth that I had never seen
it like this before. History was once again being made in it. That
old, old obelisk brought by Caligula to Rome, which has
reached our generation intact—what horrors of orgies and bloody
games it has seen!—the bony fanatic Christians dressed in skins
and devoured by wild dogs (the first hot breath, stinking, of the
dogs upon the withdrawn cheek!), the living torches, for Nero
to bite his nails to the quick in restless pleasure, the actual
crucifixion and death of St. Peter, at last its removal by Sixtus
V from in front of the sacristy to this center of the Square,
where it became of all ironies Christian, and has been venerated
by millions of pilgrims from 1586 until now.

I looked at this old obelisk and watched the kindly gentle
faces stretching from side to side of the Square. Cruelty of man to
man, how strange, how illogical—for we are a freak, a "sport"
from Nature's pattern. We are Nature and something very much
more as well. For us to return to Nature, as the cry of the poets
and philosophers once was, is to go back altogether on our tracks,
to return to the living torches lighting ruddily the writing on the
obelisk. There can be no return.

On every side of me they began to sing a psalm in somber-
measured Gregorian. Next to me, his face raised under his black
felt hat, his mouth smiling, was a young ruddy-faced priest. He

seemed little more than a boy. He had the shoulders of a prize-
fighter. He was singing and smiling, both at the same time.
Next to him was a long, tall, towering monk, thin, fanatic. His
lips were moving in prayer, his large coarse-skinned hands
raised, clasped together. I have seldom seen so strained, so acute a
sense of anxiety in any face.

The sound of the singing grew stronger and stronger. It was
picked up and enforced on the very outskirts of the crowd. Pink
streamers of cloud floated into the pale green sky as though someone were hanging out banners.

The singing stopped. A figure appeared on the balcony. What
a stillness that was! The whole of Rome, nay, the world beyond it,
was stilled. The little boy-priest caught my sleeve with his hand.
I could feel the beat of his heart against my side. He was staring
forward as though he would *force* truth from the Universe.
Somewhere in that vast crowd a baby cried and was instantly
hushed.

The voice of the man on the balcony came with happy fresh-
ness—you could feel how joyful he was. He said, in Latin, "I
am happy to tell you that we have once again a Pope . . ." He said
some more words. Then, isolating it from the surrounding words,
the name—"Pacelli."

Oh! what a roar broke out then, what a shout, what a cry!
"Pacelli! Pacelli! Pacelli!"

And to show his kinship with Pius XI, whom he had dearly
loved, he would himself be "Pius XII."

"Pacelli! Pacelli! Pacelli!" I found that I myself was crying. I,
who was no Catholic, who had seen Pacelli but once, to whom
this must surely be an outside affair, was joyfully happy as though
my dear friend had received his heart's desire. I felt it so personally that I had to speak to the young priest: "I *am* so glad. That
makes me so happy. *Now* things will be better. . . ." And he,
knowing no English at all, smiled and laughed and looked at me
as though he loved me.

Down the furrowed brown cheeks of the tall monk tears were trickling. He stared in front of him, rigid, carven. The American priests were chattering like birds in an aviary.

"That's bully. Who said it wouldn't be Pacelli? Of course it had to be, the state the world's in. And he's *clever*. He's a diplomat. He'll keep the world straight. He's a good man, too, although he's so clever."

We had to wait, some half-hour or so, while Pacelli was arrayed in his white robe, and it was during this half-hour that I participated, for the second time in my life, in the conscious, active, glorious happiness of the Brotherhood of Man.

I remember that, at that very moment, I said to myself: "I must drink this deep into my spirit. I must realize that this is happening—truly and actually happening, and that, whatever things of hatred and terror the future holds, this also is true."

I have said something already, I think, of those days at the beginning of the March Revolution in Petrograd in 1917 when we all walked along the streets, arm in arm, singing, loving one another, and, what is more, *trusting* one another. So it was now. For half an hour three hundred thousand of us stood, hand in hand as it were, joyful and happy, believing in God, believing in Peace, and *trusting one another*.

Had we who stood there been given the ruling of the world, and *stayed permanently in the spirit and temper that we then experienced*, there would be no more fighting, no more lust of selfishness and cruelty of desire. For an instant, believing in God, being willing to put His precepts into practice, we saw clearly, we knew the only Law:

"Jesus said unto him, Thou shalt love the Lord thy God with all thy heart, and with all thy soul, and with all thy mind. This is the first and great commandment. And the second is like unto it, Thou shalt love thy neighbor as thyself. On these two commandments hang all the Law and the Prophets."

At that single moment of time it seemed ridiculously easy. Love

God? Love your neighbor? Why, of course, what is there to prevent it? Let us all share and share alike. Let us meet in a World Conference and say: "What do *you* want? What are *your* needs? . . . Certainly you can have that piece, even more if you like it. And instead of bombs let us make new schools with shower-baths and halls of song."

Everyone was singing again. The stars were breaking into the sky.

The thin white figure appeared on the balcony. All we, his children, received his blessing.

—*Roman Fountain.*

V

To the Consummation of the World

IT IS surprising to read how often the idea of the Papacy's early extinction is hopefully expressed in the diaries and the letter books of nineteenth-century writers, whether the coup de grâce was to be delivered by malaria from the Campagna, or the slow enlightenment of mankind, or the march of honest republicanism. Alfred Austin, Queen Victoria's poet laureate, perhaps remembering his history classes at Stonyhurst and Oscott, had no such illusions.

It is safe to say that never since the sixteenth century has the Papacy mattered as much as today. Scientific developments in transportation and communication, which the amateur Isaiahs of a century ago were confident would make the papal office an anachronism, have only brought the words of the Shepherd more clearly to every part of the world, and gathered his children in their millions to take his blessing.

This final chapter of the book gathers a sheaf of impressions of the last two Popes: Pius XII, the Roman prince crowned in the basilica where he had been baptized, whose life burned with an incandescent energy; Pius XI, a monarch who had added to Lombard stolidity a touch of the Romana grandezza, yet was still the father who could find his fortresses of reserve stormed by tenderness or laughter.

Macaulay's familiar vision of the future has lost none of its edge or resonance. It will still be the one clear prospect in the mysteries of time when an Eskimo or a Nigerian may sit upon the Chair of Peter and wear his beautiful and immortal crown.

THEIR ANCIENT PLACES

❦ Nothing strikes one more, in renovated Rome, than the increased relief, in the sculpturesque sense of the word, into which the invasion of the modern spirit has brought its ecclesiastical monuments and basilicas, as compared with the subordinate interest they aroused when one came here first. Then Pagan Rome, the Rome of the Republic and the Empire, the Rome of Livy, Suetonius, and Gibbon, occupied the most prominent place, and absorbed the meditation of serious sojourners from beyond the Alps. These have suffered hurt, and been thrown into the background by the ruthless cleaner and scraper, by the disappearance of the tangled vegetation that once draped the monumental skeletons underlying it, and by the transformation of what one may call Rome Ruinous into Rome labelled as a sort of open-air Museum.

It might have been thought that the Quirinal, the Italian Court, Foreign Embassies, tramways, electrically-moved omnibuses, morning, afternoon, and evening newspapers, military bands, perpetual tramping of soldiers, in a word all the fever, fret, hurry, parade, and noisy monotony of modern city life on a metropolitan scale, assisted by the wranglings on Monte Citorio of Senators and Deputies of the People, together with continually recurring Ministerial Crises, would cast into the shade Pagan Rome and Papal Rome alike. It has done so to the first. It has not done so to the second. In vain the King and Queen of Italy are in the Palace of the Quirinal. In vain the Popes have shut themselves up in the Palace and Garden of the Vatican, and designated themselves Prisoners. In vain Cardinals no longer openly bear themselves as Cardinal Princes, but drive about Rome as unostentatiously as possible, instead of, as of old, traversing it with an air of majestic humility, doffed to by all the world, and doffing to it in turn with sovereign grace and condescension. In vain the sumptuous ceremonies of Easter at Saint Peter's, the long proud sacerdotal procession ending in the Peacocks' Feathers, the cushioned Triple Tiara, and, crowning all, the Successor of Saint Peter borne high on the shoulders of men in his Gestatorial Chair, the pompous Mass, the entrancing Silver Trumpets, the blessing conferred on the City and the World from the External Balcony of the Basilica, the illumination of the dome, from circle to summit, by tens of thousands of oil-fed lamps and cressets, in vain, I say, these magnificent spectacles have been suspended, and equally in vain has the reproduction of them at the Lateran on June 29, the Feast of Saints Peter and Paul, suffered the same fate.

Saint Peter's, the Vatican, the façade of the Lateran, and all they represent, tower above modern Monarchical Rome, and are more conspicuous than ever, because Pagan Rome has been robbed of much of its former significance. The Papacy, not the Kingdom of Italy, nor yet Hapsburg or Hohenzollern Emperor, is the Heir of the Caesars; and whose is the inheritance is now more clear and incontrovertible than ever. The successor of Augustus is at this moment Leo XIII, the Pontifex Maximus is he who has during the last thirty years restored and embellished all the most ancient churches of the Eternal City; and the Roman Senate of today is not that unmajestic and powerless Body posturing as such at Monte Citorio, but the College of Cardinals.

I set this down, not to glorify the Papacy, but to indicate the fact. Never in its history of so many centuries has such a stroke of good fortune befallen the Papacy as the abolition of its Temporal Power; and its shrewdest councillors well know it, though openly they may avow it not. Only the other day, I was walking in the Vatican Gardens with a well-known English Roman Catholic who lives in Rome, and he confirmed me in this suspicion by informing me that so it is. The Protest against Spoliation, for spoliation of course it was, is still maintained, for certain diplomatic and likewise certain financial reasons. But it grows fainter and fainter, and will in time, without explicit disavowal, die away; and then the Papacy, the true Heir of the Caesars and the Pax Romana, will, I believe, be stronger than ever. I remember, on returning to England after that first Winter I passed here, being informed by an English lady of extreme anti-Papal piety, that Pius IX, then reigning, would be the last of the Popes. I smiled, and said nothing.

"*La Papauté est finie,*" exclaimed a French Deputy in the Chamber, a few years later. "*Elle vous ensevelira tous!*" shouted in reply M. Paul de Cassagnac; and, not very long afterwards, it beheld the interment of the Second Empire. It will see many more sepulchres. "I shall never go to Canossa," Bismarck proudly declared. Withal, he went. There is no more striking illustration of the fundamental distinction between the Passing and the Permanent than this distinction between any other Institution and any other Dominion one can name, and the Papacy. Everyone knows the closing passage in Macaulay's Essay on Ranke's *History of the Popes.* I believe the British Empire will live to bury some States of younger origin than itself. But, much as I may desire it, I cannot venture to think it will survive the Papacy.

—The Poet's Diary.

NO SHADOW OF PRIDE

❧ I SAW HIS HOLINESS Pius XI three times; the first time in private audience; the second in a semi-private assembly of various notables; and the third time among the crowds that thronged St. Peter's on the day of the Beatification of the English Martyrs. On the first occasion a dignitary who was the head of one of the National Colleges kindly helped to introduce me; and I have seldom been more grateful for human companionship. It is altogether inadequate to say I was nervous. I was nervous when I saw Signor Mussolini, chiefly because he talked French so much better than I did. But it is perhaps curious to note that, while my nervousness in the presence of Il Duce drove me madly on to talk French and more French, merely because I could not talk French, I found in the presence of the Pope that I could not talk English, or talk at all.

He came suddenly out of his study, a sturdy figure in a cape, with a square face and spectacles, and began speaking to me about what I had written, saying some very generous things about a sketch I wrote of St. Francis of Assisi. He asked me if I wrote a great deal; and I answered in fragmentary French phrases that it was only too true, or words to that effect. The clerical dignitary nobly struck in in my support by saying it was my modesty. As a matter of fact, my head was in a whirl and it might have been anything. Then he made a motion and we all knelt; and in the words that followed I understood for the first time something that was once meant by the ceremonial use of the plural; and in a flash I saw the sense of something that had always seemed to me a senseless custom of kings. With a new strong voice, that was hardly even like his own, he began *"Nous vous benissons,"* and I knew that something stood there infinitely greater than an individual; I knew that it was indeed "We"; We, Peter and Gregory and Hildebrand and all the dynasty that does not die. Then, as he passed on, we rose and found our way out of the Palace, through knots of Swiss and Papal Guards, till we were again under the open sky. I said to the clerical dignitary, "That frightened me more than anything I have known in my life." The clerical dignitary laughed heartily.

One touch may be added to the scene, which is not so irrelevant as it looks. When we left the Vatican, one of the party discovered the loss of an umbrella; I believe somebody else's umbrella. With all respect to the umbrella, I thought it unlikely that it would be used as a Papal canopy and carried in state in any of the gorgeous processions. But we made the obvious jest about the highest church dignitaries having a weakness for stealing umbrellas, or having a little horde of parasols. Then someone more native to the spot said firmly that the Pope would certainly give it to the niggers. "At this moment," said my informant solemnly, "a little nigger is walking about in the sun with your umbrella." In this slightly exaggerative form I first fully realized the quality to be added to the obvious qualities of Pius XI; it is called an enthusiasm for missions, but it is in fact a very strong antagonism to the contempt for the aboriginal races and a gigantic faith in the fraternity of all tribes in the light of the Faith. "We have not only to save Christendom, but to save mankind." A distinguished Scandinavian, whom I met later, was so warm an upholder of this humanitarianism that he said, with shining eyes as one who beholds a vision, "We may yet have a black Pope." In a spirit of disgraceful compromise, I suggested meekly that (if not quite ready for that) I should be delighted to see a black Cardinal. I was conscious of some shadowy pleasure in the image; and I recalled the imperial bust of black marble with the red robe, and wondered if there is something prophetic or significant in our fancies. Then I remembered the great King who came to Bethlehem, heavy with purple and crimson and with a face like night; and I was ashamed.

The second time I saw the Pope with more detachment, and heard him at greater length; when the documents of the Beatification were finally read for his approval. I heard the very long list of those English heroes, who resisted the despotic destruction of the national religion, read in due order; and listened to a number of names that sounded like Smith or Higgins pronounced with a perfect Italian accent. Then the Pope himself spoke, in a manner rather conversational than rhetorical, but with not a little Italian gesture and vivacity, by the standard of English conversation. What moved me very much, as an Englishman and an exile, was that he spoke with peculiar warmth and vividness in praise of England, and like one who had seen it rather than heard of it. He dwelt even more strongly on the words, "So beautiful a country," than on the words "So great a nation." He also emphasized strongly the fact that the last witnesses in England were men of every class and condition, poor as well as rich, and agricultural laborers as well as the first noble of the land. He spoke in Italian; but so clearly and with such exact gesture that I could understand nearly every word.

Lastly, as I have said, the last time I saw him was in the fullest blaze of publicity when he came to consummate the Beatification before a colossal congregation, and to conclude it by celebrating Benediction at the High Altar. Here indeed there was, admittedly and openly, the full torrent of pomp and popular excitement; but it seemed to me as if I already knew enough not to trust merely to the effect of these. Pius XI will always be to me a real man whom I have met; with all the intense but indescribable difference that that fact makes in our judgment of men. I should always know that certain things said about him were nonsense; it is true, in that sense, that pageantry proves nothing one way or the other; and he might be enthroned on the top of St. Peter's, with populations lying prostrate round it for miles, and I should still know that there was not in him any shadow of pride.

—*The Resurrection of Rome.*

FATHER AND SON

🌷 AT LAST I find myself in the city made eternal because a Galilean fisherman came to die here. The very first thing I did on arriving was to go immediately to the tomb of that fisherman, St. Peter, the first vicar of Christ, whose successor, Pius XI, I made this journey to see. Our party, following a Catholic custom, knelt before the tomb and recited the Creed, and then arising, the first sight to greet my eyes was the golden inscription on the dome bearing the words of the Saviour to Peter, over nineteen hundred years ago: "Thou art Peter, and upon this Rock I will build My church."

I shall venture no description of St. Peter's, for my style of writing is quite unequal to that task. It is something you must see to appreciate.

Within eighteen hours after my arrival in Rome it was my happy privilege to be received in private audience with the Holy Father. I have never before been at a loss for anything to say during my long public life. I have been interviewed and have given interviews to the great and near great, but today was the first time I was ever speechless in the presence of anyone.

I was particularly at a loss in view of the fact that the sole and only reason for my trip to Europe was to receive the blessing of the Holy Father. Since I had no other purpose, it was only natural for the Holy Father to do most of the talking. It pleased me greatly to hear him speak so well and so affectionately of

America, and I was indeed embarrassed by the tribute he paid me as "a loyal son of the Church."

. . . As he spoke I glanced about the room at the dozen or more nationalities represented. This thought came to me. On the outside, nation was divided against nation and people against people, whereas here before this great man in white they all were one in mind and in heart. Certainly if the nations of the world are ever to be drawn together in peace and concord, it must be by and through someone who is outside the nations themselves, just as a man who packs a bag must be outside of the bag. To me there was no escaping the fact that if civilization is to have one spokesman who will talk for the peace of the world and for the good of all, it must be the man who in this very audience drew together the only real League of Nations that can be made to work.

In order to escape the heat of Rome the Holy Father has left the Vatican for the summer and is now about fifteen miles outside of Rome in what is called Castel Gandolfo. As our car drew closer to the castle we passed through narrow and winding streets of what was a village of the poor. Suddenly the castle emerged without the least detachment from the village.

I had heard and read much about castles and I expected this one to be one of those great elaborate affairs the like of which one sees in pictures, but his home was to me anything but a real castle. I would describe it as a comfortable country home, typical of the Italian countryside. The houses of the village were hardly distinguishable from his own, for they all seemed to huddle together as if there were in fact as in spirit but little difference between the two.

As I made my way down from that village built on a hill I could not help but think that Gandolfo was a symbol of all that he stands for; a humble man of God, living in the middle of a humble peasantry from which he took his origin.

I have always been proud of being a Catholic. I was never prouder than I was today, when I could call him "Father," and he called me "Son."

—*The Boston Sunday Globe*, May 30, 1937.

THE POPE AMID STORMS

POPE PIUS XI assisted recently at the Memorial Mass cele-brated annually in the Sistine Chapel for the Cardinals who have died during the year. Around him that morning were grouped most of the living Cardinals of the Curia. Beyond the lovely marble screen of Mino da Fiesole they sat in two rows facing one another, their bent white heads and crimson capes overshadowed by Michelangelo's "Last Judgment"—in a world of dark signs perhaps still the greatest handwriting on the wall. The Pope himself sat apart, on a throne beside the altar, a hieratic figure that nothing overshadowed. In his stiff, bell-like cope, his tall miter, he looked rigid and symbolic as the rock of Peter.

At public functions Pius XI has this quality of immobility that makes everyone around him appear fidgety and nervous. His vigor is extraordinary for a man of seventy-eight. His strong-featured face is still bronzed after a summer spent at his villa on the terraced hills above Lake Albano. His black hair is only sprinkled with gray. As he intones the benediction his voice is firm and resonant. His step is heavier but as decisive as on the June day in 1921 when he entered the nearby Hall of the Con-sistory to receive the red hat.

Even more extraordinary than the Pope's vigor is his quietness. It is not the quiet of serenity; there is too much iron in it for that. In the Vatican they speak of him as "a born Pope," meaning that his character is as papal as his office. In a period so over-

whelmed by shouting rulers, he is the only one I have seen who
suggests force in repose.

Those who know the Sistine Chapel remember it for the
splendor of its frescoes. There the greatest artists of the Renaissance outpainted one another in the procession of masterpieces
running like a frieze around the side walls. From the ceiling
Michelangelo's prophets and sybils brood over the ineluctable
mystery of man; and on the end wall he left that blackened
judgment and revelation which must have startled his time as
much as the indictments of Rivera shock ours. To recall in that
place the murals of the Detroit Museum, of Dartmouth College,
of the just-opened Aula Magna of Rome's new University City,
is to wonder if the moderns of today will remain after four
hundred years as timely, or as timeless as these.

Really to see the Sistine frescoes, however, they must be seen
as the backdrop of the pageant for which they were painted.
When the officers of the Mass move before the altar, when the
Supreme Pontiff and the princes of the Church, the Swiss Guard,
the papal chamberlains, files of clerics in purple and scarlet,
people the choir, then the sober-colored walls and the scene below
become part of one picture, blurred alike by incense and the
sense of crowding centuries. And really to hear the Sistine Choir
one must listen to the disembodied voices issuing from the little
gallery and filling like one ineffable voice the space for which
the choir was created.

But though choral and spectacle help, they do not of themselves produce the atmosphere which struck one observer most
that morning. I had hardly realized how tense and troubled and
super-heated is the air of Rome when suddenly, here in the heart
of Mussolini's straining capital, I found myself in a place where
everything was slow and calm. It was not peace exactly—this
strange relaxation. If any spot is seismological, sensitive to every
spiritual tremor that shakes the earth, it is the Vatican. It was not

detachment, for the Holy See, and particularly its present occupant, is intensely interested in the events and movements of the time. After a time one perceived that it was perspective; mounting the Scala Regia out of St. Peter's Square, out of the Rome of sanctions and militant resistance, one passed out of the short into the long view of things.

Everything presses on the Vatican that presses anywhere, but the very walls repeat that everything passes, too. Mussolini must do what he has planned to do this year, this hour, so he believes, or it will be forever too late. Combinations alter so quickly that no political ruler today can count on tomorrow. In the Vatican there is not only all the time there is, but a kind of continuum which makes the interval called Now both longer and less important than it is in the Fascist era, the Roosevelt administration, the life of the British Government.

The reigning Pontiff is the 260th of his line. Beholding him surrounded by the old Cardinals who will choose his successor, one saw not only that the Holy Father himself is always venerable but that he is an old man elected by old men. Most Popes are well over sixty before they begin their pontificates; Pius XI was sixty-five when he assumed office in 1922, the year the Fascists marched on Rome. The See of Peter will never be stormed by a youth movement, and there is something oddly steadying even in that hierarchical fact—at least, if you have traveled over Europe surveying the effects of youth movements and revaluing the ripeness and tolerance of age as a guarantee against the violent reaction of adolescence.

Individually the Pope is seasoned by a lifetime of priestly experience before he becomes chief pastor of his world-wide flock; officially he is one link in a lengthy chain. The attitude toward current problems of the most contemporary of pontiffs is thus in a sense non-contemporary. He comes from further back in time and looks further ahead than other rulers. His authority and

responsibility are of an order so different that even when he pro-
nounces on the same questions he speaks with another accent and
another purpose.

A recent visitor found him with a pile of letters from England
on one hand, a book describing the new political tendencies of
France on the other, and in front of him the *London Times*,
which he reads every morning. After a perfunctory inquiry as to
the visitor's health—and Pius XI has little concern for the ills of
the flesh, in himself or others—he plunged without preliminaries
into a keen discussion of world affairs.

In character he is not so much austere as habitually serious.
He seldom smiles or relaxes. His thoroughness and tirelessness
are proverbial at the Vatican. He knows the dioceses under his
charge as well as he knew the books on his shelves when he was
librarian of two of the greatest libraries of Italy. He has organized
the administration of his handkerchief-size kingdom to the last
detail with the most business-like precision.

The Vatican has been completely modernized during his reign,
and many of its great art collections have been rehoused. He has
built enormously, for use rather than beauty, in the space at his
disposal since Vatican City became the smallest independent
State in the world. It is due to him that it is so small; he de-
liberately cut out of the final settlement the adjoining Villa Doria
and its park which Mussolini wished to cede. "The Church wants
independence," he said, "not territory."

"Everything this Pope touches he tidies up," remarked an old
monsignor rather somberly, and you can see his passion for order
and system in the arrangements of Vatican City and in the model
dairy farm he has constructed at his country villa at Castel
Gandolfo, where the scrubbed "papal briefs," as the dairymen call
the newest calves, swagger in blue-tiled stalls that are the marvel
of the countryside.

Stronger still is his passion for order in the world. Political order, social order, moral order. The Pope is terribly anxious as he looks out upon the gloomy confusion of the secular scene. Through his thick spectacles the policies of contemporary states-men seem above all discordant and short-sighted, concentrated only on the immediate.

In the effort to chart a Christian course for the social revolu-tion, he resurrected and brought up to date a famous encyclical of Leo XIII, *Rerum Novarum,* and embodied its principles in his own encyclical, *Quadragesimo Anno.* Last year the sociolo-gists seeking to reform the Swiss Confederation were studying this document. The late Chancellor Dollfuss drew on it in planning the Austrian Guild State he did not live to inaugurate. Father Coughlin asserts that he found there the inspiration for his Union for Social Justice.

Above everything Pius XI has worked for peace. In 1933, see-ing the thickening clouds on the horizon, he proclaimed a "Holy Year," inviting to Rome the faithful of all nations to form a spiritual union for peace. Ever since his every public utterance has been an appeal and a warning. Before the Italian military concentration in Africa became war—supposing it is war—the Pope spoke out strongly on at least three occasions, condemning unprovoked aggression as a crime against the moral law.

On August 27th, in addressing an international congress of Catholic nurses, he said, in words since frequently quoted, that a war of conquest is "an unjust war, something inexpressibly sad and horrible." Referring to the Italian argument that the war was justifiable as a defense of frontiers against incessant dangers, and necessary for the expansion of a population increasing day by day, the Pontiff declared it should and must be possible to reach a solution of such difficulties by means which do not in-volve war.

"One thing seems to us certain," he concluded. "If the need of expansion is a fact of which account must be taken, the right

of defense itself has certain limits which must be observed if
defense is not to become guilty. In any case we pray to God that
He may second the activities and the efforts of men of clear
vision who understand the exigencies of the true happiness of
the peoples and of social justice; that He may bless the efforts
of all who do their best, not by means of threats, which do
nothing but irritate the spirit and aggravate the situation, ren-
dering it every day more difficult for those who work for pacifica-
tion with the sincere intention of avoiding war."

—*New York Times Magazine*, December 15, 1935.

THE ONE MAN IN ALL
THE WORLD

🌷 WEDNESDAY, March the 6th, was a day that I hope I shall never forget. Because that day at noon I had the great privilege of an audience with the Pope. I am not a Catholic; I am not even very religious; but like all human beings who are not utterly lost to Grace, I am humble and respectful and awed and ashamed, too, before very good men who do God's work greatly.

A Catholic friend in the Vatican had offered to arrange the audience, but partly because I am not a Catholic and partly because, as I say, the look in the face of a man of great good will is so likely to upset one for days and make one think too many painful and searching things about oneself and the whole world (which is, I suppose, why saints in their time were people to be avoided as much as possible), I was timid about going, and at first said I wouldn't. But vanity and curiosity prevailed, so I went.

There was quite a scramble about my clothes. It seems you must wear a long high-necked black dress, and black stockings, and a black veil over your head. Although I had a long black dress, the neck-line came a little below my collar-bone, and I had no lace veil at all. But the *Vogue* editor had an Italian friend, a lovely dark-haired woman, Donna Cora Caetani, and she fixed me up. She sent her maid with a new paper of white pins and a black chiffon scarf, and the maid tucked it in and pinned it and

blocked out the white patch of my throat entirely. Then she
draped a mantilla over my head, and I thought I was ready. But
the maid said:

"Signorina, where are your jewels?"

"My jewels?" I asked.

And she explained: "Always the ladies wear their great jewels
when they go to the Vatican," and I said:

"Well, I have no great jewels." But she looked so sorry for
me that I added: "I mean they're all home in cold storage." Really
I was shocked at the idea of wearing great jewels to see the Pope,
because I am a Protestant of Puritan ancestry. I can't help as-
sociating emeralds and diamonds and gold with bare alluring
backs in night clubs and fleshpots like the Metropolitan Opera.
That is one reason, I suppose, why Protestants will never quite
understand the Catholic Church. We cannot separate, as the
Catholics do, the possession of material wealth from the idea of
moral and spiritual bankruptcy. Anyway, it's only in Protestant
or non-Catholic countries that any substantial headway is ever
made in soaking-the-rich for both moral and political reasons.

The *Vogue* editor, who was also going to see the Holy Father,
and I went down in the elevator of the Rome Excelsior Hotel at
eleven o'clock in the morning, looking like something out of a
Goya. In the lobby we met Anabel, the honest and splendid
and Junoesque wife of Myron Taylor, the American representative to the Vatican.

She said: "Hello, girls. Bet I can guess where you're going."

The *Vogue* editor answered: "Oh, my dear, dressed like this,
at this hour of the morning!"

Mrs. Taylor sighed. She said: "We have a very strange life.
My husband gets up at the crack of dawn every morning and puts
on his white tie and tails to go to the Vatican. He gets home at
night just in time to change into a sack suit for a formal dinner."
She waved us gaily to the taxi. "But you'll see—the Pope's a
wonderful man—just wonderful."

We drove through a cold drizzling rain past the leafless syca-
mores by the yellow Tiber, past all the pagan ruins and Christian
churches, to the Vatican. In the center of the piazza formed by
the gigantic arms of Bernini's Colonnade, I saw the Obelisk of
Pope Sixtus X, and I remembered the inscription on the pedestal
that the guide had read to me the day before.

> *Ecce Crux Christi*
> *Fugite Partes Adversae*
> *Vicit Leo de Triba Juda.*

> "Behold the Cross of Christ.
> Flee, hostile factions—
> The Lion of the Tribe of Judah has conquered."

And I thought of the other Lion of Judah I had seen also the
day before—the great stone Lion of Judah brought by the
conquering Italians from the square of Addis Ababa and set in
captive splendor on the Highway of Triumph under the Arch of
Constantine alongside the Colosseum—which had also known
Christians and lions in its day. I said to myself: "Can there
really be room in Rome for both these lions; the conquering
Lion of the Tribe of Judah who faces all the world from the hill
on which Saint Peter died, and that other conquered Lion which
is simply a trophy on a pagan highway?" It didn't seem to me that
there could be room.

Now we were before the doors of the place where the Vicar
of Christ, the guardian of the Lion of Judah, lived. The palms of
my hands were wet and I trembled. I asked myself: "What are
you trembling for? It would be different if you were a Catholic."
But I knew what I was trembling for. I was trembling because
I was about to see the one man in all the world who perhaps had
the power that perhaps still resided in an organized Church
of Christ, the power that comes of God, to stop this war, to give
the sad world a little breathing-space of peace. I thought perhaps

I was going to see the one man who could perform the miracle, the one miracle for which millions of hearts are truly yearning.

When we came into the Vatican, we went up a long noble flight of steps guarded by soldiers in mediaeval orange and black striped costumes, who carried halberds like the Beefeaters in the Tower of London, and then we were met by a little fussy usher in a white tie and tails who whisked us down a long corridor covered with the most incredibly lovely paintings into a hall where the *Vogue* editor left her sables and I left my silver foxes, and then into a small red-velvet anteroom, in the Pope's private apartments. I'm afraid we were a few seconds late, because this room was already full of people standing in a line all around the walls. There were about forty of them, a few men in white ties and tails, three or four women dressed as we were (but with great jewels, so I knew they were Catholics), and about twenty nuns in gray, some of them young, but most of them old, with faint black mustaches, who came from somewhere in South America, as I found out later. The nuns were all talking in hushed whispers, fingering their crucifixes with white and knotted and trembling fingers and cautiously shifting from foot to foot, and looking expectantly with wide, feverishly bright eyes at the little closed door at the end of the room before which the secretaries or ushers were standing. And then the door opened and in came His Holiness, Pope Pius XII, the servant of the servants of Christ. . . .

Everybody knelt. He circled the room, his back to us first. All I could see was that he was very slim, a little bent, and wore a white cap on his head, a red sash around his thin waist, and little red slippers without heels on his narrow feet. Then as he went down the line, leaning over the upturned faces, the faces broke into such good and happy and purified smiles that I could hardly wait to see his face. And then when he came to the nuns kneeling beside me, I saw it. It was so intelligent and so beneficent. He was talking to the nuns in Spanish, and they were hardly breathing. I started to smile too, before he quite reached me. And when he did, he asked me, in very good English, if I were the American lady, and I said: "Yes."

"Ah!" he said, "I loved your country when I was there," and I knew he meant he *loved* it. And then he smiled a thin sweet smile at my smile and made the sign of the cross and said: "God bless America!" Then he went on to the few others, and afterwards he went back through the door. Then everybody got up from his knees and let his breath out in a long gasp, and suddenly we all stopped smiling and began to rearrange our ties and jewels and crucifixes and veils.

So that was the audience with the Pope.

As we went back to the hall to get our wraps, I was still bemused and didn't want to talk. I felt, for some exceedingly strange reason, so much better in my heart.

—Europe in the Spring.

THE FIFTH ARMY IN
THE VATICAN

🌿 TRUCKLOADS of young girls with loud speakers and banners toured the congested streets of Rome calling the people to Saint Peter's at five o'clock. At the appointed hour at least a hundred thousand persons jammed the great square before the cathedral as the ponderous bells opened and closed their black mouths, sending a clangorous peal across the white roofs of the city. The Pope walked out on the balcony—rather, he seemed to flow out—in his shimmering white robes, and when he raised his arms and in melodious Italian offered thanks to his Deity for the sparing of Rome, the mass of humanity knelt in a vast, rippling movement. I was, and am, devoid of any feelings of religious awe toward the Vatican, and I have always felt that as a political force it has inclined toward Fascism. Yet in this spectacle there was a medieval splendor and pageantry which, as theater alone, was profoundly stirring. In its controlled mastery the Pope's eloquence was as beautiful as any I have ever heard, and I was impressed both by his "showmanship" and by his political genius. For, by inference, he took credit for the fact that the city had been spared. As time passed, we were to realize how he had taken energetic advantage of the situation in every respect. He knew the Allies were bound to take Rome and win the war. While he had allowed very few Germans inside the Vatican grounds, we discovered that dozens of escaped Allied fliers and prisoners had found sanctuary there. He had given no general audiences to German soldiers, but every day he received and individually blessed hundreds of Allied troops, tattered and dirty though they might be. Furthermore, the Vatican at its own expense was keeping some three hundred thousand Italian refugees alive in Rome, and, when the relief administrators of Allied Military Government arrived, they simply fitted their organization in with that of the Vatican. The Pope's prestige in Italy soared to great heights.

The war correspondents, too, were received in audience. At least, the audience was intended for the journalists, but a couple of hundred soldiers, nurses, and hangers-on joined our procession into the long room and lined the walls with us as he mounted the dais to speak. In several respects this audience broke with Vatican tradition. It was the first mass meeting the Pope had ever held with journalists, and it was surely the first time he ever received a woman wearing trousers. She was an enormously fat journalist who was temporarily without other garb. As the Pope came upon her in the lineup, he retained his remarkable composure and merely smiled benignly. I suppose also that this was the first occasion when the Pope's wishes were flouted by visitors within his sanctum: while he spoke from the dais, the photographers scrambled into their mad performances. They jumped up beside him and snapped their shutters. They ran around in front of him, bending low for "angle shots." They dropped their cameras with a clatter, burst bulbs and whispered hoarse curses at one another. One went flat on his stomach before the august presence to get an even better angle shot. Several times the Pope waved them away with a brief, peremptory gesture, without pausing in his English discourse, and his tail-coated attendants gestured madly at the photographers while sweat poured down their fiery faces. The cameramen continued their antics quite unabashed. Most of us were stiff with shame and so distracted that we could not follow his words. In the immense crowd I found the chief press officer standing next to me and could not refrain from whispering: "Do you want me to dateline this story *With the Fifth Army in the Vatican?*" He shuddered.

—*Not So Wild a Dream.*

THE END OF THE HOLY YEAR

❦ THE POWER that gathered all these elements into the greatest religious demonstration of the century, which is not to say that the century has been a very outstanding one in that line, was Pope Pius XII. At the end of the year, when all over the vast spaces around the high altar in the basilica of Saint Paul you had to pick your way among kneeling pilgrims racing in Latin through their rosaries, the whole Vatican hierarchy is said to have been dizzy with success. Such numbers! such response! nobody would have dared to hope for anything approaching it. If the pope cared to consider his efforts as anything more than an operation of divine truth, he might well congratulate himself; many people had wondered if he would survive the strain, healthy though he appeared to be, until the end of the year.

For all the interest of Boniface VIII in the first Holy Year and his fame as the originator of the tradition, he was outside Rome the best part of the year, busy with diplomatic crises and in preserving the lull in his war with the Colonna family—who were excluded from all the benefits of the jubilee; remission of sins was not for political opponents. Others in the series of jubilee popes after overhauling the city would attend the most important ceremonies and let it go at that. Pius XII was dedicated body and soul every minute; even at his summer residence in Castel Gandolfo there was scarcely any let-up in his exhausting number of private audiences, and he continued to appear twice a week in Saint Peter's for the mass ones, which drew a near-capacity crowd every time; this on top of twelve beatifications and canonizations and a number of large special occasions, such as the epoch-making celebration of the Greek rite in Saint Peter's, at which he assisted in December; plus the regular political, financial and theological business of his huge, peculiar empire.

The "Mystical Body of the Church," on which he had written an encyclical in 1943, depended by definition on the health and participation of all its members. An impression even more striking than the aesthetic one from the year's exhibit of missionary art was of the ubiquitousness of that body; jungles, lake dwellings, obscure Asian plateaus were suddenly to be seen, really seen, not just known about, as parts of one organism with Rome; an unfriendly term for the impression would be tentacles—in those rooms the word lost its pallor from overuse, the image was brand new; the head with its never-sleeping eyes was a block from where one stood. In orthodox imagery the body is more like a human one, and no sacrifice undergone by any pilgrim could have compared with the grueling labors of the pope in giving it its year-long blood transfusion, and making unforgettably dramatic for every participant its fabulous unity.

The most publicized fact regarding his mass audiences was that he was able to address the pilgrim groups in five or six languages. It was impressive, but no more so than the welcoming gesture of his arms, alternating to left and right, as of a dancer, and his keeping that and his thin earnest smile, as he was borne across the "sea of faces," from becoming mechanical through so many repetitions. The great slow single wave of cheering that breaks around the progress of all popes down that aisle is a standard awe-rouser; in this case there was uncommon personal charm at work too, whether or not it were felt as emanating from uncommon holiness; it had warmth and what seemed even a real humility, not incompatible with an autocratic office and a character suited to making the most of it.

But that was not the main point. There was one grandeur in these enormous gatherings that was not a matter of taste or opinion. It was a fact, for this century the most thrilling possible. For an hour each time many thousands of people, of many nationalities, stood together under one roof and were not asked to make war on anyone, neither a communist nor a Colonna nor a Turk; the pope's little speech of welcome and blessing, addressed to each group by name and repeated in all the languages he could pronounce, contained not a word of anything but affection and respect for the whole human race. It was moving; it was queer; it produced goose-pimples. It was likely to blind many people to various practical activities of the "Mystical Body," aimed at binding the whole human race with something more dependable than love. Nevertheless for one hour of their lives people had heard the words, and stood together hearing them; they had had at least one experience of peace, perhaps strong enough to turn some of them some day even against the Church if the memory were betrayed; the pope had risked that, perhaps more than any of his predecessors.

According to reports, he was truly convinced of the spiritual benefits of the year, whatever the worldly ones might be, and truly grieved when the day came at last to close the Holy Door. The wooden stands were up again in the portico; only now there was a trowel instead of a hammer. Inside, Saint Peter's was lit up, not with the big vulgar lights of some churches but very beautifully with a Milky Way's worth of little ones, drawing forth other golden reflections from the tremendous barrel-vault ceiling, less Gothic, more celestial than ever, from the ribs of the writhing baldaquin pillars under Michelangelo's dome, and the huge sunbeam horse-collar ring, Roman archetype for all holies of holies, around Peter the Apostle's chair. His bones had been found down below, it was said, during the year; it was important that they should be, to settle any lingering disputes about the vicarage, and the excavations in the Vatican grottoes had been too exten-

sive not to come up with them if they were there. Through the
golden haze the inside of the dome was sufficient for the eternal
glory of papal architecture whatever might be added or taken
away, if only that were left, with its thin rib-lines gathering upward toward the lantern modeled on the eye of God; outside for
miles around, appearing in all its uncanny ways and perspectives,
it was proclaiming, aside from what it always does, the triumph
of this particular jubilee. Another work by Michelangelo but
of his youth, not yet Roman, the dead Christ and mourning girl-
mother of the Pietà beside the Holy Door, the only great work
of pity in all Rome, looked utterly forgotten and dismissed afterwards, with the door rubbish heaped up around it. There had
been signs up for several weeks, there and in the other basilicas,
saying that one could give money for a brick for one of the four
Holy Doors, which would be removed on Christmas Eve, 1974.

It was not a golden day, as it had been a year earlier when the
door was being opened. It was chilly and gray; in fact it had been
raining most of the time for two months, which is not the kind of
thing anyone seems to report about the Holy City. There was
only a loosely formed little crowd in the square, carrying umbrellas, waiting to make a dash for the upper corner where the
parade of the guards would pass, and another one back to the
center to cheer the pope when as the really last gesture of Holy
Year he appeared, a small figure in white high above them, at one
of the Vatican windows. With the mystique of numbers still not
altogether superseded, some might be thinking more of the year
2,000 than of 1975, possibly with something of the terror that
the world of the Middle Ages felt at the ending of the first Christian millennium, and with somewhat better reasons.

—*Rome and a Villa.*

THE POPE WHO REMAINS
A PRIEST

❧ IT IS STRANGE to come on a monument to a living man, for even the greatest usually appear only on tablets and tombstones after death. But if we suppose a close observer wandering in Rome through the churches, the yellow squares and the *trattorie,* among the fountains and flower stalls and broken columns, he would notice here and there about the city the memorials to a man still living, Eugenio Pacelli. He would see them, in an obscure side street, on the wall of a house that has come down in the world—"In this house was born . . ."; in the hall of a school—"Student of this Lyceum during the years . . ."; at the entrance of a church—"Here he meditated upon the choice of his vocation . . ."—Pope Pius XII mummified in marble before his death.

Our imaginary observer might well wonder at this great harvest of tablets. For it is not enough to say that Pacelli is the Pope. There have been so many Popes. They stretch away like a column of ants, busy about affairs that have often seemed to the world of small importance. An odd anonymity shrouds the greater number of them—we don't remember them as we remember kings, or even as we remember presidents. Their titles, stiff and un-original, have a kind of textbook air. Pacelli becomes Pius XII and already he seems fixed on a page of history (rather dull history) with all the other Piuses (who were they?), fixed like a butterfly on cork, pinned out for dusty observation.

A few Popes—even to such a Protestant schoolboy as I was—broke through their anonymity. Generally this happened because they clashed with kings or emperors who were the more interesting characters since they wore armor and swore great binding oaths and made wars and memorable sayings. The only memorable saying of a Pope that we learnt at school was far too smug—Gregory the Great, remarking, "Not Angles but angels" at the sight of the young blond British slaves. One remembered, too, Innocent III fulminating against King John, though his victory over the king seemed a bit underhand; corpses lying unburied because of the interdict did not seem to compare in chivalry with burning lead. The Emperor Henry knelt in the snow at Canossa and our sympathy was always with the emperor (already I have forgotten which was the Pope he knelt to). Pius V (was it?) excommunicated Queen Elizabeth. Pio Nono fled rather absurdly before the conquering army of Garibaldi and his romantic Red Shirts. And there were the wicked popes like Alexander VI (the Borgia).

In England in those days just after World War I, one knew very little about the living Pope. He was associated rather disagreeably with a peace offer the Allies had rejected. We were the victorious powers, or so we thought, so there was a somewhat disreputable air about premature peace offers, and in any case peace has small appeal to the young. Our history books dealt mainly with wars, and as for any peace that passes understanding, it was not in any university curriculum.

I don't think it ever occurred to us that the Pope was a priest, or that he could be a saint. A priest was a small, sour man in black who had a tin-roofed church in a back street of the country town where one lived; his congregation consisted mainly, so one was told, of Irish servant girls, and he was never invited to dinner as the vicar was. But still he was a human being and had no

connection with the outdated tiaraed ruler in Rome. I remember
the shock of surprise at seeing a box inside a Roman Catholic
church marked Peter's Pence—I thought that all that had been
stopped sometime in the Middle Ages, probably by King John.

But even later, when I became a Catholic, the Pope remained
a distant hierarchic figure, and I imagine he remained so for
many Catholics, until contemporary history began to break into
our homes with the sound of explosives and the sight of refugees
and the sudden uncertainty—where shall we be next year? The
Pope became a man when we grew aware that he suffered from
the same anxieties and tensions as ourselves, only infinitely extended by his responsibility and his solitude. When in 1922
Pius XI was elected on the fourteenth ballot, the Cardinal
Primate of Hungary is reported to have said, "We have dragged
Ratti through the fourteen Stations of the Cross: now that he
has arrived on Golgotha we leave him alone." For nearly twenty
years now we have become aware of the papacy as the point of
suffering, the needle of pain, and a certain love always arises for
the man who suffers. Pain makes an individual, whether it is a
Chinese woman weeping for her dead child or the patient figure
in the hospital bed or this man in the Vatican.

We have worked slowly forward in our knowledge of this one
particular Pope, this priest, not so far removed from our parish
priest, led against his inclination into a position of responsibility.
But we cannot see him fully as an individual man unless we see
him in relation to his immediate predecessors. They have all had
the same aim—to be servants of the servants of God, to serve the
world, to temper the winds of hate, corruption, injustice, to give
us such peace as it is possible to get here. Pacelli becomes individual when we see how he differs from the others in trying to
attain this aim.

Since the days of Piux X, who was Pope when World War I
broke out, that word "peace" seems to chime through all the encyclicals and papal letters and speeches, as it chimes through

the Mass—so that we become accustomed to it in its every declension: *pax, pacis, pacem.* When he was asked to bless some armaments, he replied, "War! I don't want war, I don't bless war, I bless only peace. Gladly I would sacrifice my life to obtain peace." A fortnight after war was declared he was dead.

Benedict XV, his successor, whose peace proposals in 1917 were rejected, who was called Papa Bosch by the French and "the French Pope" by the Germans, said, "They want to silence me, but they shall not succeed in sealing my lips; nobody shall prevent me from calling to my own children, peace, peace, peace." And his successor, to whom he said these words, Pius XI, remarked to an English archbishop as the alignment for the new Hitlerian war became evident, "Peace is such a precious good that one should not fear to buy it even at the price of silence and concessions, although never at the price of weakness."

The world has darkened progressively since those days. Pius X was an old man ready to give his life, but a prayer is not always answered as we want it answered. Benedict believed in reasoned diplomacy and failed. Pius XI believed in a mixture of cunning and pugnacity, and he failed too. Now a new note sounds from Pacelli, the man who was his secretary of state and who from that inner position saw the cunning and pugnacity outwitted, and observed the limits of diplomacy. Isn't there a hint of despair, so far as this world is concerned, in Pacelli when he speaks of "Golgotha—that hill of long-awaited peace between Heaven and earth"? Sometimes we almost feel he is abandoning those vast hordes of people we call nations, the dealings with the war lords and dictators, and he seems like a parish priest in the confessional, a curé d'Ars, to be concentrating on each individual, teaching the individual that peace can be found on Golgotha, that pain doesn't matter, teaching the difficult lesson of love, dwelling on the liturgy of the church while the storm rages—for the storm will pass. In 1943, the year of the North African campaign and the final disaster to the Italian armies, he issued two encyclicals—

on "The Mystical Body of Jesus Christ" and on "Biblical
Studies." They must have seemed to the Italian people very far
removed from their immediate worries, but those are the worries
that pass, and the subject of the encyclicals goes on as long as
human life.

And yet one cannot help exclaiming, "If only they were more
readable, less staid, tight, pedantic in style!" I doubt whether
many of the laity read these encyclicals and yet they are addressed
by form "to all the clergy and faithful." The abstract words, the
sense of distance, the lack of fire make them rather like a somber
editorial in a newspaper: the words have been current too long.
There are no surprises. "As it is by faith that on this earth we
adhere to God as the source of truth, so it is by virtue of Christian
hope that we seek Him as the source of beatitude." The words
have no bite, no sting, no concrete image: we feel that a man is
dictating to a dictaphone. Compare the encyclicals with such
writing as the sixteenth century's St. Francis de Sales, using his
chaste elephant or his bees as metaphors, arousing our attention
with a startling image: "My tongue, while I speak of my neighbor, is in my mouth like a lancet in the hand of the surgeon,
who wishes to make an incision between the nerves and sinews:
the incision that I make with my tongue must be so exact that I
say neither more nor less than the truth." In the encyclicals the
incision has not been made: the words clothe the thought as
stiffly as a plaster cast on an injured limb.

Not all the Popes have been quite so dry or cautious in their
encyclicals. Leo XIII in his *De Rerum Novarum* wrote with a
kind of holy savagery on the abuse of property (didn't the Bishop
of San Luis Potosi in Mexico preserve the copies in his cellar
till the revolution for fear of offending the rich?). And Pius XI,
attacking the Hitlerian state in *Mit brennender Sorge,* allowed
the personal tone of voice to be heard.

But a Pope—or a saint or a parish priest—is not necessarily
a writer, and many, if not most, of Pacelli's encyclicals are not

personally written by himself, only very carefully revised and approved. One distinguished writer has compared the Pope's own style to the Roman fountains, formal even in their ornateness, the Latin words, colorless as water but pure and exact, falling with certainty into the ageless basins. Roman? Renaissance? In his formality closer perhaps to music than literature? Bossuet, Dante, St. Augustine—these are among the very few literary references that occur in his writing, but he speaks with real understanding of music. Again one is reminded of many parish priests whose worldly interests seem narrowed by the love of God to a few books and the enjoyment of classical music.

This is the essential paradox in a Pope who so many of us believe will rank among the greatest. Among the gossipers of Rome he is often described as a priest first and a diplomat afterwards. But how was it that with all his years of diplomatic travel—from Germany and Hungary to Argentina and the United States—he did not become a diplomat first and foremost?

Pacelli belongs to an aristocratic Roman family. Although his own inclinations seem to have been to ordinary parish work and to the confessional, he was steered by those who may have known his talents better, from a very early period in his life as a priest, toward an official career. His first major assignment was to the Congregation of Extraordinary Ecclesiastical Affairs, dealing with problems of treaty-making and international affairs. But the paradox persisted: Pacelli combines his official work with pastoral work, just as still during his public audience he has been known to go into a corner of the audience hall at a peasant's request and hear his confession.

The ecclesiastical career drove steadily on: papal nuncio in Munich in 1917 so that he could act as intermediary for the Pope in the efforts to attain peace. Here he saw violent revolution for the first time when the Communists broke into his palace. In 1919, with the formation of the German republic, he became nuncio in Berlin and later, when Hitler began his campaign for power, he maintained close ties with the Center party. (The leader of the Center party, now Monsignor Kaas, has remained the Pope's friend, is administrator of St. Peter's and is responsible for the excavations under the Vatican which have disclosed the old Roman cemetery where St. Peter was buried. He has built the Pope a private staircase, so that he can make his way alone into these caverns and talk to the workmen. Walking among his tombs, Monsignor Kaas refers with affection to his friend, pointing a finger upwards—"Him up there.")

In 1929, when Pacelli left Germany, the inevitable cardinalate followed. The parish priest was doomed, you would have said, and yet he obstinately stayed alive. We can hear him speaking in the words of Pacelli's farewell, so different from the formal encyclicals that were to follow. "I go the way in which God, by the mouth of the Pontiff, commands me to go. I go this way fully conscious of my weakness, believing in Him who uses the weak to put the strong to shame. What I was is nothing; what I am is little; but what I shall become is eternal." As the Pope placed the red hat on his head, he spoke the traditional words that in our day have taken on real significance: "Accept the red hat, a special sign of the cardinal's dignity. This means that you should be ready to shed your blood and to die, if need be, in the fearless defense of our Holy Faith, for the preservation of quiet and peace among the Christian people. . . ."

Only a little more than a month later he was appointed secretary of state to Pius XI, perhaps the most politically active Pope since the Middle Ages—the man who revived the Vatican State, who fought Mussolini so firmly that Mussolini rejoiced at his death, who began the struggle against Hitler not only by his encyclicals but by personal affront, leaving Rome when Hitler came there and closing the Vatican Museum which Hitler had intended to visit. On his death bed in February 1939 he finished his last allocution—the final words written on the night he died, his last blow, it was to have been, so they say, at the totalitarian state.

The new Pope as secretary of state had been very closely associated with his predecessor's policy, and his attitude to affairs in Germany was well known. At a party which he gave in Rome after his return from Germany, an old conservative friend of his, the Marchese Patrici, was overheard by him to remark that it was a good thing Germany had a strong man now who would deal with the Communists. Cardinal Pacelli turned on him. "For goodness' sake, Joseph," he said, "don't talk such nonsense. The Nazis are infinitely worse." We can assume, therefore, that neither Hitler nor Mussolini was gratified when the Conclave, breaking with a tradition of nearly three hundred years, elected the secretary of state Pope in March 1939 at the age of sixty-three. Perhaps the foreign cardinals turned the balance in Pacelli's favor. He was almost the only cardinal they could have met personally.

For this is another paradox of the Pope—that this priest, whom I have heard described as a Franciscan by one who knows him well, is regarded as a very traveled, very modern man. There are the new gadgets of the Vatican, from the white typewriter and the white telephone and the electric razor to the short-wave wireless station and the latest television equipment. But the television transmitter is not in operation and the programs of the much-publicized Vatican radio consist of little more than astonishingly uninspired relays of editorials from the *Osservatore Romano*, local pieces of Catholic news.

As for travel, it is true that Pacelli moved about a good deal of the earth's surface before he became Pope, but it is a reasonable guess that the only two countries that made any deep impression on him were Germany and America. For both these countries he has retained great affection. The administrator of St. Peter's is German. The Pope's personal feeling of friendship for Cardinal Spellman seems certain, though somewhat surprising considering the marked divergency of their characters. (The cynical

sometimes point out that the United States is the only country
of importance left that is able to transmit Peter's Pence to Rome:
the Catholics of most other nations are bound by their currency
laws.)

His other travels have been widespread but brief, filled with
the official duties of the Pope's representative: to the Eucharistic
Congress at Buenos Aires in 1934; to Lourdes in 1935 on the
Nineteenth Centenary of the Redemption; to Lisieux during
France's Eucharistic Congress in 1937; and to the next congress
in 1938 at Budapest. How much during such journeys does the
Pope's representative see? There is a passage in Tolstoy's *War
and Peace* that describes the travels of an army. "A soldier on the
march is hemmed in and borne along by his regiment as much
as a sailor is by his ship. However far he has walked, whatever
strange, unknown and dangerous places he reaches, just as a
sailor is always surrounded by the same decks, masts and rigging
of his ship, so the soldier always has around him the same
comrades, the same sergeant major, the same company dog and
the same commanders." The papal secretary of state moving from
country to country, Eucharistic Congress to Eucharistic Congress,
always was hemmed in by the pack wagons of the church, the
dignitaries in skullcaps, the distant crowds that hide by their
pious mass even the shape of the buildings.

One cannot believe that the journeys of Pacelli have influenced
him except insofar as they have driven him to learn many languages. One must not exaggerate his knowledge however. We
hear the gentle, precise voice speaking to us in English and we
forget the strict limits of his vocabulary. He sends his blessings
to our families "with deep affection"—that is a favorite phrase
often repeated and emphasized—but inevitably he has to address
the pilgrim in certain set formulas.

For the priest this is a smaller handicap than for the diplomat.
A priest in the confessional too is apt to speak in formulas, but
into the strait jacket of a limited vocabulary some priests are able
to introduce an extraordinary intimacy, gentleness, a sense of

love. That is Pius XII's achievement—if we can call the grace of
great charity an achievement. We become aware that he loves
the world as another man may love his only son. The enemies
whom his predecessor pursued with such vigor he fights with the
weapon of charity. In his presence one feels that here is a priest
who is waiting patiently for the moment of martyrdom, and his
patience includes even the long-drawn conversations of the nuns
who visit him. From another room one hears the long stream of
aged feminine talk while the monsignors move restlessly in their
scarlet robes, looking at their watches or making that movement
of the hand to the chin forming an imaginary beard—which
is the Latin way of exclaiming at a bore. Out comes the last nun,
strutting away with the happy, contented smile of a woman who
has said her say. And out from his inner room comes the Pope
with his precise, vigorous step ready to greet the next unimportant
stranger "with deep affection."

. . . This is the Pope whom most of us before the war regarded
as a diplomat. Even his photographs, in which the eyes seem
expressionless behind deep glasses and the thin lips suggest little
sensitivity, seem to confirm the mental image of an ex-secretary
of state. It is true he keeps that office in his own hands, assisted
by Monsignor Montini, but one who has close knowledge of
the Pope told me that diplomacy has little importance in his eyes.
In the last thirty years the Pope has seen the consistent failure of
diplomacy; since he knew so well this world of ambassadors and
ministers, he retains these contacts in his own hands much as a
man keeps the trophies on his wall of a sport long abandoned.
But he knows the world cannot be saved by diplomacy.

What can save it?

So much time for audiences public and private, so much time
for work (the light in his study over St. Peter's burns till one
in the morning), so much time like any other priest for his
breviary—and in the background one is aware of the huge
threatening world, the conferences in Moscow, the speeches at

Lake Success, the troops pouring down in Korea. He presses into one more visitor's hand a little green envelope with the papal arms containing a small nickel holy medal. Can this Thing—so defenseless it seems—survive?

Every morning at breakfast the Pope lets loose his two canaries and his favorite bird—a small bird with a green breast—I don't know its name. They walk over the table pecking at his butter, and his favorite takes crumbs from between his fingers and perches on the white shoulder. "He talks to children," my informant said, "as though they were his birds and to his birds as though they were children . . ." That was why he has been called Franciscan, and the Franciscans next to the Jesuits are his favorite order. Even in this short period of relaxation he seems to be making a hieratic gesture symbolizing charity. If a man loves enough, every act will represent his love.

I have said he gives the impression of a man patiently waiting for martyrdom. He has already barely escaped it. At his coronation the German ambassador was heard to remark, "Very moving and beautiful, but it will be the last." And a moment came during the war, under the German occupation, when the end was expected. Hitler was said to have uttered the threat that he would raze the Vatican to the ground, and it is certainly true that the administrator received orders one day from "him up there" to produce a plan for summoning the ambassadors of the powers at a moment's notice to St. Peter's so that the Pope if necessary might make an announcement of grave importance. But the threat of exile or death passed. Now again the danger threatens. The Church's borders are widespread in Poland and Korea, but war travels fast these days. Hitler was handicapped by the presence of the Church in Germany: in Russia the Church is represented only by a few priests in hiding.

Sometimes a Pope can be known by the saints he canonizes. This Pope's predecessor, Pius XI, the pugnacious priest, canonized Thomas More and John Fisher, overruling the requirements of miracles: they were men who fought the totalitarian state of their day. But Pacelli has canonized the child Maria Goretti, who died forgiving her murderer.

It is a long time since a Pope has awaked, even in those of other faiths, such a sense of closeness.

. . . One visitor replying to a polite formal inquiry of the Pope said that there were two Masses he would always remember. One was at five-thirty in the morning, at a side altar in the small Franciscan monastery of San Giovanni Rotondo, in the bleak southern province of Apulia: the Host was raised in the hands of Padre Pio—the aged, bearded priest whose hands are famed through the Catholic world for the black, ugly dried patches of the stigmata that they bear. The other memorable Mass was the Pope's Jubilee Mass in Rome—the enormous crowd pressed into St. Peter's, and men and women cheering and weeping as the Pope passed up the nave, boys flinging their scout hats into the air: the fine transparent features like those on a coin, going by, the hand raised in a resolute blessing, the smile of "deep affection," and later the Pope alone at the altar, when the cardinals who served him had stepped aside, moving with grace and precision through the motions of the Mass, doing what every priest does every day, the servant of the servants of God, and not impossibly, one feels, a saint.

But how much more difficult sanctity must be under the Michelangelo frescoes, among the applauding crowds, through the daily audiences than in the stony fields of Apulia where the saintly priest, Pio, is confined. It is the strength of the Church in Italy that it can produce such extremes, and exactly the same thought came to one while kneeling among a dozen women in the early morning in the Franciscan monastery—or while pressed among the cheering crowds in St. Peter's. It was not after all the question—can this Thing survive? It was—how can this Thing ever be defeated?

Life, September 24, 1951.

EPILOGUE

✤ THERE IS NOT, and there never was on this earth, a work of human policy so well deserving of examination as the Roman Catholic Church. The history of that Church joins together the two great ages of human civilization. No other institution is left standing which carries the mind back to the times when the smoke of sacrifice rose from the Pantheon, and when camelopards and tigers bounded in the Flavian amphitheatre. The proudest royal houses are but of yesterday, when compared with the line of the Supreme Pontiffs. That line we trace back in an unbroken series from the Pope who crowned Napoleon in the nineteenth century to the Pope who crowned Pepin in the eighth; and far beyond the time of Pepin the august dynasty extends, till it is lost in the twilight of fable. The republic of Venice came next in antiquity. But the republic of Venice was modern when compared with the Papacy; and the republic of Venice is gone, and the Papacy remains, not in decay, not a mere antique, but full of life and useful vigor. The Catholic Church is still sending forth to the farthest ends of the world missionaries as zealous as those who landed in Kent with Augustin, and still confronting hostile kings with the same spirit with which she confronted Attila. The number of her children is greater than in any former age. Her acquisitions in the New World have more than compensated for what she has lost in the Old. Her spiritual ascendency extends over the vast countries which lie between the plains of the Missouri and Cape Horn, countries which, a century hence, may not improbably contain a population as large as that which now inhabits Europe. The members of her communion are certainly not fewer than a hundred and fifty millions; and it will be difficult to show that all other Christian sects united amount to a hundred and twenty millions. Nor do we see any sign which indicates that the term of her long dominion is approaching. She saw the commencement of all the governments and of all the ecclesiastical establishments that now exist in the world; and we feel no assurance that she is not destined to see the end of them all. She was great and respected before the Saxon had set foot on Britain, before the Frank had passed the Rhine, when Grecian eloquence still flourished in Antioch, when idols were still worshipped in the temple of Mecca. And she may still exist in undiminished vigor when some traveller from New Zealand shall, in the midst of a vast solitude, take his stand on a broken arch of London Bridge to sketch the ruins of St. Paul's.

—"Ranke's History of the Popes," *Macaulay's Essays.*